LESSONS FROM "TAKE ME HOME, COUNTRY ROADS"

LESSONS FROM "TAKE ME HOME, COUNTRY ROADS"

Identity, (Be)Longing, and Imagined Landscapes

SARAH L. MORRIS

WEST VIRGINIA UNIVERSITY PRESS
MORGANTOWN

Take Me Home, Country Roads
Words and Music by John Denver, Bill Danoff and Taffy Nivert
Copyright © 1971 BMG Ruby Songs, My Pop's Songs, Dino Park Publishing, JD Legacy Publishing and Reservoir Media Music
Copyright Renewed
All Rights for BMG Ruby Songs Administered by BMG Rights Management (US) LLC
All Rights for My Pop's Songs, Dino Park Publishing and JD Legacy Publishing in the U.S. Administered by Kobalt Songs Music Publishing
All Rights for Reservoir Media Music Administered in the U.S. by Reservoir Media Management, Inc.
All Rights Reserved Used by Permission
Reprinted by permission of Hal Leonard LLC

The Lost Verse of "Take Me Home, Country Roads"
Written by Bill Danoff
Used by Permission
Reprinted by permission of Bill Danoff

"West Virginia Chose Me"
Words and Music by Colleen Anderson
Copyright © 2020 Colleen Anderson
Used by Permission
Reprinted by permission of Colleen Anderson

"If You Love My West Virginia"
Words and Music by Colleen Anderson
Copyright © 2006 EDNA Records
Used by Permission
Reprinted by permission of Colleen Anderson

Other copyrighted material referenced in this has not been specifically authorized by the copyright owners but are within "fair use" as referenced and provided for in section 107 of the US Copyright Law and are acknowledged in References.

Copyright © 2025 West Virginia University Press
All rights reserved
First edition published 2025 by West Virginia University Press
Printed in the United States of America
ISBN 978-1-959000-47-1 (paperback) / ISBN 978-1-959000-48-8 (ebook)

Library of Congress Cataloging-in-Publication Data

Names: Morris, Sarah L., author.
Title: Lessons from "Take me home, country roads" : identity, (be)longing, and imagined landscapes / Sarah L. Morris.
Description: First edition. | Morgantown : West Virginia University Press, 2025. | Includes bibliographical references and index.
Identifiers: LCCN 2025004004 | ISBN 9781959000549 (paperback) | ISBN 9781959000556 (ebook)
Subjects: LCSH: Denver, John. Take me home, country roads. | Danoff, Bill. Take me home, country roads. | West Virginia—Songs and music—History and criticism. | Nostalgia in music. | Place (Philosophy) in music.
Classification: LCC ML410.D3634 M67 2025 | DDC 782.42164092—dc23/eng/20250320
LC record available at https://lccn.loc.gov/2025004004

Cover design by Emily Sokolosky, Base Camp Printing Company.
Book design by Than Saffel

NO AI TRAINING: Without in any way limiting the author's exclusive rights under copyright, any use of this publication to train generative artificial intelligence (AI) technologies to generate text is expressly prohibited. The author reserves all rights to license uses of this work for generative AI training and development of machine learning language models. For EU safety/GPSR concerns, please direct inquiries to WVUPress@mail.wvu.edu or our physical mailing address at West Virginia University Press / PO Box 6295 / West Virginia University / Morgantown, WV, 26508, USA.

CONTENTS

Acknowledgments	vii
Chapter 1 *The Song Is a Memory (an Introduction)*	1
Chapter 2 *Hiraeth, Home, and West Virginian Rhetorics of Identity*	21
Chapter 3 *Placing "Country Roads" in Context*	64
Chapter 4 *A West Virginia State of Mind*	103
Chapter 5 *Evoking (and Marketing) Belonging and Home*	131
Chapter 6 *The Window, the Mirror, and the Lens: Pedagogical Implications*	178
References	211
Index	239

ACKNOWLEDGMENTS

This book was originally grounded in a teaching need and in lessons designed for my undergraduate writing students at West Virginia University, who embrace and use "Take Me Home, Country Roads" in varied and expressive ways. Their inspired thoughts, engaged questions, and enthusiastic feedback allowed me to be a writer alongside them and for this project to grow beyond the classroom. It has been a long process, but this book could not have come at all without the generosity and kindness of so many, the first of whom are my students.

I am grateful to the West Virginia Humanities Council, who supported this project with a summer grant, and the West Virginia University Humanities Center, who provided fellowship funding. This extra support allowed me time to write that I would not have otherwise had.

Many people freely gave their time to talk with me about "Country Roads," West Virginia, and music. I am especially thankful to Bill Danoff, who talked with me about the song's origins and impact, the lost verse, and many other topics; who kept me alerted to new ideas; and who connected me to others who share an interest in the song. I am equally grateful to Taffy Nivert, who talked openly with me about her West Virginia connections, her memories, and the power of music to "connect the dots in our brains."

Many West Virginian songwriters and musicians shared their thoughts with me not only about "Country Roads," but also about their experiences, their own West Virginia songs, and their sense of place: Colleen Anderson, Aristotle Jones, John Ellison, and Michael Lipton, as well as others, less formally.

I was lucky to speak with fans of Fat City and John Denver from the days when "Country Roads" was still in draft form, including William Brustein, Andy, Ridenour, Bill Wilkinson, and Mary Ellen Griffith. Other folks, including West Virginians, writers, and teachers, such as Barbara MacLennan, Sarah Mullens, David Hoyt, as well as those who completed my research survey, shared thoughts with me. Many others reached out with their own connections and experiences. These conversations expanded my understanding, and I wish I could have included every story.

This project transformed itself many times during the writing process, and I would have been lost without kind and thoughtful friends and readers, including Mary Kay Weimer, Amanda Berardi Tennant, Beth Nardella, Laura Brady, Rosemary Hathaway, Anne Pancake, Debra Lattanzi Shutika, Amanda Hayes, Rebecca Rider, and Marguerite Avery, who joined WVU Press late in my drafting stages and provided immediate help.

A few special people have listened to me talk about this project for years, providing encouragement, laughter, commiseration, and love: Beth, Mary Kay, Rose, Melissa, Darin, Nick, Natasha, Eugenia, and J.

Finally, I learned many unexpected lessons while writing, perhaps the most important of which is persistence, modeled by my mother, Linda (Dunmire) Morris, who has never stopped fighting through challenges much harder than writing a book. My father, Frank Morris, found time to read my drafts and offer encouragement to me, even while he was fighting alongside my mother. I am grateful to the way my parents, proud West Virginians, instilled in me a sense of home and an understanding of place, one where I belong.

LESSONS FROM "TAKE ME HOME, COUNTRY ROADS"

1

THE SONG IS A MEMORY (AN INTRODUCTION)

AS IF IN PRAYER
One August evening in 2011, I exited my shared office in Cole Field House at the University of Maryland, where I was a graduate student and teaching assistant. I had recently left my job teaching high school English in Morgan County, West Virginia, to begin a doctorate. I sold my home, left a life I loved, relocated to urban Maryland, and began living outside West Virginia for the first time in my adulthood. That night, my head full of theory, I stepped into the warm dusk. The sky was turning from pink to purple; campus was green and quiet. Buildings reflected lights from the stadium, where a soccer game was on, and announcers' voices drifted on the air. As I crossed campus, seven unmistakable guitar notes echoed, and John Denver's voice sang, "Almost heaven, West Virginia..."

Holding a heavy stack of books, I stopped, listening. Soon, more voices chimed in; a chorus of spectators, players, and students from both teams (I imagined) singing:

> Country roads, take me home
> To the place I belong
> West Virginia, mountain mama
> Take me home, country roads

I stood moved and unmoving, eyes wet, homesick, lonely, and hopeful. As if fixed in prayer, I waited until the end of the song. Then, I headed to my car and to a basement apartment, a place that housed me but did not feel like home.

"COUNTRY ROADS" AS A CALL TO HOME

I have never known a world *not* shaped by "Take Me Home, Country Roads." Written by Bill Danoff, Taffy Nivert, and John Denver, "Country Roads," from Denver's album *Poems, Prayers, and Promises*, reached number two on the Top 40 chart on August 28, 1971, three years before I was born. Embraced by a nation in flux during the Vietnam War, "Country Roads" was an easy anthem for deployed and drafted service members and their families because of its nostalgic longing for home. Its popularity rocketed Denver to international fame, and he recorded many versions and performed it worldwide. In West Virginia, the song was an immediate success, an honor to be called by name in a way that felt true—recognition instead of ridicule.

The song presented an image of a region peculiar to mainstream America and offered a counternarrative to dominant conceptions. Characterized by images of poverty and depression, as in the 1965 CBS special "Christmas in Appalachia," national impressions of West Virginia were set amid misery and insufficiency. A 1971 pamphlet by activist James Branscome lamented the way popular media colored Appalachia in narrow, disparaging terms; for instance, CBS's 1970 Tuesday night included "The Beverly Hillbillies," "Hee Haw," and "Green Acres," composed of images meant to "belittle, demean, and otherwise destroy" place and people (1). In the early 1970s, these images represented what America knew about Appalachia, if it knew anything at all.

These persistent stereotypes dehumanize and make acceptable regional prejudice and ridicule, with West Virginia, the only state entirely within Appalachia, at the center. Rhetorician Todd Snyder, a West Virginia native, discusses the hillbilly stereotype as a socioeconomic, cultural construction, "well-documented, bought, and sold for a profit...," a story told "from the perspective of others." Appalachia's history consists of economic exploitation from outside—extraction of resources, capital, and people, "a story crafted by wealthy northern elites who attempt to use their privileged positions to shape and mold a national identity for the people of the region." This makes Appalachia a "conceptual place," and the hillbilly an "imposed cultural identity" tied to consequences of a layered othering created by social, political, and economic invention (Snyder, *Rhetoric* 1, 5, 22–23). Named from the outside, West Virginians struggle to see themselves and their identities accurately reflected in American consciousness. This remains as true today as in 1971.

Framed by cultural context, "Country Roads," climbed the charts. It was, and still is, as described by one Denver biographer, "an anthem with the power to speak to those who will never know West Virginia," a song for "any country lover, forced to be 'long in city pent,'" that evokes "the feeling of the heart lifting as one sloughs off the urban streets and heads for the hills" (Collis 83). "Country Roads" presents a positive image, a vision of home West Virginians can own. It has special resonance for those who left to find work, seeking jobs far away. A 1970 *New York Times* article documents statewide population loss of more than one hundred and fifty thousand people in the '60s and quotes the state schools superintendent as saying "outmigration of young people was 'overwhelming,' especially in the southern coal counties and the central mountain counties, where there simply were no jobs for high school graduates. In the hollows, only the old, the infirm and those on welfare remained" (Bigart). Amid an exodus fueled by lack of opportunity, "Country Roads" became a swan-song when leaving seemed the only option for young West Virginians. My parents were two of those migrants.

"COUNTRY ROADS" IN UTAH IN 1975
My father worked for a mining equipment repair and manufacturing company, Morgantown Machine. An airman first class,

honorably discharged in the '60s after four years of service, Dad started by tarring roofs and doing maintenance at the industrial shop. His background in aircraft mechanics and hydraulics helped him move up, and in the early '70s he was sent west as a regional representative for the expanding company. In 1975, he, my mother, and I moved to Price, Utah. I was a year old. I remember little beyond vague images of dry, red dirt and red shag carpet in our Utah house, just like the red shag carpet in our West Virginia home, which my parents built just before I was born. They rented it out when we went to Utah. The move was never meant to be permanent.

Dad ran a truck route from Price, to Helper, to East Carbon, to Rock Springs, Wyoming. He was home a few days, gone a few days, in a cycle of sales visits and equipment transfers. The roads, he remembers, were straight and empty with hypnotic sameness. His truck did the work of staying on the road while he nodded at the wheel, and he listened to the radio when he could get a signal. "Country Roads" was in regular rotation; I imagine that he always turned the volume up and sang along.

My parents remember "Country Roads" in an "everytime, always" frame as a call to return. Once they found a reliable sitter in Utah, they would occasionally take a night out. One evening at The Hollow Bottle, an upscale bar in downtown Price, a band was playing cover songs, with "Country Roads" in their repertoire. As they played the first notes, my parents, a few drinks in, were immediately wracked with homesickness. My mother says, some fifty years later, "I thought we were going to die." I remember the song as continually present, an eight-track plugged into the stereo. When we moved home to West Virginia in 1977, "Country Roads" remained present, and continues to be, for me and for others across the state, nation, and world.

PERIPHERAL RELEVANCE, PERENNIAL RESONANCE

The origin story of "Country Roads" has been well documented, with embellishments and controversy, over the years. The recorded version was performed for the first time by Danoff, Nivert, and Denver on December 30, 1970. It was mostly complete before that, though, as "original inspiration for the song came one day while [Danoff and Nivert were] driving down a little country road in Maryland, and it was totally written in [their] basement apartment" in Washington, DC (Danoff, website). In an interview, Bill Danoff told me that he and Nivert "had the whole song done when [they] played the song for John.... It was already a song."

Taffy Nivert confirmed this account, explaining, "I was driving, and Bill was playing the guitar. He's just sitting there watching the sheep, and the goats, and the cows, and we're on a two-lane blacktop, up and down, up and down. And he just starts strumming: 'Country Roads, Country Roads, Country Roads' and nothing else happened." The pair kept working, Nivert explained: "We sang for months in our basement apartment, 'Country Roads, take me home . . .' and then we would add a line, or subtract a line, or try something that did or didn't work, because we were working on other songs too at the time." When it started to "feel right," it came together quickly. Danoff expressed this too, saying that he knew that it was a hit "because it had the elements of a hit: It had a repetitive chorus, it had a nice beginning, it had a story, to me, it had all the things that I wanted to have in a song."

Performing as Fat City, they played "Country Roads" in clubs as they polished it. One person with whom I spoke tended bar at a club where Fat City regularly played and confirmed hearing different versions over several months (Brustein). When they shared it with Denver, the trio worked together over one night to shape it into what we know today, replacing a verse and modifying the bridge. They finalized the song in about three hours and played it live that same evening at The Cellar Door. It received a standing ovation, fueled in part by a group of West Virginians at a table in the front of the room (Ridenour, Wilkinson, and Griffith). The next week, the trio recorded it in a New York City studio. The single was released in April 1971 and was number two on the Billboard charts by August.

It is widely reported that Bill Danoff had never been to West Virginia. An account on Danoff's website elaborates: "It was a song the inspiration for which had first come to [Danoff] when he was driving through the countryside of Maryland to visit his wife's [Nivert's] family. On those drives, his feeling for the land tapped into feelings that he'd had for the countryside of his youth—the hills and valleys and country roads of Western Massachusetts and Western New England." Besides having listened to bluegrass on a radio station out of Wheeling, West Virginia, he had little connection beyond fans, friends from the state, and news accounts. In an interview, Danoff told me that he knew about West Virginia but did not visit until after the song was released.

It is also commonly reported that John Denver had never been to West Virginia, but this is not true. Denver visited West Virginia several times with his band, The Mitchell Trio, with whom he performed from 1965–68, stopping at several state campuses, including West Virginia Wesleyan and Marshall University; he also performed solo at Concord College's homecoming celebrations in 1970, months before his collaboration with Danoff and Nivert on "Country Roads" ("New Homecoming..."). However, it is difficult to find a sense of what he knew or felt about West Virginia prior to the song. Denver devotes pages in his autobiography (and much of his music) to elaborating on the theme of home, and while he writes in detail about Colorado, where he lived, as well as other places he toured (China, Russia, Germany, Australia) and visited (Alaska, Hawaii) he never addresses West Virginia as a place beyond the image of it in "Country Roads" (Denver and Tobier).

Of the songwriters, Taffy Nivert had the most experience in and knowledge of West Virginia. She attended college in Steubenville, Ohio, a stone's throw from the border. Nivert told me "I spent my leisure time there. I would get my hair done in West Virginia when I was in college. And there was a great restaurant in Wheeling that we went to on special occasions." Her daydreams held the West Virginia hills as a landscape. As she explained to me, Nivert knew part of the state, the Northern Panhandle, and felt affinity for what she knew. For the rest, she used "imagination and *National Geographic*," as well the encyclopedia, as she did for other songs about places, including "I Guess He'd Rather Be in Colorado," which Denver also recorded.

Counter to some lore, the songwriters knew of West Virginia and had fans and friends who lived there, though their knowledge was shallow—gleaned from letters, books, current events, and Taffy's recollections. As they worked the tune, the state's name had syntactic fit; it just sounded right. "Country Roads" is only peripherally about West Virginia, though. The Blue Ridge rests along the eastern border with Virginia, and the Shenandoah River crosses through Harpers Ferry, a presence in the state for only about twenty miles. In fact, an article in the *Daily Athenaeum*, WVU's student newspaper, claims, "When John Denver performed the song at Morgantown High School in 1977, he changed the 'Blue Ridge Mountains, Shenandoah River' lyric to 'Appalachian Mountains, Monongahela River,'" more appropriate geographical markers ("9 Things . . ."). The name of the state fits rhythmically, but the song is inaccurate geographically. Written by outsiders, it resonates deeply with insiders, despite its peripheral relevance to the place it names. Even so, it felt right, still feels right enough, for West Virginians and many of the rest of us.

AN IMAGE OF IDENTITY

"Country Roads" was written from an "outside" perspective; it is a cultural artifact that refers indirectly to the tradition of extraction in West Virginia by defining and naming from the outside looking in. Still, West Virginians embrace this outside naming and its "take me home" lyrics, which they display on cars, in homes, on clothing. Despite geographical problems and somewhat disparaging descriptions of "miner's lady/stranger to blue waters," the "dark and dusty" sky, and the "misty taste of moonshine," West Virginians take up the song as a symbol of who we are and where we come from; it holds resonance that transcends actual meaning.

In 2014, the West Virginia legislature formally adopted "Country Roads" as an anthem, the state's fourth. In 2017, the West Virginia Office of Tourism purchased rights, making "Almost Heaven" a trademark, employed in publications and marketing. On the state tourism page, the words "Almost Heaven" scroll across the screen over photographs of people fishing, hiking, and gazing at panoramic mountain views. The same script adorns the cover of a free vacation guide available on the website. The inner text of this guide references Denver's "famous ode to West Virginia" (11) and conjures up his ghost, claiming visitors can "almost picture John Denver at Almost Heaven—The Decks at Winterplace crooning out tunes about the Blue Ridge Mountains" (19). Winterplace is not a vantage from which one can see the Blue Ridge.

Folks at West Virginia University (WVU) take it up, too. "Country Roads" is used in promotional and fan materials at WVU; it has been played at football games and graduations since 1972 and is used for recruiting and marketing. Statewide, traces of the song are everywhere. It touches themes present in Appalachian culture, literature, and history. "Country Roads" represents what scholar Boyd Creasman identifies as "quintessential concerns" present in West Virginian literature: "the role of tradition, connection to the land, and leaving the region in hopes of better economic opportunity" (15). "Country Roads" taps into place-based identity rhetoric for West Virginians and Mountaineers, even as it conjures an idealized, transcendent sense of home for listeners completely unconnected to the state.

"Country Roads" makes an argument about who we are even as it misnames. In her work on identity, Amanda Hayes argues that explorations of Appalachian rhetoric lead to a clearer sense of self among Appalachians and empower self-naming. That is one aspect of what this book seeks to do, too: examine a deeply resonant, charismatic text that is part of the rhetoric of West Virginian identity despite its inaccuracy and outside origin. I follow Hayes's model of incorporating story as illustrative and evidential, as well, for "narratives (often nonlinear) demonstrate the speaker/writer's process of thinking about a subject; in other words, demonstrating how one has come to knowledge or belief, without overtly insisting on similar beliefs from the audience" (106). I will explore nuanced ways "Country Roads" serves a range of purposes for a range of audiences, how it represents naming, both the taking-up and rejections of that naming, as well as pedagogical possibilities for critical engagement.

"COUNTRY ROADS" AS WEST VIRGINIAN IDENTITY RHETORIC

"Country Roads" is part of a rhetoric of identity for West Virginians. Made up of a set of complex interactions that may shift based on context, relationships, and tensions, identity affects how we present ourselves in social spaces. Writing scholar Robert Brooke describes identity like a melody; it is "viewed in the same way a piece of music is viewed: as a series of transformations and variations on a small set of enduring themes" (16). In this way, self-concept is mediated through stories we tell and hear, including music we listen to and love. Identity is connected to symbols and markers: For West Virginians, a consistent marker of identity is "Country Roads." Every state has symbols, and West Virginia is no exception: Rhododendron (state flower) and cardinal (state bird) are markers that many West Virginians know and love. We are reminded of home when we wind our way through thickets in a state park in May, rhododendrons full, or in February, when the redbird is the brightest color against dark trees and white snow. We are taught these symbols in school, but if you are not West Virginian, they will not signify West Virginia to you. "Country Roads," however, likely will, even if you have never known West Virginia.

"Country Roads" is a familiar marker of West Virginian identity, one that transcends state borders. When I was traveling in Japan and told strangers I was from West Virginia, many people responded, "Oh! Country Roads." My interviews, survey research, and conversations hold similar anecdotes. Nearly every West Virginian I know has had the experience of being identified by

"Country Roads" at one time or another. Some embrace it; others do not. Regardless of how the song makes us feel, it is integral to cultural identity rhetoric. It identifies us to others and to ourselves. I wonder how "Country Roads" represents us, affecting the stories we tell. How does it inform how we and others know who we are? These are existential questions, fundamentally tied to how we understand ourselves and each other, places and space, and how "Country Roads" provides a soundtrack for that understanding. My thinking about its relationship to identity and place is influenced by ideas from a range of disciplines: rhetoric, writing studies, history, Appalachian studies, and social sciences, all of which are woven through this book and contribute to understanding how "Country Roads" has become local and global cultural rhetoric. Voices from these scholars provide information about how larger cultures talk about West Virginians and Appalachians, how we talk about and present ourselves, and how we use "Country Roads" to add to, resist, or divert that conversation.

"Country Roads" is a song connected to and descriptive of place, but West Virginia is more than that. The individual West Virginian, despite taking it up, is more than the song. For example, I am not just a West Virginian; I am also a woman, a white person, a teacher, an academic, a first-generation college student, and so on. As philosopher Judith Butler explains in her foundational work on identity and gender, our identities are dynamic, tied to discourse and context, and continually reconstituted through repeated patterns of enactments and performances. Even amid common rituals and patterns, though, identity is complex and discursive in that we are never just one thing, so "Country Roads" can mean something different for a Black woman who is also a West Virginian than it can for me, as was demonstrated by my students upon hearing "Country Roads" sung by Black men's voices. This challenged their understandings of West Virginian identity, and one person exclaimed, "You would never hear a Black man sing 'Country Roads' where I am from!"

Identity is intersectional and multilayered and exists in contextual tension. The choices we make within that tension are rhetorical, tied to purpose and audience; they make an argument about who we are. As Amanda Hayes explains, rhetoric is "the process and means by which identity and values are shaped and conveyed" (13). When tied to place, identity becomes more complex; Appalachian studies scholars Stephen Fisher and Barbara Ellen Smith claim "the concept of 'place' bundles together cultural memories, practices, and beliefs with social relations to generate the potential for powerful, unifying identities. Once again, however, the meaning of place and any associated identity is produced, not received" (274). We construct and perform our identities through presentations of self when we speak and through our bodies in spaces and places. Some markers of our identities are choices, like wearing a "Country Roads" T-shirt. Some are not, like the colors of our skins, our ages, our accents. Regardless, we exist in space in a rhetorical way: Our very existences make an argument about who we are and where and how we belong. This argument takes specific shape in Appalachia and West Virginia.

We are able to construct parts of our identities based on social, cultural, and economic factors, but these factors limit us, too. Others' impressions affect our perceptions and performances of our identities. Erica Abrams Locklear, in her work on Appalachian literacy, discusses how some identity markers, like dialect and mannerisms, define Appalachians in ways we cannot control. This explains why so many Appalachians lose their accents. Influenced by cultural texts that make an argument about place, "American audiences have been schooled by literary and popular media to imagine Appalachia as a repository for socially undesirable hillbillies, those who are among other things drunken, ignorant, and illiterate" (Locklear 144). Appalachians, and West Virginians, may find themselves subconsciously—or consciously—distancing from aspects of identity that align with stereotypes, especially in situations where we may be judged or seen as "other." However,

"Country Roads" is a safe cultural text that speaks inclusion rather than exclusion, evoking a different imaginary. It provides for West Virginians a way to perform and express place-identity that is affiliative rather than othering.

Identity, and how we express it, brings us into affiliation with some groups and differentiates us from others. Assumptions that shape Appalachians' relationship to the world frequently come from outside, influenced by conversations spoken *about* us rather than *by* us. Historian Henry Shapiro documents how the earliest public conversations about the region brought Appalachia into being through rhetoric, so that it became a "subject of discourse" (122). Stereotypes about Appalachia are well-documented and persistent, and, as Carissa Massey explains, codify into "essentialist structures of identity" that become socialized into "material truth" through cultural artifacts and texts, like news media, literature, art, and music (13). Cultural anthropologist Clifford Geertz analyzed how texts shape our perceptions of communities and identities, writing that "the culture of a people is an ensemble of texts, themselves ensembles, which the anthropologist strains to read over the shoulders of those to whom they properly belong." Texts belong to people, and people are shaped by texts we value—pledges, vows, themes, anthems. Social reality is experienced through these symbols, and so is self-perception, through a "symbolic framework" that is part of a constructed, learned system that provides social order (Geertz, 452). When West Virginians identify as "mountaineers," or as "mountain mamas," we actively participate in a system of symbols, connected to identity and embedded in culture.

Appalachians are characterized in a number of ways that generalize, both negatively and positively; regardless, all stereotypes flatten and distort. While the otherness that Appalachians and West Virginians experience is complex, obvious markers of identity differentiate Appalachians from "in-groups" and require social and rhetorical negotiation. For West Virginians, "Country Roads" assists in that identity negotiation. Kathryn Trauth Taylor discusses language and identity as performative and defines "*literacy performances* and *identity performances* in a rhetorical sense, to mean public language performances that represent, challenge, conjure, or negotiate conceptions of Appalachian identity, community, and culture" ("Diverse" 119). Taylor claims that when we publicly claim an identity, we open up a rhetorical space where that identity can be taken up and performed by others ("Naming"). While she discusses this specifically in terms of Affrilachian (African American Appalachian) identity, we can apply a similar concept to West Virginians who take up "Country Roads." In it, West Virginia is imagined in a way that evokes deep longing and softens negative perceptions, even as it glosses over complexity. When West Virginians claim this naming, the choice is rhetorical; it makes an argument about who we are and where we come from and expresses pride detached from shame or negative stereotypes.

It is not only that West Virginians like "Country Roads"; it is also that we use it to make meaning, as part of cultural traditions. We enact identity through shared symbolic frames—like songs—that tell us who we are and create affiliations among us. Artifacts and symbols help us put a constriction upon events and lived experiences so that we can find our bearings in the world. Geertz tells us that "emotions, too, are cultural artifacts," shaped by an essential "existence of cultural resources, of an adequate system of public symbols" that constitute a constructed understanding of our feelings. Shared artifacts help us understand ourselves and our place in the world, as "the public images of sentiment that only ritual, myth, and art can provide" (Geertz 51, 82). We take up these images to evoke emotions and express who we are.

Considered rhetorically, as argument, "Country Roads" becomes more than a song for West Virginians or Mountaineers to sing in a bar, in a stadium to celebrate a football win, or at a wedding. The meaning changes when we consider the song as identity performance because, "as a practice of interpreting and generating awareness of language choices, rhetoric offers strategies for harnessing the emotive and symbolic powers of Appalachian literacies [so that] literacy performances are capable of establishing and generating respect for difference" (Taylor, "Diverse" 119). If we think of singing "Country Roads" as a literacy performance, an identity performance, and a rhetorical performance, it means more: It is a declaration of person and an argument about place and people, one that includes rather than excludes. It is contextually bound and shifts based on the place where the performance occurs. Not just about a place, it is about belonging to place—one that is general for many outside West Virginia, but one that is specific for West Virginians themselves.

FOREVER COUNTRY (ROADS)

I have never not known "Country Roads." It was one of only a handful of songs our father would sing to my brother and me. I have memories of it at bonfires, parties, reunions, weddings, funerals. "Country Roads" played in Mountaineer football games on the radio; because West Virginia has no professional sports teams, WVU sports belong to everyone. On the mantel above the fireplace in our living room sat a copper music box shaped like an old Model T Ford that plunked out "Country Roads" in offkey, bell-like tones. My brother and I were allowed to play with the music box, a gift from my grandmother, but it occupied a special place in our home.

"Country Roads" is about homecomings. After we moved back to West Virginia, my grandfather retired from the mines and moved to North Carolina's Outer Banks, where he lived in a trailer park on an island, fishing, smoking his pipe, and reading crime novels. We visited every summer, traveling state roads and then, after it was built, the interstate highway. At the end of our visits, Dad woke us before dawn, packed us in the car, and we began the journey home through North Carolina, Virginia, and Maryland. My brother and I napped in the back seat, while Dad drove and Mom navigated. In Western Maryland, we passed under a huge sign on I-68: "Wild and Wonderful West Virginia." That crossing over was a moment of celebration, every time. Sometimes we sang "Country Roads." Other West Virginians tell me their families do this, too. But the song signals belonging beyond West Virginia, as well.

Like many West Virginians, I have heard "Country Roads" in unexpected places. I taught high school English for several years in West Virginia's eastern panhandle, and during that time I participated in a summer teacher exchange in Japan. At a middle school in Tokyo, I sat with a group of American teachers for a performance by the school's marching band, who played "Country Roads." I heard it in a curry joint in Bangkok, performed by a Thai band, sandwiched among other American '70s era covers. It is not as much a song about West Virginia as it is a song about home. "Country Roads," as a text, transcends sense of place to capture the feeling of home for a global audience. It served the initial purpose of its authors (to achieve commercial success) yet moves beyond that purpose: It remains an anthem across time, space, and context, even after fifty years. It is used in public rhetoric, marketing, politics, and protest. Not only has it become an anthem, but it has also taken on a hymnal quality. It is played at celebrations and memorials. It calls to us, whether we have a state connection or not: It calls to anyone longing for home. This deep longing can be translated through the Welsh concept of *hiraeth*, which evokes yearning for a metaphorical, sometimes never-existent place. Hiraeth saturates "Country Roads."

Bill Danoff, in an interview quoted on his website, recognizes the song's international power, discussing how fans have shared connections with him, "starting with back in the Viet Nam War when the song was a hit, and it was very popular with the troops over there because it mentioned coming home." Danoff further acknowledges that "'Country Roads' didn't particularly apply to West Virginia; it applied to coming home, period. It meant a lot to a lot of people around the world, but I've become especially aware of what it means to West Virginians." I have heard "Country Roads" all over the United States, in bars and cafes, at barbecues and parties. The song always stirs me, but it is different when I hear it at home.

In June 2019, I ran a marathon in Hatfield and McCoy territory, through sites of feuds and mine wars, across golf courses, and among crumbling towns. Located at the heart of the hillbilly exodus and the opioid epidemic, this race is one of a series of health-related and tourist-focused events and commodifies the hillbilly stereotype and local history to attract runners from all over the world. The Hatfield McCoy Marathon, established in 2000, includes a performance from Hatfield and McCoy descendants, who play roles of the patriarchs in the famous feud, hillbilly- and history-themed aid stations, and post-race moonshine. During race weekend, "Country Roads" is everywhere. The course, hilly and hard on winding roads alongside and crossing the Tug Fork River, twists through both West Virginia and Kentucky, looping through Matewan, center of the infamous mine war massacre, and ending in Williamson, home of the "Coal House," a landmark building constructed entirely from locally mined coal. At mile 19, I passed three women who were casually running together, carrying a music player and chatting. As I approached them, their playlist echoed one of many cover versions of "Country Roads," the 2016 hit mashup "Forever Country," which includes Nashville legends singing a medley of "Country Roads," Willie Nelson's "On the Road Again," and Dolly Parton's "I Will Always Love You."

The music video for "Forever Country" opens with West Virginian Brad Paisley singing, "Almost heaven, West Virginia." In a heavily computer-generated scene, Paisley looks wistfully out a cafe window toward a street not unlike ones in the small towns on the race route. When discussing "Country Roads," in an *Entertainment Weekly* feature, Paisley confesses: "It was one of the first [songs] I learned because at any event you did in West Virginia, it works. But it works everywhere. It's truly boundary-less" (Finan). This boundarylessness makes "Country Roads" appropriate in a song intended to be about the music industry, to celebrate fifty years of country music awards. But for West Virginians, "Forever Country" took a different meaning. Remixed, the new song develops a story of perpetual departure and return, longing for beloved home after a long time on the road, only to feel compelled to leave again.

With seven miles left to run that day, I was energized and moved by the song as it pulled me along. The three women were singing, running together, and when I passed them, one of them shouted, "You get it, Sis!" When I crossed the finish line, I ate a banana and stretched against a brick wall painted with butterfly wings and the words "Almost Heaven, Williamson, West Virginia." Despite having grown up in another part of the state, I was home. Teaching at West Virginia University, too, I am home, and "Country Roads" has a place in the classroom, too.

"COUNTRY ROADS" IN THE CLASSROOM

In Morgantown, home of West Virginia University, the song surrounds us. "Almost Heaven" is printed on T-Shirts, decals, notebooks, stickers, bags, and jewelry. "Take Me Home" is an ever-present slogan on a range of products. A friend who recently shopped for houses told me she was astonished by how many on-the-market homes were staged with "Country Roads" lyrics embroidered on throw pillows or painted on walls. On campus, it rings out from carillons in buildings and is played in formation by the WVU marching band, The Pride of West Virginia. Students sing it, arms linked, at sporting events, orientations, and graduations. If you do not know all the words to "Country Roads," you cannot consider yourself a Mountaineer. Still, I want my students to think critically about this song—in fact, any text—that gives such shape to our identities and is used so ubiquitously.

In Spring 2019, while teaching first-year written composition, I struggled to find a common text with which to help my students understand and practice rhetorical and textual analysis. I wanted something resonant, something that had cultural significance and that we could view from multiple perspectives and analyze with complexity. I settled on "Country Roads." My students, who came not just from all over West Virginia, but also from surrounding states and other countries, scribbled in their notebooks as we moved through different versions and variations, watching videos, considering movie clips. When I asked, "What calls to you here?" the conversation exploded. We discussed purpose, audience, speaker, voice, and how meaning of the song shifted based on these aspects. We uncovered sentimentality, a sense of connection we all felt, but in different ways. West Virginian students talked about the ever-present soundtrack of the song in their lives, like mine. Non–West Virginian students connected to football games and tailgating, official school events. An international student shared that he learned the song in eighth grade as part of the Japanese national curriculum, but he had not realized that the song was about an actual place until he found himself studying at WVU. But West Virginia is a real place, one with complex social, political, and economic issues, fractured identities, and complicated history; it is a place named in song, yet still invisible and unknown. This phenomenon is worth exploring, so this book has pedagogical implications, too.

THIS SONG IS MORE THAN A SONG
Based on an imagined conception of West Virginia, "Country Roads" nevertheless speaks lyrics resonant to West Virginians, wrapped in a melody that has continued to captivate national and international audiences for more than half a century. "Country Roads" is an artifact of identity rhetoric, but also, as Benedict Anderson says of anthems, "a cultural artifact of a particular kind" that arouses "deep attachments." This anthem, tied so intimately to place and person, suggests we can learn something from looking closely at how its meaning came into being, changed over time, and "command[s] such profound emotional legitimacy" (4). Untangling the attachments that bind "Country Roads" to culture uncovers implications for how we relate to place and who we are.

In a 2010 *Appalachian Journal* article, David Whisnant lists defining qualities and principles related to Appalachian identity. Whisnant posits that *Appalachia* has many definitions, used for differing rhetorical and political purposes, which require additional interrogation. He recommends new ways of thinking about and strategizing Appalachian identity, rather than continuing to rely on past concepts. This meditation on "Country Roads" is meant to answer this call, to present a range of ways of thinking about identity and belonging and how it is reflected in this deceptively simple text.

"Country Roads" is a love letter. Carrying international resonance and popularity, it has presence and shifting meaning for people the world over, regardless of where they actually call home. Voices in my survey research reveal interesting thoughts about the place, meaning, and experience of "Country Roads." This book considers what it is like for West Virginians to experience the song at home and in other places. Likewise, it explores what it means to others outside the state who take it up—especially those who have no connection with or conception of West Virginia as a place. It also examines contexts and purposes for playing and performing "Country Roads" and how it shifts in meaning and shape.

This book is about a place that names itself by taking up a song that summons into existence a sense of place. "Country Roads" touches on what it means to be from West Virginia or to go to college in West Virginia, to identify as a Mountaineer, to imagine a conception of place and self in place; so this is a book about identity rhetoric, community, and the ways we take up texts to help us see who we are. But "Country Roads" is, of course, just a song, one resonant and popular from a global perspective. This book discusses conditions in West Virginia that allow us to adopt a song that is not really about us, including circumstances in the 1970s and situations today that contribute to its enduring presence. It also explores other songs about West Virginia and why they have not carried the same meaning or gained the same popularity.

This book considers "Country Roads" as a cultural artifact and living text, present in public, political, and commercial discourse across the world. It is problematic as well as a source of pride. It harnesses the concept of home, idealized and transcendent, even in the midst of uncertainty and bleak reality, as evidenced by its renewed popularity and numerous new recordings during the COVID-19 pandemic. This is a book about a song that spread across the world yet that names a specific place. "Country Roads" is anthem and advertisement, used to market the feeling of home, leveraged to sell all manner of products and ideas. It is a source of comfort in dark times, a coping tool for responding to sadness and isolation, and a way to find connection. It resonates with those of us who find meaning and visions of home in it, even if we have never set foot in the place to which the song calls.

Lastly, "Country Roads" is a window, a mirror, and a lens. Because I come to all my work from a teacherly stance, we will discuss pedagogical implications for the song, exploring how it is situated within wider place-based rhetoric. How does it show a perspective of West Virginia from without, from within, distorted, enlarged, reduced, and reflected back? What can we learn? What is worth teaching? And why is this important, despite the complications? This book is not a work of music theory; rather, it is an exploration of identity rhetoric and belonging manifested in a common text that shifts in different communities, for different purposes and audiences. Because much of my understanding of the world is deeply grounded in who I am as a teacher and West Virginian, this story is my story, too. I hope to construct a vision that uncovers multiple perspectives, recognizing that understandings are always partial, particularly when the central item of study, a simple song, is still evolving. I hope, also, that the teaching and learning insights I share here will help others make sense of a text that is more than a text, a song that is more than a song, a song that is sung for different reasons by different people all over the world, but which has special significance to West Virginians. Reality of place is mediated through memory and charismatic rhetorical texts like "Country Roads." In this book, we dismantle the imaginary from the materiality and consider how it is possible to reject and embrace, to understand the reality and love the anthem, both at once.

2

HIRAETH, HOME, AND WEST VIRGINIAN RHETORICS OF IDENTITY

"COUNTRY ROADS" IN MEMORIES AND MEMORIALS
In the summer of 2019, in a church on a hillside in Buckhannon, West Virginia, we celebrated the life of my mother's brother. A mining and highway engineer, Uncle Harry spent much of his working life out of state. He finally came home to West Virginia but suffered a stroke at age seventy-five while driving himself to work on a highway project. He passed away some months later after living under hospice care with my cousins in Maryland. At his funeral, my cousins' children led a heartfelt rendition of "Take Me Home, Country Roads." Standing surrounded by family, I looked around the chapel to see a congregation in tears, but singing. Everyone knew the words.

Later that same summer, a friend was buried at the top of a ridge in a country cemetery in a different part of the state. He was a transplant who had left and returned several times, whose children had been raised in West Virginia, and who felt a deep connection to the state despite living elsewhere when he died. The view from the cemetery was breathtaking, a three-hundred-sixty-degree view of rolling mountains, a city in the distance, under the vaunted blue sky—a common sight atop a West Virginia hill. Graveside, a small group of people gathered to share stories and memories. When the urn was lowered into the ground, it was to "Country Roads," played on someone's phone.

Twice in one summer, I experienced "Country Roads" as a funerary dirge, yet before that, and since, I heard it at weddings as well. I am not alone in noticing this seemingly paradoxical use. During my research several respondents recalled hearing "Country Roads" both at weddings and funerals. One person wrote: "I went to a wedding and everyone linked arms in a circle and swayed and sang to 'Country Roads.' Just a few months later I attended a funeral for my Aunt who had moved to Florida but wanted to come home to be put to rest and during her services 'Country Roads' was again played and took on a new meaning of being brought home."

More than an anthem, the song is liturgical, public worship, an expression of longing and of joy—a call beyond the literal. "Country Roads" symbolizes a profound sense of longing for the place we belong, whether we are from West Virginia or not. This is due to a felt sense: *hiraeth*, a deep existential longing. Hiraeth exists in versions, variations, translations, and complications, and through many interpretations of "Country Roads." The hiraeth imbued in the song makes it powerful as rhetoric, expressing not just longing for home and belonging in general, but also an argument about what it means to be from West Virginia in particular. In this chapter, I define hiraeth as a concept and explore its presence in "Country Roads." I also focus not only on the ways the song evokes (be)longing, but also how it expresses identity, affiliation, resistance, and tellability.

HIRAETH AS A FRAMEWORK FOR CONSIDERING "COUNTRY ROADS"

A Welsh concept, hiraeth is a helpful framework for considering "Country Roads" in that it calls to us and calls us to, regardless of our place of origin, an idealized home. The home of "Country Roads" is West Virginia in name, but it is also not West Virginia, as it conjures a dream space in its depiction, lacking the substance and shape of the actual state. The home of "Country Roads" is flexible and general enough that it can be substituted for any longed-for place, any space, any loved and lost home, or even a spiritual home in the afterlife. The term *hiraeth* has no direct English translation, but, as one writer describes, it is "an unattainable longing for a place, a person, a figure, even a national history that may never have actually existed. To feel *hiraeth* is to feel a deep incompleteness and recognize it as familiar" (Petro). "Country Roads" depicts an imaginary place, one simpler and softer than the factual place of West Virginia, and that generalized picture draws us in and creates a flood of longing.

It is fitting that a Welsh term so neatly applies to something experienced in relation to West Virginia. Like West Virginia, "Wales is a poor, rural place of mountains and ribboning hills with empty underground pockets where its coal used to be" (Petro). Similar nostalgia pervades similar landscapes. Though the notion is problematic, the image of an Appalachia populated solely with immigrants from the British Isles persists despite evidence of more diverse realities. Nonetheless, this presumed heritage shapes understandings about and within mountains of West Virginia. As described by the travel writer Jan Morris, "the old Welsh emigrants [who] had left Wales because their lives there were poor and miserable," found themselves implanted in a foreign land that was not enough like home, "yet nothing could suppress the hiraeth within them." That kind of longing is pervasive, universal.

Likewise, in the history of the mining industry, risk is intertwined with work, and labor is infused with loss; when someone leaves to go to work, they may not return. This is another kind of longing, akin to hiraeth. Hiraeth is a heritage; a memory of those immigrants who made their way into West Virginian mines, seeking a better life. It is the same longing of those who left West Virginia as part of a history of outmigration, or those who served in Vietnam at the same time "Country Roads" was released, many of whom never returned. Hiraeth resonates in "Country Roads," and West Virginians can hear it deeply. But anyone pulled toward home, real or imagined, experiences hiraeth in the simplicity of the song.

In evoking hiraeth, "Country Roads" is placeless. In his work on invisible landscapes, Kent Ryden explains that folklore serves a purpose in "vivifying" landscape, making space into story. This is true of "Country Roads" in the way it has spread to other landscapes and lived experiences. Behaving like folklore, songs like "Country Roads" imbue belonging, and can be "artifacts of human intelligence first and foremost; they are created and repeated for a reason, because they encode and carry important personal and cultural messages; they are deciphered the same way. The messages behind the patterns finally matter more than the patterns themselves." We create the world through story, and as Ryden so tellingly explains, "here never is a world for us except the one we sing and, singing, make" (57, 58). So, then, "Country Roads" is a product of an imaginary world that makes meaning and community in realities it names and in other worlds, as well. Unlike folklore, though, which arises out of an attempt to understand and explain phenomena rooted in place and community, a text like "Country Roads" works in reverse—it is universally applicable, and yet applied to place, imposed upon rather than arising from. Folklore draws power from the universal in the particular. "Country Roads" draws power from its generalizable applicability, its ability to tap into hiraeth and a sense of belonging.

ALMOST HEAVEN AND ALMOST HYMN

Many songs evoke a sense of belonging and homecoming, so "Country Roads" is not unique in calling forth hiraeth. Church hymns describe passing over: "Going Over Home," "Beaulahland," "In the Sweet Bye and Bye." While hymns refer to heaven as the destination, other songs name tangible places. "The West Virginia Hills," for example, completed in 1885, was published in West Virginia church hymnals in the early 1900s, and was made an official state anthem in 1961. Like "Country Roads," it captures the feeling of deep longing for home from afar:

> Oh, the West Virginia hills! I must bid you now adieu.
> In my home beyond the mountains I shall ever dream of you;
> In the evening time of life, If my Father only wills,
> I shall still behold the vision Of those West Virginia hills.

Also like "Country Roads," this song names an actual place but attributes otherworldly qualities to it, distancing symbolic longing from material reality. The West Virginia of "The West Virginia Hills" is compared to "our Prince Immanuel's land" with mountains that are "bathed in glory" and reach toward "the Great Almighty's Land." Like the West Virginia of "Country Roads," this manifestation, too, is almost heaven, infused with hiraeth.

Both are state anthems verging on hymns; they stretch toward the ineffable, just out of reach. "The West Virginia Hills" was popular at state functions as well as in churches and at 4-H gatherings. What makes it different from "Country Roads," though, is that it calls us home to a state that is known and unmistakable, one that cannot be substituted for any other place, even when inscribed with heavenly qualities. It is an anthem that is also a hymn, a paean to place infused with a spirituality, but the place is real. "Country Roads," on the other hand, is an anthem with a nod to the spirit, "almost heaven," which makes it almost a hymn, a public expression of faith. Its liturgical quality makes it appropriate for settings where one might hear a hymn—like funerals, memorial services, weddings.

These sentimental and semireligious uses can be found in a range of settings, some unexpected. *Fallout 76*, an online roleplaying game released in 2018, is set in West Virginia and features a version of "Country Roads" that evokes similar responses as the original. One thread in the *Fallout 76* Reddit community discusses experiencing the song at funerals. The original poster writes,

"'Country Roads, Take Me Home' was my grandfather's funeral song. I grew up visiting my grandpa's home in West Virginia. I miss walking through the woods and going hunting with him," and elaborates that the video game version brought comfort in those memories. Many other Reddit users respond, remembering the song at funerals for their own loved ones, some with West Virginia roots, some not. Another poster adds, "It's a song I sing to my newborn that's currently in the hospital in the NICU, 97 days now and counting..." Home, for this person and their baby, takes on a more literal meaning, and the song becomes a prayer of hope. "Country Roads" represents peace, remembrance, and faith for the participants in this online conversation.

This use of the song is perpetuated by the memorial industry as well. Funerary service providers take up the "Country Roads" theme, directly and indirectly, in planning, marketing, and products. These uses are not limited to providers or clients from West Virginia. Tranquility Cremation and Burial, in Ontario, Canada, recommends "Country Roads" as a "funeral or cremation song." Wilbert Funeral Services, an Illinois-based manufacturer of burial vaults, cremation supplies, and other funeral products, offers a "Country Roads" vault applique decal. In reference to the song, a country road is a metaphor for the afterlife.

Unsurprisingly, "Country Roads" was played at John Denver's funeral on Friday, October 17, 1997 (Collis 171). The song should take on a memorial quality at a service celebrating the life of the man who recorded it, but it is used for memorials of all kinds. For example, C-SPAN footage of long-time West Virginia Senator Robert Byrd's funeral in 2010 shows those in attendance singing as the casket is carried up the steps of the state capitol building in Charleston. Byrd's service ended with "Country Roads," which followed both "Amazing Grace" and "Taps." Bill Danoff recounted to me that he performed "Country Roads" at the Vietnam Veterans Memorial in Washington, DC, as part of a wreath-laying on Memorial Day, 2001. He sang a more subdued version, "the type of version that comes out when you're standing on top of the

Veterans Wall." It was moving and well-received, Danoff said, but most meaningful is his claim that he sang "for all the people that didn't come home." Homecoming and homegoing, to both material and spiritual homes, are represented in the song.

Respondents to my survey research reported hearing "Country Roads" at funerals and memorials for siblings, grandparents, friends, and others. The appeal of hiraeth, combined with the liturgical uses of the song in West Virginia specifically, makes it a quasi-religious text, characteristic of some Appalachian music. In her work on faith and music in Appalachia, Heather Ann Ackley Bean discusses Appalachian religious narrative as having a particularity that serves to "express a view of life as troubled but basically good, although death is seen as better, a release from painful existence, a rest from labor, and a reunion with loved ones and god" (158). Consistent with Bean's conclusions, people use "Country Roads" and its sense of home as a release from suffering; home may be West Virginia, the ancestral home where the body rests, but it is surely heaven, with or without the "almost."

Some writers argue that all of Denver's recorded songs have a religious quality. John Collis ascribes to his music "a spirituality, a mysterious force, that somehow informs the harmony of the whole—including, presumably, the universe," describing "environments that hint at a greater spiritual mystery" (32–33). This hymnal quality is infused into much of Denver's catalog so that "a sense of pantheistic mystery is undeniably one way into his songs...." (Collis 33). Even the album title on which "Country Roads" was initially released, *Poems, Prayers, and Promises*, alludes to spirituality.

As much as "Country Roads" is used in memoriam, it is as often used in celebration. At least twice as many of my survey respondents wrote about its use at happy occasions, often sharing that it was played at their own weddings. One was of the opinion that "it's a tradition to end a West Virginia wedding with 'Country Roads'!" If you are from West Virginia, the song may be special and relevant to homebuilding in a new marriage, or it may be a nod to a family or ancestral home, even if you no longer live in West Virginia. Stranger still is the phenomenon of the song at weddings without an obvious West Virginia connection. For example, one survey respondent wrote, "I have very good friends not from WV who have requested the song be played at their own weddings in CO because of how magical the song is and how they enjoy hearing it when I am with them." In this respondent's interpretation, the friend from West Virginia provides the entry into loving the song's magic. Whether the home in "Country Roads" is the afterlife or the one you intend to build with your newly wedded partner, the song is aspirational, hopeful, and taps into hiraeth.

Easy to sing, "Country Roads" invites a sense of togetherness that people feel when they sing in unison. Many respondents described a kind of circling up, to link elbows, hold hands, or wrap arms around shoulders to sway and sing, with "all of our family and friends in a big circle," as one person remembered. This phenomenon is common and happens at every West Virginia University graduation—students link arms and sing "Country Roads," swaying together—and at many high school dances, sports events, and parties, too. In these moments, togetherness connects with timeliness, synchrony in the moment. One respondent expressed that the power of singing "Country Roads" in these celebratory settings creates a sense of shared vision and tangible connection, even when participants may not know each other. In that person's experience, ritual singing of this song allows us to feel " like we are a united community rather than individuals," and at a gathering, especially, "it's a blend of various friends and families and everyone is united singing together a song that's important to our culture." For this person, the memory of the sense of home found in collective song is deeply associated with "Country Roads." It is a tribute to love, and family, not just homecoming, but homemaking.

This, combined with the warmth of singing together, makes this experience holy in the same way we feel a spiritual togetherness when singing any song in a group. Songwriter Taffy Nivert speculated that the magic in "Country Roads" comes from a combination of chords and harmonies that taps into something instinctual, suggesting that "it makes you feel good when you hear it or sing it. It somehow changes the arrangement of the little dots in your brain." Nivert's hunch about how music touches something primal is backed by science. The pleasure and connection we get from singing together may be biologically and socially significant. Researchers Chris Loersch and Nathan Arbuckle define music as a "universal human phenomenon," consistent across every documented human cultural group and hypothesize that music is a tool for communal living, communicating group moods, and binding people together in community because it can set a tenor for many people at once. They conclude that "music is a group process, a special form of social cognition that may have evolved to serve the intense social needs of our species" and that "the powerful psychological pull of music in modern life may derive from its innate ability to connect us to others" (Loersch and Arbuckle 777, 792). We can think about this deep connection through the theory of entrainment, a process that occurs in many physical systems in nature but that is manifest in human bodies in the ways we adapt to circadian rhythms, for example, or the way lovers' heartbeats and breathing harmonize as internal systems attune. When we coexist with other people, our rhythmic systems synchronize.

Entrainment, George Leonard writes, "is the stuff of life itself, echoing the essential connectedness that defines existence. Different cultures speak and move in different specific rhythms, but the process of rhythmic connectedness is the same for all cultures" (35). Ethnomusicologist Martin Clayton claims this rhythmic synchronization is an embodied, biological, and social process that is always present when we make music. When we sing together, we tap into primal togetherness, the material of shared existence. No wonder it feels like we are speaking to a power beyond our surface understanding. Singing together is universal and holy. Singing "Country Roads" together taps into primal knowing, belonging, and togetherness, both through a sense of hiraeth and through entrainment.

"COUNTRY ROADS" IN THE TIME OF COVID-19

"Country Roads" was especially significant for expressing togetherness within the indelible context of the COVID-19 pandemic, which began in March 2020 and during which entire countries were locked down. Quarantine opened a range of ways to communicate while distancing, and some of those connections coalesced around "Country Roads." References to this song appeared in videos, online concerts, public information bulletins, and other publications. It appeared for audiences within and outside West Virginia, providing comfort and creativity as people kept space in their homes but reached out to others. "Country Roads" represented a sense of shared values and togetherness in a time of necessary but frightening separation.

Its use was specific to place in West Virginia, as one might expect. The song drew West Virginians together as it has for fifty years, but the unseen threat of a deadly virus added a layer of resonance. As COVID-19 spread across the eastern seaboard, West Virginia held out. A meme (see Figure 1) in early March 2020 showed the entire nation blocked in red, except West Virginia, with no confirmed cases, and read "Corona virus apparently fears the following: pepperoni rolls, John Denver, guns and Jesus" (E. Fisher).

On March 17, West Virginia became the last state in the nation to recognize a first COVID case. In following days, Governor Jim Justice declared a stay-at-home order that limited nonessential activities, closed nonessential businesses, and outlined prohibited activities, such as group recreation and social gatherings. At the end of March, Justice signed another executive order, requiring visitors or travelers from out of state to quarantine for fourteen days. Justice's language, consistently, related that we are "all in this together," but separately, at home. Not surprisingly, "Country Roads" was used in many official communications. For example, West Virginia Coronavirus Czar Clay Marsh frequently signed blog posts and updates with "Almost Heaven," and also reminded readers to sing the chorus of "Country Roads" while handwashing to get to twenty

FIGURE 1 A meme from early March 2020, showing West Virginia as the last state in the nation with a confirmed COVID case, references John Denver (and "Country Roads")

---

seconds. US senator Joe Manchin tweeted the lyrics for use in proper handwashing in March 2020, as well (Figure 2).

West Virginia had the most vulnerable population to COVID-19 in the nation. Many were elderly, health-affected, and immunocompromised, and "Country Roads" was used as a point of connection to protect the entire population in official and popular ways.

Country musician Brad Paisley performed live on Facebook and Instagram on March 19, asking folks to stay at home. The archived performance and comments show many requests for "Country Roads." In response, Paisley reiterates the risk for West Virginia's aging population and references Manchin's tweet, saying, "why I want West Virginians to be diligent right now is our population is a disproportionately large portion of people over 70 and are really,

🎼 Country Roads
🎵 Take Me Home
🎶 To The Place
🎵 I Belong
🎶 West Virginia
🎵 Mountain Mama
🎶 Take Me Home
🎵 Country Roads

Sing along while washing your hands so we can all do our part to stop the spread of #COVID19 & other diseases. Find more information at manchin.senate.gov/coronavirus.

HELP PREVENT CORONAVIRUS IN WEST VIRGINIA

WASH YOUR HANDS OFTEN FOR AT LEAST 20 SECONDS, OR ABOUT THE TIME IT TAKES TO SING THE CHORUS OF "TAKE ME HOME, COUNTRY ROADS."

3:01 PM · Mar 10, 2020 · Twitter Web App

FIGURE 2 A tweet from Senator Joe Manchin uses "Country Roads" to promote proper handwashing

really high risk. So, we really want to make sure that the young people in the state do their best to distance, and at the same time we want people to stay home in that state, and let the thing burn out." Paisley then moves into "Country Roads," embellishing on the guitar. As he begins to sing, the comment thread explodes: "Mountaineer strong," and "my favorite song," in a cascade of identified cities, gold and blue hearts, and memories of loved ones who also loved West Virginia. After finishing, Paisley references the way "Country Roads" captures home for everyone, "Boy does home mean different things to all of us now. It's always been something that's a big deal to people, I think, getting to go home when you haven't been there in a while, or connect with your family in your house, or in your home, but wow, this is something right now." The "something" to which Paisley refers is hiraeth.

As communities continued to quarantine, Zoom videos of "Country Roads" spread almost as quickly as the virus. Alderson-Broaddus University's acapella singing group released an alumni video in May 2020, for example. Of course, WVU's response to COVID used "Country Roads" as a uniting text. Another video reference to handwashing posted in early March 2020 shows the Mountaineer, WVU's mascot, entering a public restroom. He checks his beard in the mirror above the sink as a voice instructs him to wash his hands for at least twenty seconds to mitigate the spread of disease. "For reference," the voice says, "try humming the chorus of 'Country Roads.'" The Mountaineer pumps several squirts of soap from a dispenser labeled with the trademarked "Flying WV," turns on the water, and commences scrubbing his hands and humming while a timer ticks from twenty down to zero in the corner of the screen. The video ends with the Mountaineer exiting the restroom, grinning into the camera, and offering a double thumbs-up. "Great job, Mountaineer," says the voice.

West Virginia University posted another video on March 28, 2020, after campus had officially been closed due to COVID. Entitled "Mountaineer Nation Sings COUNTRY ROADS!" it begins with a clip borrowed from Brad Paisley's living room concert, and features other prominent Mountaineers, each singing a line or two. These singers, some with more confidence and/or talent than others, all decked in WVU gear, include coaches and their families, administrators, the Mountaineer, athletes, alumni, celebrities, police officers, state senators, and others. The song ends with Paisley, once again, strumming his guitar, Mountaineer football helmet in the background.

Other versions of "Country Roads," with people singing together but apart, originated beyond the boundaries of West Virginia. One purports to show a neighborhood in Italy singing "Country Roads," and while the video's authenticity is questionable, hiraeth remains, so much so that the video went viral. British opera singer Jonathan Antoine used the clip as an introduction to his sweeping, orchestral version, "Country Roads (A Music Video for Our Time)" in April 2020. Antoine's video begins with ten seconds of that viral one: Denver's version of the song plays over the video footage of Italians on balconies, purportedly singing together, with a caption and the hashtag "#AlmostHeaven." The scene then transitions into images of medical professionals in hospitals, masked families, empty city streets. As music builds, images of the pandemic fall away as people embrace, dance, climb mountains, and hold hands in front of sunsets. These suggestions of a return to normal life are interposed with video of Antoine performing "Country Roads," backed by a choir before a full theater audience. The suggestion of togetherness and perseverance is clear in the choice of both the song and video arrangement; the longed-for home in this version is a return to safety and community.

Others, including YouTubers and celebrities, used the song as well, resonating with audiences worldwide. These examples show that "Country Roads" is about hope, community, and a longing for the normalcy of a post-pandemic world, one in which West Virginia is neither origin nor destination, but a space of hope and imagination. Singing together is powerful; singing "Country Roads" together takes us home, wherever we are.

PASTORAL ROMANCE AND WEST VIRGINIA AS A COUNTRY MUSIC EVERYPLACE

This is a song that can serve many purposes: It helps us mourn and celebrate, it offers up solace and hope, it gives us words, and it leaves us longing. This function of music is characteristic of how we might see many songs used in West Virginia and other parts of the region, as well as around the world. Heather Ann Ackley Bean addresses process philosophy as part of Appalachian musical culture, explaining that "God and the world, the sacred and secular, are deeply interrelated" so that "the ordinary and the extraordinary, the natural and the supernatural," are deeply interrelated in Appalachian belief, with music being a way of tapping into spirit. That is exactly what "Country Roads" does, but in a way that transcends region and resonates across the globe. "All popular music is theological, since religion pervades every aspect of culture," and this makes popular music an important lens for studying not just history but human values (Bean 13, 45). Certainly, we can use "Country Roads" as a lens to understand what is important not just to West Virginians but also to any listener from any place who feels called home, the ubiquitous experience of hiraeth.

In more direct reference to the song, Carissa Massey, in her research on Appalachian identity, addresses the overarching themes in "Country Roads" explicitly in terms of created space and "a return to place of origin or identity. The mythical landscape—with its winding roads, mountains, and misty horizons—is a place of family, love, and longed-for cultural practices." West Virginia in the song is a substitute for the listener's home and "an extension of this myth of a transcendent landscape," which contributes "to a new myth of Appalachia," one of natural settings, a return to the land and a fantasy of the ancestral home (C. Massey 128). Tied to this sense of romanticized rurality, as Massey and others point out, Appalachia is perceived as a preserved pocket of unique culture, where people speak variations of "old English" and continue forgotten traditions in backwoods hollows. These impressions exclude certain voices and deny the complexity of actual lived experience.

Likewise, Emily Satterwhite finds the literary vision of Appalachia is traditionally pastoral, non-threatening, and grounded in both solitude and community (*Dear*). Similarly, Parks Lanier distinguishes Appalachian poetic characteristics through three areas of concern, including "the political, the pastoral, and the personal." The political stance is taken "in the service of a cause," the pastoral stance is "intensely lyrical in celebrating the mountains and mountain people," and the personal stance is one of the poet's own experience within the Appalachian setting (Lanier 191). As we will discuss in later chapters, musicians and writers in and from Appalachia may tend to take up political and personal stances, writing for narrower audiences and developing their work for functional purposes. Lanier argues that the "risk" of the pastoral stance is "too much nostalgia and sentimentality" (191), but it is exactly this sentimentality that evokes hiraeth in "Country Roads."

These themes are particularly prevalent in country music, so "Country Roads" calls upon this tradition, too. In his book *Country Roads: How Country Came to Nashville*, music historian Brian Hinton explores the theme of pastoralism, tracing tropes back to Cecil Sharp and others who traveled throughout Appalachia collecting folk music recordings in the early 1900s. Songcatchers transposed music they extracted into books and pressed it into records, all the while making money, assumptions, and claims that did not benefit the people and places they encountered. These records influenced American perceptions about Appalachia and shaped a foundation for a musical genre. Hinton refers to these published collections of oral tradition as "a songbag that continues to be raided to this day," full of "echoes of the future" (59–60). Books and records of folk songs, with their pastoral themes of love, mountains, and human resonance, lay the foundation for modern country music.

"Country Roads" takes up these themes, as does much of Denver's music, continuing a tradition grounded in the conception of the mountains (and mountain people by extension) as both beautiful and complex, a space of independence and, to early settlers, "a new Eden" (Hinton 26). Of "Country Roads" specifically, Hinton explicitly draws a parallel, writing, "it is not too great a leap of the imagination from [the folk collections] to John Denver's song, 'Take Me Home, Country Roads,' written two centuries later but with much the same message." However, Denver adds another layer, "a modern note of regret and exile. Like Wordsworth's daffodils, the 'misty taste of moonshine' is recollected in the city, brought back to his mind by a song on the radio" (Hinton 26–27). The added theme of placelessness, loneliness, is part of what makes the song so flexible. Barbara Klemt, who wrote her dissertation on Denver, also compares his lyrics to Wordsworth's poetry. Denver told her in an interview, "The nature references are consciously incorporated," and Klemt shows how those references contribute to the universality of the tunes, adding romanticism to rurality and nostalgia for daily living (58). The romance, pastoralism, and perceived simplicity of rural spaces provoke intense longing.

Home is in the natural world in country music as well as in the pastoral tradition, and rurality is reflected as a space of return as well as escape. Music scholars Connell and Gibson characterize the country pastoral as a landscape of redemption, refuge, and salvation: "Home and homecoming, the essence of yearning, is the charter of country music." The call to home found in country genres invites us to sit a spell, to warm up by the fire, to be comforted within idealized homecoming. The home to which the speaker returns in country music generally is one of green fields, simple purity—pastoral space—but one so romanticized that the difficult realities of the day simply do not exist. Regarding Denver, Connell and Gibson write, "Nothing epitomises (sic) this perspective more than various saccharine lyrics" and, "above all, the bestselling 'Country Roads, Take Me Home'" (81, 79). The repeated refrain of "take me home" emphasizes return and belonging, the deep longing of hiraeth rather than West Virginia as a tangible, actual, and complicated destination.

"Country Roads" is a quintessential country song, despite its pop packaging, which continues to make it a crossover success. The song represents three qualities, or "staples," characteristic of country music, including a "sense of the mountains holding an ancient wisdom, unavailable elsewhere," a loved one embodied by landscape, and pilgrimage or "journey" that happens on literal country roads (Hinton 27). These elements make the song modern and timeless, sacred and secular, general and specific. "Country Roads" combines pastoral and natural themes of the earliest country music with more modern concerns of destination and return, of longing for home and homecoming. These themes are particularly relevant for listeners who moved away from home as part of migration patterns in the years leading up to the song's release. The emphasis here, of course, is the mountain home, but the space described in "Country Roads" is symbolic of an imagined space. As in literature, Satterwhite discusses, the "Mountain setting functions as an aesthetic feature more so than as a cultural or material landscape" (*Dear* 185). The Blue Ridge Mountains of "Country Roads" are poetic and nostalgic, vivid in image, but mostly absent geographically from the materiality of West Virginia.

The magnetic pull of hiraeth evokes a journey of return, along country roads real or metaphorical. Dreams of pilgrimage in popular music, grounded in modern mobility, allow listeners "voyages of escape and discovery," into "open space" and "freedom, restlessness, and divorce from dreary conventional lives," especially in country music. When a charismatic tune combines with memorable lyrics, a song about a place can impress upon us a perception of that place. As a cultural product, "Lyrics, often enhanced by the music … provide both reflections on the past, contemporary and future worlds, and escapes to them. These 'other worlds' through alternative imaginary spaces, arise from existing worlds" and can shape everyday realities of place (Connell and Gibson 83, 72). "Country Roads," with its flexible imagery and nostalgic words, creates an imagined world where things are not so hard, where we are loved timelessly, where home is a mothering, nurturing space of belonging and longing.

"Country Roads" moves us to return home, even if it is not West Virginia, even if that home is imagined rather than real. This is a common trope in popular and sacred music. It is a product of the way music represents cultural geography, creating and always renegotiating space, so that "nostalgia for lost and distant places, dreams of making it elsewhere, concerns over problem places . . . or simply evocations of idyllic landscapes . . . are all part of the ability of music to transport listeners away from their ordinary lives" (Connell and Gibson 73). The sense of the pastoral in "Country Roads" is evocative of simpler times, natural space, beauty and ease, and it exists within a larger pattern of musical and literary traditions, one that is manifest in the way we write and speak about Appalachia. "Country Roads," then, mentions West Virginia, but it is not *about* West Virginia. It leverages a tangible place to evoke a sense of nostalgia and myth, as well as a felt homesickness, tapping into places both material and symbolic. This is the kind of longing described by one writer as "a call to go to the place that brings him as emotionally close as possible to the place his spirit lives" (Kielar). Hiraeth compels us not to an actual place, but to existential home. Nonetheless, "Country Roads" names a real place, and in its fifty years, it has become an integral component in the rhetoric of West Virginian identity, an outside naming that West Virginians embrace for a range of purposes and audiences.

THE VIEW FROM JEFFERSON'S ROCK

The small town of Harpers Ferry predates West Virginia's statehood by one hundred years. Established in 1763 and now a National Historic Park, Harpers Ferry hosts a mix of monuments, museums, boutiques, restaurants, and outdoor recreation. Visitors can hike Maryland Heights and see Civil War artillery mounds; clamber down rock outcroppings and watch trains cross the river and vultures circle the sky; visit the John Brown Wax Museum; read the history of Storer College; put in a kayak; ride a bike on the C&O Canal; sip local microbrews; and wander across the cobblestones with hand-dipped ice cream in a fresh waffle cone. It is a space of contradictions, full of DC day-trippers and history buffs, home to the Appalachian Trail Headquarters and several adventure outfitters. Traces and echoes of insurrection, education, and civil reconstruction are tempered by candy shops and craft stores, international tourists, and foodies sampling local wine and honey.

High above cobbled streets, at the top of a set of irregular rock-carved steps, stands St. Peter's Church, a gothic structure of stained glass and stone, survivor of the Civil War. Its pointed spires reach toward open sky. Behind St. Peter's is a second steep climb to Jefferson's Rock, where one can see the Shenandoah below and Virginia's Blue Ridge rising in the distance. It is not difficult to imagine this space two centuries ago, when Thomas Jefferson looked out in awe and wrote, in his *Notes on the State of Virginia*,

> The passage of the Patowmac through the Blue Ridge is perhaps one of the most stupendous scenes in nature. You stand on a very high point of land. On your right comes up the Shenandoah, having ranged along the foot of the mountain an hundred miles to seek a vent. On your left approaches the Patowmac, in quest of a passage also. In the moment of their junction they rush together against the mountain, rend it asunder, and pass off to the sea. (17)

To Jefferson, this view of the Blue Ridge at the confluence of the Potomac and Shenandoah was a call to explore, "inviting you, as it were, from the riot and tumult roaring around, to pass through the breach and participate of the calm below. Here the eye ultimately composes itself; and that way too the road happens actually to lead" (18). Jefferson's Rock remains a scene of rugged beauty, where the road leads in one direction toward Maryland and DC and in the other farther into West Virginia. This is the only place "Country Roads," is geographically accurate (Figure 3).

FIGURE 3 Jefferson's Rock at Harpers Ferry (photo by author)

Harpers Ferry, with its mix of historic and modern buildings, the pay-by-credit-card parking meters alongside John Brown's Fort, is a complex place. Standing at Jefferson's Rock, I can look out and consider Jefferson, himself a complicated figure, an unrepentant slaveholder, amid a space known for antislavery insurrection. I can imagine his unbroken view, at least until a line of traffic crosses the bridge, or several teenagers crowd around the overlook taking selfies. Bill Danoff described to me a moment he experienced in Harpers Ferry a year or so after "Country Roads" came out. He was wading in the Potomac, and a girl with a guitar started playing "Country Roads" on the riverbank. The place, the naming of the place, the creation of a space happened in that moment. For Danoff, it felt like magic more than coincidence.

All places have complicated stories to tell. Landscape itself is an authored space when people inhabit it, and narratives of place affect our perceptions. The appeal of the simplistic, sweet story wins in "Country Roads." The place shaped the song, but also the song has shaped the place (perhaps more so). "Country Roads" redefined West Virginia, made it more visible, but it is just a projection—not reality. "Country Roads" shaped West Virginians, too; it became part of the language of our identities.

A PORTABLE REMINDER OF IDENTITY IN PLACE

The sense of identity and belonging in "Country Roads" shifts depending on context, speaker, and listener. In certain situations, it is used to declare identity and include us as listeners. We can see this in situations of affiliation, as when an out-of-town band plays "Country Roads" for a local audience, and the crowd goes wild. Several years ago, I saw Old Crow Medicine Show, a Grammy Award–winning string band, play in a nearly full concert theater at West Virginia University. After performing many original favorites, they played "Country Roads." From the first notes, the audience was on their feet, singing along. Many listeners were even visibly moved, hands on hearts, eyes tearful.

West Virginia musician Aristotle Jones, whose album *Appalachian Soul Man* contains a version of state anthem "The West Virginia Hills" that incorporates "Country Roads," told me that he thinks "Country Roads" appeals to West Virginians because of the explicit naming of place combined with generality:

> As far as the rhetoric goes, it works. It works on a very basic level of what West Virginia is. The inclusiveness of it—it works for West Virginians because it has our name in the chorus. You get to sing it several times. You can be in a bar anywhere in the world, and somebody's singing 'West Virginia,' you know? It's great. It's exciting. Who doesn't love that? It gives you an ice breaker.

As an "ice breaker," the song provides a glimpse of recognition, a glance into a mirror. It is also general enough that anyone can relate so that the West Virginia of "Country Roads" becomes everyplace. This affirmation tells us we are not alone, that there are others like us here, experiencing hiraeth, looking homeward.

This identity performance, affiliation, and affirmation also occurs when West Virginians hear the song traveling outside West Virginia. Nearly every West Virginian who has traveled out-of-state has a story to tell about hearing "Country Roads." For example, a 2012 *Charleston Gazette* article documents places West Virginians reported hearing "Country Roads," including in a German restaurant in Connecticut and in a pub in Ireland, where the singer claimed it was "an unofficial Irish National anthem." The article goes on to reference performances by a Swiss Oompah band, at "a baggage claim in a Chinese airport, by a gondolier in Venice, in an amusement park in Australia, and on a boat in Mexico" (Robinson 1F).

My research prompted stories of "Country Roads" in Korean Karaoke Bars, street fairs in London, festivals in California, on a train in France, in Scotland. Survey participants reported hearing the song in Greece, Hawaii, Wisconsin, Italy, Sweden, Germany, Niagara Falls, Russia, China, Honduras, the Caribbean, the Philippines, Cyprus, South Africa, Hong Kong, and Holland. One person claims to have heard it in "every freakin' bar in the tristate area," and another at "every piano bar, ever." A single respondent sums up the experience in general, reporting the song in "Rome, Prague, Oaxaca, Tulum, all over Mexico really, Costa Rica, Panama, Guatemala, Belgium, London, Wales, Ireland, Hungary, basically all over Europe, Nova Scotia, [and] all over the US."

Beyond stories of hearing the song, many of my survey respondents recounted being gifted with (or perhaps subjected to) spontaneous performances when people discovered they were from West Virginia. One person told a story that illustrates this well:

> I was an exchange student, and I met some other exchange students from Spain. When I said that I was from WV, one goes "COUNTRY ROADS!!" and started singing it! That actually became my nickname. Then, one night the Spaniard told me

he wanted to show me something—he had 3 other Spaniards, 3 Frenchman, 2 people from Botswana, and a few friends from Asia all sing Country Roads to me. I asked one of them after if they all knew it previously, and he replied with "No, but he paid us in beer to learn it!"

"Country Roads" is a marker of home, a declaration of love of home away from home, and a way of making connection that also taps into longing.

Another respondent recounted hearing "Country Roads" performed "at the Clark County fair in Nevada by a man with a guitar." She was stricken with emotion: "I was pregnant and I cried." Like my parents in that bar in Utah, this woman felt called home, and, unable to return even while carrying the next generation, she was awash with longing. Stories like this illustrate the power of song to transport. A portable reminder of identity and place, "Country Roads" brings home to us when we are far from home, and, at the same time, it helps us to identify who we are and to find our people, including those we elect to office.

POLITICAL IDENTITY RHETORIC AND PUBLIC PERFORMANCE

Identity is to some degree defined institutionally—birth certificates, passports, drivers' licenses, and other official documents identify us and tie us to place legally. Current West Virginian drivers' licenses have "Almost Heaven" embossed on the back in pale blue block text surrounded by stylized silhouettes of blue mountain ridges; the lyric of the song is integrated into official government documents, taken up by state organizations.

In political rhetoric, Appalachia is depicted as a land of men, miners, and working-class whites, and "Country Roads," aligns with that depiction. However, "The real forgotten working-class citizens of Appalachia," Elizabeth Catte claims, "much like the rest of the nation, are home health workers and Dollar General employees. They're more likely to be women, and their exemption from the stability offered by middle-class employment is not a recent phenomenon." Media and popular culture perceptions of Appalachia are imagined, fueled by dependency narratives, economic exploitation, and outside descriptions, "a monolithic 'other America' that defies narratives of progress" (Catte 12, 22). This is true in political representations of West Virginia, and "Country Roads" is used to further these perceptions, across the political spectrum, in national, statewide, and local events.

There is no better identity rhetoric for romancing West Virginian voters. Local candidates hold potlucks where bluegrass musicians sing it; state representatives allude to it in their social media posts and campaigns. The Mountain Mamas Political Action Committee supports progressive women candidates in the state of West Virginia; on their website contributors can buy a women's fit "Mountain Mama" t-shirt. The Country Roads Political Action Committee, based in Charleston and affiliated with former senator Joe Manchin (whose boat is named "Almost Heaven"), contributes to candidates with diverse party affiliations across the country. President Barack Obama used the song in a Charleston town hall meeting in 2015 (McKelvey). Outside West Virginia, Mike Pence's campaign played the song during a 2020 campaign rally in a Florida retirement community (Wilder and Weber). The song is also used to comment on West Virginia's politics, as in a 2021 *The Late Show with Stephen Colbert* video, which criticized senator Manchin for opposing a climate package in the wake of monumental flooding. The video parodies "Country Roads" and depicts Manchin accompanied by a cartoon crab aboard the senator's boat, singing "Almost SeaWorld" and "Wet Virginia, Mermaid Mama."

Contemporary media portrayals of West Virginia draw from historical patterns in literature and cultural texts advocating Appalachian exceptionalism dating back at least one hundred years. "Country Roads," with its romantic portrayal, is part of that rhetorical tradition. The song came to consciousness in a particular way during the 2016 election cycle and was used by both sides to create affiliations with West Virginians, whose votes mattered. In that election, Appalachia became "Trump Country" and a "Mecca for journalists wanting to commune with Trump's people," many of whom "came armed with hillbilly stereotypes that constrained their view and deeply shaped the stories they told" (Hathaway 193). The song accompanied speeches and enhanced political rhetoric on every side during 2016, focusing attention on West Virginia arguably as much as the Kennedy-Nixon race in 1960. Sometimes, it was initiated by the audience, as in a rally in April, ahead of his primary win in West Virginia, when Bernie Sanders spoke to a packed arena. One account describes how Sanders's supporters "sang 'Country Roads' like a mega church choir" (Nash). Other times, it was taken up by candidates' language, as in references to the state as "Almost Heaven," which Hillary Clinton made in campaign visits. After losing in 2016, Clinton published a memoir, *What Happened*, with an entire chapter dedicated to Appalachia; that chapter is titled "Country Roads." While these examples show supporters and candidates using the song in reference, we also see it used as intentional and explicit rhetoric, played at rallies for the purpose of creating affiliation.

On May 5, 2016, presidential candidate Donald Trump used "Country Roads" as an entrance theme in a Charleston Civic Center rally. Footage of the event shows Trump climbing a set of metal steps onto a stage, waving to a cheering crowd, pumping his fist, and pointing at adoring attendees in acknowledgment of their "Trump Digs Coal" signs. As he approaches the podium, about a minute and a half into the song, the music stops, but the crowd keeps singing. In response, Trump raises his hands like a choir director conducting the audience. Within the first minutes, the content of the speech turns to coal, coal miners, and how Donald Trump "has always been fascinated by the mines." Later, representatives from the West Virginia Coal association present him with a hardhat, which he dons for a moment, picking up an imaginary shovel and pantomiming digging imaginary coal. Trump promises that if he is elected, coal miners will be "working their asses off." After speaking for more than forty-five minutes, Trump tosses the hardhat somewhere off camera, and disappears into the crowd as "Country Roads" begins to play again. Attendees can be seen taking photographs, waving signs, and (of course) singing.

It is impossible to ignore the way the song bookends Trump's rally and the way participants join in singing it naturally, almost automatically, as an expression of celebration, support, and identity. At political events, "Country Roads" is an expression of hope and longing for a better future, tied firstly to identity of place. In a 2018 article, rhetoric scholars Will and Krista Kurlinkus discuss Trump's speech specifically as part of a "rhetoric of nostalgia" that helps to form a "model for who we think we wish we were." In their analysis of Trump's speech, they show how imagery and constructed ideas create nostalgia as something culturally experienced rather than personally lived. They discuss the rhetoric of Appalachia as influenced by nostalgic story that is constructed, generational, and "an inescapable part of all identity formation and memory" (Kurlinkus and Kurlinkus 90, 108). Surprisingly, the authors do not mention "Country Roads," either in their analysis of Trump's speech or in their discussion of the literatures of Appalachia that contribute to cultural constructions of a nostalgic sense of place.

The day after Trump's speech in which "Country Roads" was featured so prominently, administrators on the John Denver Facebook page posted: "In response to the comments and calls received since Donald Trump's campaign played 'Take Me Home, Country Roads' at a rally in West Virginia yesterday, John Denver's Estate would like fans to know that though politicians are not required to ask permission for music they use at public rallies, Denver's Estate requests that all candidates refrain from using his music." Despite this statement, West Virginians felt seen and heard. Political use of the song is a way of speaking the language of West Virginian identity. As Bill Danoff explained to me, musicians have little say in how their songs are used politically, and taking a stand for or against a song's use amounts to taking a position on the candidate or generating publicity for the artist. "The thing's around, people can use it," but artists "don't have any legal recourse to say, 'you can't play' whatever the song is" (Danoff, personal interview). Artists do take positions about how their music is used, as when Denver's estate attempted to distance his legacy from a politically divisive candidate romancing the state the song purports to be about. The effort had little measurable effect on voters' perceptions of the candidate or the song, however.

"Country Roads" is an integral part of the rhetoric of West Virginian identity, bringing forth nostalgia for what we think we may have been, hope for what we could be, and hiraeth for what we wish we were. As such, its use is flexible and can be applied by any candidate. Geographer Marco Antonsich's review of the literature suggests that an individual's sense of belonging in place is determined by awareness of the self, relationships with others, shared culture, participation in economy, legal citizenship, and time spent in place; it is the individual's sense of connection to place and others there. But politics of belonging incorporate more complex relationalities, including those of power and the ability of people to be accepted and granted belonging. Belonging politics imply that there are in groups and out groups: those who belong and those who are "other." Furthermore, Antonsich shows how belonging is constructed, dynamic, and collaborative among people engaged in shared community. "Country Roads" is interesting in belonging politics in West Virginia because it signals shared place-identity for those who are used to being othered; it is known cultural rhetoric. The use of the song in political arenas adds another layer by evoking both a sense of togetherness and a sense of affinity, incorporating the politician or group using the song into the in group, even if temporarily.

In campaign music, the best theme songs inspire hope and evoke feelings of universal connection. The trend of using popular music for political campaigns, which began in the 1970s and 1980s, saw hopeful candidates using preexisting songs in their entirety. The use of already well-known and well-liked songs creates an association with the candidate in voters' minds, especially when they are played strategically at different points in a campaign (Schoening and Kasper 163–64). In the instance of "Country Roads," the association becomes less about policy, more about place-belonging—the feeling of hiraeth in general, and to West Virginia specifically. This resonates especially in the context of the state as imagined by voters and candidates, "for places are always imagined in the context of political-economic determinations that have a logic of their own" (Gupta and Ferguson 11). A candidate who loves our anthem will surely do what is best for the state.

Political use of a song like "Country Roads" in West Virginia reflects what folklorist Tim Cresswell describes as places within discourses of power "[that] express themselves as discourses of normality." Some aspects of this discourse, like those in the media, or in this case, politics, have more leverage than others and can "ascribe meanings to place in the language of common sense," and these discourses can be "ideological insofar as they attempt to define what is good and true, what exists, and what is possible (the limits to change) and insofar as they serve the interests of powerful groups." Control of the conversation directly affects who can "participate in the construction and dissemination of meanings for places and thus places themselves. The meaning of place, then, is (in part) created through a discourse that sets up a process of differentiation (between us and them)" (Cresswell 60). This "us" and "them" differentiation is especially relevant in political campaigns, particularly as conversations have become more divisive and partisan. "Country Roads" signals that a candidate sees a West Virginian "us" that includes the candidate as an affiliated identity. This use also ties directly to legacies of outside naming and ownership in West Virginia and Appalachia.

The political narrative suggested by the use of "Country Roads" interweaves a historical pattern of stories about West Virginia and Appalachia, one that resists the power of people to name themselves or decide their best interests. Amanda Hayes, in her book on Appalachian rhetoric writes, "the story we are so often told, by the extractive industries, media, and even the schools, is that those politicians who 'get' us have our best interests at heart." Persuasive messages conveyed through these stories prevent us from being able to "evaluate closely what those interests, both the politicians' and our own, actually are" so that we need to "think about what our rhetoric is, what it indicates, and how it can be used for, or against, our interests" (Hayes 186). Certainly "Country Roads" is part of that rhetorical pattern that relies on emotional connections and political invisibility and about which we must think more critically.

Some scholars imply a vision far more sinister. Heather Ransom argues that, viewed through the lens of Stockholm Syndrome, economic and political movements controlled by outside forces leave victims (here, West Virginians) powerless to respond productively. Ransom documents the ways in which outside interests in Appalachia have controlled the economy, government (through lobbies and campaign contributions), and educational structures to promote extraction industries, owned from the outside. This, too, is part of the historical pattern West Virginians face (Ransom 109–10). To feel seen by a candidate is persuasive in a media environment that so often brushes West Virginians aside, or worse, depicts us as caricature or stereotype. When a candidate captures hearts using such a familiar text, West Virginians feel seen, despite the candidate's agenda. However, as Elizabeth Catte reminds us, "The shared story and analogues at work are not about people, but about power" so that "credibility falls easily to those given the privilege of defining *who* or *what* Appalachian is. It also shows the rewards that fall to individuals, universally men and exclusively white, regardless of the company they keep" (93). When "Country Roads" is used as state narrative, it perpetuates political legacies and soundtracks a historical story of silence. Still, West Virginians participate in using the song as an expression of political identity—even at the statehouse.

A June 16, 2017, video clip posted by WOWK13 News in Charleston shows a two-and-a-half-minute performance by a seven-year-old boy and his grandfather, who play together an instrumental rendition of "Country Roads." The accompanying news piece identifies the duo as Liam and Phil Farley, from Chapmanville in Logan County (Fitzwater). Papaw Phil, in jeans and a blue T-shirt, strums his guitar, swaying gently. Liam, dressed in khaki pants and a striped polo shirt, hair carefully parted, furrows his brow in concentration as he coaxes the melody out of his fiddle, which seems huge in his small hands. As the song ends, the room fills with applause, and the boy, seemingly self-conscious, looks to his grandfather, who bends at the waist, makes eye contact with the boy, says something unheard by the camera, and nods. The boy moves to begin another song, but his grandfather motions for him to wait. The applause continues. The grandfather smiles broadly, lifts his own hands to clap, and stretches them out toward Liam in a gesture of pride. Standing behind the pair are officials of the West Virginia House of Delegates, including then-Clerk Stephen Harrison, who reaches for a tissue, and wipes his eyes. Other members of the House rise in standing ovation. This is the power of "Country Roads" to move West Virginians: It signals belonging.

Human sense of belonging in place is more than physical; it can be spiritual and emotional, too, since "locales are not necessarily limited by the physical world but can be bounded cognitively through perceptions of belonging and exclusion" (Shutika 11). Belonging is constructed not only through being and identity in place, but also through rituals and cultural practices. In this sense, collective singing of a place-anthem like "Country Roads" does not just create an event; the song pools into a liminal valley of place-making, in which West Virginians can come together in community and recognition of shared identity. This anthem is a single familiar text that denotes place and people, mostly devoid of negativity. It is no wonder West Virginians embrace it, but it is important to explore the implications of an identity symbol that misses complexities of person and place. I wonder whether we can use "Country Roads" not just as cause for celebration, but also as an invitation for dialogue about what it means to be West Virginian, to be from a place (or in a place) that some people know and see only through song, even as we embrace that song to help the nation know us. This speaks to the need to better understand rhetorics of place.

Political scientist Benedict Anderson writes that the widespread acquisition of literacy made possible an imagined community devoid of specific location in time, but centered in place through local texts like newspapers, bulletins, et cetera. Although Anderson frames this affiliative tie to place in terms of shared print language, like nationalist documents, pledges, or publications, we can apply this underlying argument to other texts, like songs and anthems. This multilayered, affiliative community is constructed and imaginary, yet we feel it in real and powerful ways. The text "Country Roads" ties us to place and community, globally and locally.

The prevalence of an international music industry makes this deeply felt but imagined landscape and community wider by tapping into the notion of the local and distributing it for global audiences. "Country Roads" as a school anthem at West Virginia University creates a common experience on campus, a shared map of understanding and identity as Mountaineers. Widening out, "Country Roads" as a state anthem creates a common text through which West Virginians can experience belonging and home, even an inaccurately described one. It is infused into the rhetoric of West Virginian identity, and this meaning is revealed when we look at how West Virginians use it to respond, to resist, and to simply exist.

"COUNTRY ROADS" AS A WEST VIRGINIAN RESPONSE TO NEGATIVITY

Cultural conceptions and produced images affect people's lives. To illustrate, an anecdote: In November 1954, Jamison Coal and Coke Company's No. 9 mine in Farmington, West Virginia, was rocked by an explosion caused by a buildup of methane. Sixteen men died. My grandfather, Harry Dunmire, was among them. In the hours that followed the explosion, rescue teams from around the region, community members, volunteer groups, and press flocked to the town. My newly-widowed grandmother, Mercia Dunmire, was a teacher at No. 9 in a one-room schoolhouse. She told the painful story of being visited by national press, who, among other questions, wanted to know why so many of the children were wearing shoes.

A 1959 article in *The Nation* documents a similar school visit in southern West Virginia, describing "shaggy, shoeless children of the unwanted—the 'hillbilly' coal miners who have been displaced by machines and largely left to rot on surplus government food and the small doles of a half-hearted welfare state" (Ernst and Drake 3). This vivid description, meant to evoke sympathy, perpetuates stereotypes that existed then and persist today in what Todd Snyder calls a "rhetorical tradition" that "profoundly affects the way Appalachians view themselves and the connections to the outside world.... To be West Virginian is to be Appalachian, which is to be *othered*" (Snyder, *Rhetoric* 31). This otherness creates contrast, a comparison that tells West Virginians we are separate, unfortunate others, the object of jokes. We West Virginians know these jokes from T-shirts and bumper stickers, movies, Halloween costumes, and reality TV; they leave a cultural and rhetorical residue that settles on our daily lives. "Country Roads" is part of that "dark and dusty" residue.

West Virginians illustrate how this rhetoric sifts into everyday conversations. My friend Beth tells a story about the first time she realized that being from West Virginia made her something other. As a teenager, she visited a sleepaway camp with attendees from all over the country. During an introduction session, when she told the group she was from West Virginia, another camper said, derisively, "I'm sorry." Everyone laughed, and Beth learned, in that moment, that such laughter was acceptable. These interactions are not limited to childhood. Sarah Mullens is a West Virginian entrepreneur and journalist who has written about "Country Roads" and its complicated relationship to the state. In an interview with me, she recalled a meeting "in a Fortune 500 office in Manhattan," where she faced a hillbilly joke. She explained, "I was the last one to sit down, and a guy had asked me where I was from on the walk in. I told him I was from West Virginia, and he's like 'we don't have any moonshine, but can I offer you some water.'" Mullens was incredulous and embarrassed, and this feeling was amplified because the speaker felt justified. She told me, "if it were any other identities, like any other part of my identity . . . [l]everaging those stereotypes in that context would be wholly inappropriate but, for whatever reason, the Appalachian identity has just not risen to that level." West Virginians are the butt of jokes in all kinds of contexts.

I, too, have been in professional settings where, when people find out I am from West Virginia, they jokingly check my feet for shoes, or ask about my accent, or wonder whether my teeth are real, or casually drop a hillbilly joke. And almost as frequently, upon learning I am from West Virginia, someone might ask "Do you live near Richmond?" or some other city in Virginia. When West Virginians reveal our identities, the jokes follow. The alternative is invisibility—West Virginia becomes "western" Virginia—unrecognizable as its own state.

A cultural example: In October 2019, comedian Whitney Cummings appeared on *The Late Late Show with James Corden* and discussed her recently discovered West Virginia roots. Although CBS has since deleted this video, it is still available on the internet. Cummings says that the big difference between Virginia and West Virginia is "four chromosomes," that West Virginia is "the skin tag of Virginia." Cummings goes on to blame "hillbilly DNA" for her dental problems, attraction to greasy beards, and penchant for aggression, explaining that West Virginians are "pure crazy in the woods." As she speaks, show host Corden and fellow guest Bradley Whitford laugh. Perhaps the worst part of the segment is this: At the beginning, Cummings asks Corden "Do you know West Virginia?" Corden says, simply, "no." Cumming's sentiments, combined with Corden's ignorance, illustrate two ways West Virginians are perceived by American media at large: hilariously repugnant or completely invisible. We embody offensive stereotypes, or we simply do not exist.

Following the appearance, social media posts directed at Cummings, Corden, *The Late Late Show*, and CBS in general expressed public outcry from West Virginians. CBS removed the clips from their social media, and Cummings issued hollow apologies, indicating that it was "just a joke." Within a week or two, the incident appeared to be forgotten, but for West Virginians, it is just another incidence of the same preconceived imagery to which we have been subject since 1863.

Similarly, in December 2021, singer and actor Bette Midler, in response to West Virginia's senator Joe Manchin's vote on a congressional act, tweeted that Manchin, "wants us all to be just like his state, West Virginia. Poor, illiterate and strung out." Adding a more recent layer to the stereotype, Midler referenced the current issue of opioid addiction: Hillbillies are addicts. Public response included West Virginians who defended the state, invited Midler to visit, and condemned the use of disparaging stereotypes. Within an hour, Midler issued an apology, but the damage was done, the disconnect and tendency to jump to stereotypes and tropes clearly visible (see Figure 4).

In these situations, we see West Virginians leveraging "Country Roads" as a response to negativity. Many posts directed toward Cummings and Midler used hashtags #AlmostHeaven or #takemehome. One Twitter user responded to Cummings by posting a meme of John Denver singing "Country Roads." In these responses, "Country Roads" declares public visibility, claims positive identity, and shows that someone sees us favorably (since 1971, if not since 1863). "Country Roads" is a consistent marker of cultural rhetoric by which we can be identified (mostly) positively. It echoes in the gap between the hillbilly stereotype and cultural invisibility.

Stereotypes about Appalachian people in popular culture are "crafted in the entangled process of creativity, subjectiveness, misinterpretation, and social signification that comprise image production, dissemination, and reception" (C. Massey 16). In other words, how cultural artifacts present truth becomes truth, whether it is or not, and those perceptions influence how we see the world.

> **Tweet**
>
> **bettemidler** ✓ @BetteMidler · 21h
> What #JoeManchin, who represents a population smaller than Brooklyn, has done to the rest of America, who wants to move forward, not backward, like his state, is horrible. He sold us out. He wants us all to be just like his state, West Virginia. Poor, illiterate and strung out.
>
> 💬 15.8K   🔁 8.2K   ♡ 17.8K   ↑
>
> **OSU Football**
> @OSUFootball4
>
> Replying to @BetteMidler
>
> **Almost heaven, West Virginia**
> **Blue Ridge Mountains, Shenandoah River**
> **Life is old there, older than the trees**
> **Younger than the mountains, growin' like a breeze**
>
> 3:26 AM · Dec 21, 2021 · Twitter Web App

FIGURE 4 A reply to Bette Midler's tweet about West Virginia uses "Country Roads" as a response.

West Virginians, with limited options for positive perceptions, choose to present identity using "Country Roads" to point out "truth" that we can accept in the face of "truth" we cannot. When we are represented as shaggy and shoeless, deviant, drug-addled, and depraved, or simply invisible, we can call up "Country Roads" as a way of declaring a positive identity.

"Country Roads" as a Cultural Product and Expression of Resistance

The West Virginia joke draws consternation these days, but criticism of the hillbilly joke has been around longer than "Country Roads." The same year that the song was released, James Branscome argued the goal of American cultural and political institutions is assimilation and that Appalachian resistance to conformity makes us a target for ridicule so that "America is allowed to continue laughing at this minority group because on this, America agrees: hillbilly ain't beautiful" (1). Branscome argues that Appalachian independence and difference is resistance to definitions that promote homogeneity. Similarly, Appalachian studies scholar Phillip Obermiller documents the history of the urban hillbilly stereotype from the 1950s through the 1990s, finding that tropes remained persistent and prevalent, despite changing times. Obermiller writes that stereotyping urban Appalachians specifically is seen as acceptable, so "we might as well blame 'rednecks' and 'hillbillies,' because we can say whatever we want about them with impunity. In fact, reprimands for such behavior are usually mild, unspecific, and infrequent" (253). These stereotypes and behaviors persist.

Layered in is a perennial struggle for power in American culture—one that plays out in language and texts. Todd Snyder discusses the characterization of Appalachia from the outside as "connected to economic, social, and political domination that contain both overt and subversive rhetorical structures." Like Branscome, Snyder argues that the culture industry "manufactures rhetoric designed to promote and produce sameness." He goes on to write that uncritical adoption of "dominant characterizations" impacts real lives, that "Appalachianism is the history of a people subversively marketed by the rhetorical agenda of dominant social groups," and accepted "histories of Appalachia, are, therefore, suspect and must be called into question." These histories impact popular culture, extend into school curriculum, and pervade thinking in West Virginia (*Rhetoric* 26, 38, 27, 99). "Country Roads," within these frameworks, is symptomatic of uncritical subscription to a rhetoric of place that is a product of centuries of extractive practices. By this definition, "Country Roads" is a supremely successful cultural product. If Appalachia is a constructed social identity tied to economic and political discourse of place, "Country Roads" takes up this underlying practice or tradition of outside naming that West Virginia already accepts. Nonetheless, it is also part of a rhetoric of resistance and requires complex negotiations of behavior and response.

The energy it takes to resist outside naming takes a toll, personally and collectively. West Virginians may resist by fighting directly or indirectly, by drawing upon familiar resources and themes, by embracing stereotypes in part or even in whole. Kim Donehower writes that "Appalachians' resistance to the ways in which they have been written about and read by outsiders can take the form of seemingly confirming those representations. This is ultimately not an effective rhetorical strategy to change these tropes, but it is nonetheless a common reaction among the Othered" (23). Embracing stereotypes is a kind of resistance that can be defeating and reductionist since it conceals truths. This is relevant with both positive and negative stereotypes as neither recognizes complicated human identity. Embracing "Country Roads" is resistance to negative stereotypes and imagery. What it lacks in complexity it makes up for in familiarity. It is simple, recognizable, and globally visible.

My friend Rose tells a childhood story in contrast to Beth's experience at camp. During a family visit to Arizona, Rose wandered into a courtyard, where a band was playing "Country Roads." She felt, for the first time, a sense of place: They were singing about her home. She was seen and special rather than singled out and shamed. Many West Virginians feel this way when "Country Roads" plays, and we extend the feeling by playing it more. We learn the rhetorical move of embracing "Country Roads" early. Artifacts inspired by the song, made specifically for children, like onesies and nursery decorations, illustrate the power of impression and show clearly how much the song is fused with West Virginian identity rhetoric. It is in storybooks and in YouTube videos for and of children. It is a lullaby as well as an anthem.

For West Virginians, "Country Roads" resists the hillbilly stereotype by providing an alternative, but it exists within the tropes, too. The song is an imperfect, inaccurate expression of West Virginia, with powerful nostalgic energy: an energy that creates acceptance of the othered and constructs new conceptions of place. Cresswell argues that "geographical classification of society and culture is constantly structured in relation to the unacceptable, the other, the dirty," and analysis of transgressions that misalign with expectations of space and culture reveals that place is always constructed. Furthermore, these constructions of place are perpetuated by popular media, as "the reaction of the media has involved an unavoidable and always already existing linkage of the spatial, the social, and the cultural."(Cresswell 149). When we look at portrayals of West Virginia and Appalachia by the media generally, we see this structural, place-based othering. That is, until media culture discusses "Country Roads." As an emblem of the accepted, the "geographically central," as Cresswell describes, "Country Roads" is ideologically acceptable. However, it also exists "out of place," as a product created from outside, yet taken up. In some ways, it in itself is a transgression, and yet, it is the frame most often applied to the state, inside and outside. Cresswell defines some actions and artifacts as "geographically appropriate" or "inappropriate" in their connection to how they are used and interpreted in place (153). "Country Roads" is interesting because it is geographically and even artistically misaligned with the actuality of place, and yet it is taken up as geographically appropriate, more so than songs of and from and more accurately about West Virginia.

But what is it, exactly? Is "Country Roads" a reproach? A declaration? Identity is constructed—economically, socially, geographically, and historically—so that "any study of Appalachian culture is actually a study of national structures of culture and power" (C. Massey 82). "Country Roads" as an artifact of cultural rhetoric is reclamation of identity and power, an argument for inclusion and understanding, a flag of visibility. Appalachian culture and values tie deeply to place, and, as Amanda Hayes argues, "It is this value for place and our ability to see it as part of our families, part of ourselves, that I would posit our rhetoric preserves and promulgates" (158). Place is part of our literacy, our awareness of the world. It makes sense that a song that names us specifically, despite its flaws, ties so deeply to West Virginian identity. It is difficult to separate self from state in a place where "boundaries between self and community, land and people, history and future, are routinely nudged or outright collapsed" (Hayes 161). It is an acceptable, "tellable" narrative, one that can "move beyond the perceived space, or geographic understandings, of Appalachia [but] can sometimes trade in the types of stereotypes" in order to counter them (Webb-Sunderhaus, "Keep" 24). By trading in stereotypes, West Virginians leverage "Country Roads."

Like a letter from a new lover, "Country Roads" portrays us in the best possible perspective. Framed by romance, it does not see us as we are, but for its purposes and functions, that may not matter. As identity rhetoric, "Take Me Home, Country Roads" serves a particular function. For West Virginians, it is integrated into how we portray ourselves and each other. Applied to place-based knowing, "Rhetoric is . . . how we tell and use our stories and the stories of those around us to decide who we are and what we stand for. Thus, telling our stories can be the way we solidify knowledge for ourselves" (Hayes 9). Without visible public stories of our own making, "Country Roads" fills a specific need, solidifying knowledge, declaring existence.

Recognized worldwide, "Country Roads" is visible, even when West Virginia is not, and presents a reflection of identity, albeit a distorted one. In her reception study of literature about Appalachia, Satterwhite explains that "regional identity is . . . a result of a conversation between the outside and the inside among writers and readers with a cosmopolitan awareness but a familiarity with both the local and the global—with the especial assistance of readers who live within, or have at some point lived within, the region" (*Dear* 215). As a text, "Country Roads" is perhaps the loudest example of this kind of conversation in West Virginia: crafted by writers from the outside and taken up by those within. And yet, West Virginians must make cultural calculations in order to take up "Country Roads" despite its inherent flaws. At a surface level, appropriation of the song for West Virginians as identity rhetoric resolves misunderstandings about place. Beneath the surface, however, it creates more misunderstanding. Every time West Virginians embrace "Country Roads," we assist in conveying an incomplete impression. This impression is local and global and shapes the way we are seen as well as the way we see ourselves. We assist its recognition by embracing it, singing it, using it for a range of purposes and audiences.

Amid stereotypes, powerlessness, and disparaging definitions of West Virginians, the image presented by this song is a way to soften pain. "Country Roads" is the answer to the incest joke, to depictions of darkness and despair, to pity and misunderstanding. It is also a marker of visibility for an identity accustomed to invisibility. When we face the ugliness of what they say about us, we can cue "Country Roads," and suddenly we are recognizable as something besides poor hillbillies. It is a resistance to othering, evidence that West Virginians are just like everyone else. When West Virginians are exhausted, we can wrap ourselves in the quilt of "Country Roads" to rest. Adding to its power, the anthem as an international text expands the concept of hiraeth by reaching out to anyone longing for place, with West Virginia as an imaginary stand-in for the listener's own home, which we will discuss in later chapters. But for West Virginians, the song's power rests not in its reality, but in its tellability, which resides in a larger narrative about place and emplaced people.

"COUNTRY ROADS" AS TELLABLE NARRATIVE WITHIN HISTORICAL AND CULTURAL CONTEXT

"Country Roads" has local power, in part, because of its tellability. Sara Webb-Sunderhaus borrows the folkloric concept of "tellable narrative," and applies it specifically to Appalachian stories told by students, like mine, in college composition courses. Webb-Sunderhaus explains that "tellability is a lens for evaluating which narratives are worth telling and for further assessing who can tell which narratives in what contexts." The narratives we hear (and tell) about Appalachia reflect "common assumptions about, and stereotypes of, Appalachians" through emphasis on familiar themes (Webb-Sunderhaus, "Keep" 12). These narratives are socially, politically, and publicly constructed, and they fit within frameworks that are easily read as "true" because they align with cultural expectations. Untellable narratives are ones that defy the commonly accepted categories of experience; these "untellable" stories are often closer to individual experience (and perhaps closer to the truth) but do not fit within acceptable public discourse. "Country Roads" is tellable because it is familiar, accepted, and aligned with expectations about West Virginia.

The romantic tenor of "Country Roads" makes it not just tellable, but also a benign description of a conceptual place. Many Appalachian studies scholars define the region as a constructed rhetorical space rather than a real space, because even its boundaries are in dispute based on definitions from different stakeholders and organizations. Despite being depicted as "a monolithic group of rural people living in the hills and hollers of their respective states," Webb-Sunderhaus reminds us, Appalachians are distributed and diverse so that "there is more to Appalachian identity than where one lives" (16). Enacted through self-identification, cultural affiliation, and heritage, Appalachian identity is regional and cultural, connected to place, but not bound by it. Seen from the outside, though, Appalachia is flatly represented through commonly accepted tellable stories. "Country Roads" is one of those stories.

West Virginians and others with affiliated identities use "Country Roads" to express who they are within accepted public rhetoric. The "interplay among tellability, narrative, and identity performance" means that public discourses of Appalachia are performed through the stories we take up and tell (Webb-Sunderhaus, "Keep" 16). Music is performative, and "Country Roads" tells a resonant and believable story, even if it is not quite the truth, and West Virginians can accept and employ it because it is mostly devoid of negative stereotypes so prevalent in public discourse. When our story is told with love and longing instead of disdain and deficit, we easily embrace that narrative, even if it is told from the outside.

We are used to other voices telling our stories. Narratives about West Virginia can be framed within larger cultural narratives that include a history of being defined and discussed in scholarly and public discourse from the outside rather than from within. This outside naming of Appalachia as a distinct cultural region shapes American perceptions of people who live here, as well as perceptions of how we see ourselves. Dominant images of the region are present in historical and academic writing, policy, politics, literature, and popular culture. These multiple discourses converge to create and perpetuate imagery rife with inaccuracies and stereotypes, but they persist. These are reductive and imposed upon the region. Some of these images harmfully reinforce stereotypes, while others, like "Country Roads," romanticize. In order to fully understand how "Country Roads" works as imagery and identity production, we must explore the song in the context of West Virginia: history, culture, and music.

3

PLACING "COUNTRY ROADS" IN CONTEXT

"COUNTRY ROADS" IS (ALMOST) EVERYWHERE

The West Virginia State Museum in Charleston holds varied exhibits related to history, society, arts, industry, development, and people's lives. In the entryway, a recording of the Governor's voice welcomes visitors down steps leading into a gallery where a screen displays scenic images including flyovers of the New River Gorge, Coopers Rock, and other breathtaking vistas, soundtracked by the West Virginia University Marching Band's medley of "The West Virginia Hills," the Quaker Hymn "Simple Gifts," and "Take Me Home, Country Roads." During a recent visit, this is the only reference to "Country Roads" I found in the museum. I searched twice, exploring exhibits on the Civil War, the state's founding, river and timber industries, glass, schools, desegregation, coal (of course), and road building. On this same trip, I visited the West Virginia Music Hall of Fame. I did not find "Country Roads" there, either, even though, during his appearance at the Capitol in 1971, John Denver was made an "honorary West Virginian," and in 2014 "Country Roads" was made an official state anthem.

Despite its absence in these two places, "Country Roads" is present almost everywhere else. It is incorporated into quilts on display in the Cultural Center gallery and embossed on T-shirts, mugs, and crafts in the gift shop; the words "almost heaven" are incorporated into state materials, signs, tourist promotions, and memorabilia. "Country Roads" signifies West Virginian identity and musical identification, obscuring songs that are more accurate and more relevant to lived experience. What is it about "Country Roads" that makes it identity rhetoric in West Virginia? What factors contributed to its popularity at its release? How do Denver, Danoff, and Nivert's voices speak in chorus with other state songs? What makes it resonate so deeply as a state anthem and theme?

To make sense of why "Country Roads" was and continues to be so popular, it must be placed within the frame of regional and state history and culture. It exists within a context of Appalachian stereotypes and a discourse of rhetorics of identity. It evokes a sense of longing for home and place, but the regional conditions and context of West Virginia in the years before and after the song's release make it an anthem born of a specific time and cultural conversation, one that continues to generate meaning.

In this chapter, we discuss regional and state history specifically related to the production of Appalachia and extractive industry and outmigration in West Virginia. We focus on particular aspects that inform the origin and legacy of "Country Roads," as well as specific cultural and historical contexts that existed before, during, and after the song's debut. Other scholars have written extensively about the history, culture, and folklore of Appalachia and West Virginia; I draw from their work to provide perspective on and context for "Country Roads." Themes infused into culture, rhetoric, relationships, and infrastructures include patterns related to a history of extraction both material and cultural, and a legacy of outmigration and displacement in which folks leave with little hope of return, colored by homesickness and hiraeth. These themes shape perceptions of Appalachia as well as West Virginian identity and contribute to embracing "Country Roads" as a point of pride, resistance, and identification.

A HISTORY OF OUTSIDE NAMING IN APPALACHIA

We cannot talk about "Country Roads" without first acknowledging its place within larger cultural discourse and rhetoric of Appalachia, shaped by history, culture, politics, and economy. "Country Roads" is derived from a context that allows for oversimplification and emerged into an imagery hundreds of years in the making, and it is important that we unpack that history briefly. Pernicious images of mountain people as poor, lazy, and dirty trace as far back as explorer accounts in the mid-eighteenth century, as well as in academic work that suggested that Appalachia was a separate space culturally as well as geographically (Harkins). These early texts depicted Appalachian people as toothless, shoeless, unmotivated, unclean, and uneducated—a persisting perception.

Popular culture sensationalism fed this separateness in tabloid coverage of feuding, bootlegging, and sexual deviance (J. Williams, *Appalachia* 197). News accounts documented dissent in the West Virginia coalfields, the rise of labor unions, strikes, and rebellions throughout the 1870s and continuing throughout the twentieth century in West Virginia's "mine wars" (J. Williams, *Appalachia* 262–63). By the 1920s, Appalachia became defined not just by location, geography, and natural features, but also by assumptions about people, so that "after 1900, the mountains and mountaineers were conventionally viewed as a coherent region inhabited by a homogenous population" (Shapiro 115–16). The population was seen as one of deficiency, but ironically also as one of pure preserved culture and nobility, one worth saving. Charitable workers from outside flooded the region, motivated to rescue the hillbilly from himself, to reform the primitive people, and to educate impoverished residents. In West Virginia in the 1930s, for instance, Eleanor Roosevelt pioneered an effort to move unemployed white miners from the coal town of Scotts Run to a planned community, Arthurdale, where, once relocated, citizens were taught subsistence farming, craftwork, and trades, traditions already endemic to the region, in an effort to both redesign and preserve ways of living.

Still, negative conceptions persisted in historical and critical writing that described Appalachians as culturally regressive "savages" who were "mastered" by the wilderness (Higgs and Manning 386–87). Scholarly publications and social science continued blame and exploitation of Appalachian people, depicted as depraved and genetically inferior, into the 1940s and '50s. By the 1960s, social science was recognized as an academic field, and funded research studied the "Appalachian problem" to shape public policy, reinforcing stereotypes in doing so (J. Williams, *Appalachia* 326–27). In the midst of a period of outmigration, Appalachia "was on every well-informed American's map" (J. Williams, *Appalachia* 333). Academic experts "focused more attention on the dysfunctional hillbillies" who had moved to cities and the hills and hollows from which they came (J. Williams, *Appalachia* 334). This resulted in a popular culture image of Appalachians in comics, films, books, and other media and led to a heightened political awareness, too. This distortion affected policy in the 1960s when President Kennedy took special interest in West Virginia, which allowed him to first win the state's primary in 1960 against the odds and then, once he was president, begin a range of social and economic programs. The 1963 establishment of the Appalachian Regional Commission responded to a renewed interest amid the "War on Poverty" and funded education, highways, timber management, and tourism, further concretizing the imaginary perception of Appalachian West Virginia in American culture.

Also relevant is the legacy of extraction not just of land and mineral resources but also art, music, and people in the region and in West Virginia specifically. A pattern of absentee land ownership predates statehood (J. Williams, *Appalachia* 76). Legal, political, military, and other factors established a state resource rich but still impoverished, as "thousands of actual residents were later forced to transfer the ownership and/or the rights to the timber on and the minerals under it to nonresident corporations in the industrial era" (J. Williams, *Appalachia* 76). Even before the industrial revolution,

West Virginia was characterized by a "colonial economy," which included "a high degree of absentee land ownership," dominated by "large corporations [that] displaced the smaller firms and individuals who pioneered in industrial development; heavy dependence on extractive industries oriented to distant markets; and a relative lack of those manufacturing industries that provided the greatest stimuli to material growth and welfare" (J. Williams, *West Virginia* 130). Materials and products went out, but money did not come in. This pattern persists, including not just physical resources, but people and ideas.

Our resources are not our own, and neither is the rhetoric of the region. Government officials and other interests use stereotypes to promote aid, tourism, and attention through cultural imagery like literature and photography and to justify exploitation (J. Williams, *Appalachia* 304–5). A past example is the 1939 *New Deal Guidebook* controversy, which pit then-governor of West Virginia, Homer Holt, against the Federal Writers' Project in a struggle to shape the message. This kind of dispute "illustrated West Virginia's social landscape, like its mountain terrain, looked different according to who made the observation and from what angle" (J. Williams, *West Virginia* 163). Stories like this contribute to the sense that the rhetoric and place-narrative, like the land, is not ours.

Written in 1970, "Country Roads" emerged into a historical and cultural context that contributed to an entrenched and actively distorted discourse of Appalachia, with West Virginia at the center. The only state entirely within this politically and economically defined region, West Virginia's place in Appalachia is singular. Other Appalachian states have larger metropolitan areas and counties lying outside the region's borders, but West Virginia is "unique among the states in the region in that the federal government classifies every one of its fifty-five counties as Appalachian" (Creasman 3). A concentration of space has translated over time into a concentration of perceptions so that when an arrow lands in Appalachia, West Virginia is the bullseye. "Country Roads" is an arrow that landed so deeply that we still feel the impact, even after fifty years. It continues to pierce our consciousness, exists within and resists cultural perceptions, and adds to the distorted rhetoric and produced imagery about West Virginia.

Imagery Production and Cultural Rhetoric: The Conversation in West Virginia

Stereotypes become infused in cultural rhetoric. The regular and historically repeated "discovery" of Appalachia is well documented—in the late 1800s, in the 1950s (due to outmigration), in the 1960s, in the 2000s (with the opioid epidemic)—as is the resurfacing of the same stereotypes and general responses at each "new" exploration (Biggers; Satterwhite; Shapiro; Straw; J. Williams; Webb-Sunderhaus and Donehower). In 1990, cultural anthropologist Allen Batteau claimed that Appalachia is politically and culturally constructed, based not just on stereotypes but also on public and government policy. Rhetorician Todd Snyder discusses Appalachia as a "conceptual place," with stereotypes representing "imposed cultural identity" tied to the consequence of a layered othering of a region created from outside (22–23). A polarity of exaggeration, hillbilly versus noble mountaineer, has affected regional rhetoric.

In her book on the Mountaineer, Rosemary Hathaway discusses how popular conceptions defined Appalachia as a white, noble, ethnic group of its own standing; in need of education and enculturation; aggressive, feuding, and primitive. "The embrace of the white Other," Hathaway tells us, "led to regional interventions and ideas that had a lasting impact on Appalachian culture" (58). These images affected larger conceptions of the region so that "not only the otherness of Appalachia but the bothersomeness of this otherness had become a convention of the American consciousness" (Shapiro 121). Within this frame, Appalachia is a problem to be solved and a focal point for American cultural deficit; it is also worth preserving. Mountain culture has long been seen as a commodity, as "writers and sociologists were making forays into the mountains to alternately praise, condemn, and collect" (Branscome 10).

Passers-through and local-color writers in the 1800s created a kind of "mythical heritage" of Appalachian people characterized by "laziness, slovenliness, and love of whiskey and violence" (Higgs and Manning 55). Travel writing and literary works painted images of both dirty primitives and a romanticized wild, rugged scenery and earthy, wise residents. Exploration and popularization of local craftwork and musical traditions "provided evidence of the legitimacy of Appalachian otherness by demonstrating the participation of the mountaineers in Anglo-American culture" (Shapiro 131). Layered paradoxical portrayals hold "incredible staying power" in the rhetorical imagery of Appalachia as simultaneously "pristine," "backwater," "Anglo Saxon," and "pitiful" (Biggers xii–xiii).

Complicated imagery has continued. Magazines, the "mountain melodrama" genre of films, articles, cartoons, comics, comedies, TV shows, and music all perpetuate these conceptions and are not limited to books and other print texts, as we see in "Country Roads." John Inscoe discusses themes in films about Appalachia and cites an insider/outsider dichotomy and resulting conflict as driving the plot of popular narratives, the troubled displacement of people tied to place, attachment to place, land and family, and the desperation to return home. Inscoe relies on Batteau's concept of "holy Appalachia" as portrayed in some film: Appalachian values as "American" values, distilled to a sense of hard work, self-sufficiency, mountaineer spirit. This rhetoric has become part of place-identity over time, and we see it reflected in "Country Roads," too: a sense of romanticized hard work, a turning toward home, a longing for simplicity.

These various images exist at once, held in the American imagination, and have imprinted the people of West Virginia indelibly. Conflicting imagery of pristine landscape fraught with destruction, of hillbillies shooting each other, of a pure white region lacking diversity, and of impoverished souls in need of saving, can be traced through cultural texts like "Country Roads": life "older than the trees," with "mountain mamas," moonshine, and "dark and dusty" skies.

The discoveries, interventions, and incomplete portrayals are as much imagery production as they are anything else. Appalachia is named from the outside through repurposed narratives that characterize people as subject and object of a story, but never the *author* so that a real region "exists in our cultural imagination as a mythical place where uncomfortable truths can be projected and compartmentalized" (Catte 35). This compartmentalization perpetuates reductive stereotypes about place and people who live there. When we are used to being named, we more easily take up that naming instead of naming ourselves. And again, "Country Roads" is part of that naming, a produced imagery; even so, it is an integral part of the conversation about and in West Virginia.

In West Virginia, contradictory rhetoric is all around us: hillbilly, mountaineer, mountain mama, miner's lady. It is not all negative. In her essay on the hillbilly in comic literature, Sandra Ballard argues that the stereotype depicts Appalachians as literary fools: "mockers, truthtellers, and mirrors of culture, subversive identities that overlap and intertwine" (139). Shows like *The Beverly Hillbillies*, despite problematic stereotyping of mountain people as infantile, childlike, and ignorant, also portray these characters with an inherent sense of "essential" and "simplistic" goodness, fairness, and generosity (Ballard 139). Unlike some images, portrayals of essential goodness are ones we can embrace, as "Country Roads" shows. Still, some depictions are more sinister: Hillbilly slasher films like *Wrong Turn* are simply entertainment for most viewers, but they evoke painful stereotypes. Liz Price addresses *Wrong Turn* in an essay for *100 Days in Appalachia*, noting that a central plot feature of the film is roads—a wrong turn on a country road leads protagonists into a setting filled with inbred, cannibalistic hillbillies. America learns from films like this that "one should only find themselves navigating West Virginia's backroads by accident" (Price). At the same time, a wealth of tourist literature featuring country roads, both in imagery and in the song itself, tell readers that exploring the state is not only safe, but romantic and rewarding. Again, the contradiction: depravity and purity, devastation and beauty. These images translate from history into text into culture into rhetoric, and they impact our perception of each other and ourselves. They exist in fiction, film, and in song, echoed also in West Virginia's history and culture.

A HISTORY OF EXTRACTION, MIGRATION, AND DISPLACEMENT IN WEST VIRGINIA

The state of West Virginia was created on June 20, 1863. During the Civil War, the western part of Virginia sat on the division between Union and Confederacy, making it a natural battleground and contested space central to pivotal events, including the first land battle of the war in Philippi and John Brown's raid on Harpers Ferry. When the war ended in 1865, West Virginians came home from serving both sides; this fracturing and rejoining is part of state legacy, "symbolized on the grounds of the West Virginia state capitol, where a statue honoring West Virginia's Union soldiers stands in silent counterpoint to a statue of Stonewall Jackson, with Abraham Lincoln brooding between the two" (Snell). West Virginia is torn by history and politics and held together by relationships and community; residents live in close proximity to others who may not share the same political or religious affiliations. We believe we are accepting of differences, even when legislation and public policy suggest otherwise, and this sense of acceptance surfaces in identity rhetoric. In 1975, Loyal Jones defined "mountain values," including neighborliness and hospitality; familism; personalism (which includes tolerance instead of agreement); love of place; and sense of beauty. Jones cites tolerance and "live and let live" attitudes, along with a belief in good intentions and allowance for imperfections. These attitudes shape how West Virginians think about themselves and each other, and "Country Roads" becomes a unifying and tellable narrative to convey those beliefs.

In Appalachia, "a sense of place is not purely geographical—it is not a mere attachment to landscape. Commitment to locale comes also through relationships with other people" (Higgs, Manning, and Miller 349). Of "Country Roads," West Virginia musician

Aristotle Jones told me he believes "there's a point of pride in it, specifically... because it glorifies the simplistic values, the simpler values" of home, work, and family. The song "resonates so strongly because of those fundamental values of hard work, of self-sufficiency, of being family oriented, of being resourceful and ingenuity, and seeing farther than your own generation" (A. Jones). These values make us more tolerant, not just of those with whom we may disagree, but also with imagery, like "Country Roads," that represents a flattened view of place.

Not only might we attribute this acceptance of distortion to a supposed value system, but also to a legacy of absentee land ownership and extraction that creates power and wealth imbalances. "Country Roads," as a cultural text, has a place in a historical pattern of outside exploitation and within rhetorics of identity. In West Virginia, outside investment was enmeshed and codified legally dating back to the late 1700s, when speculator rights enabled "the emergence of an enduring system of absentee land ownership and arrested economic growth" (Rice and Brown). Laws still favor nonresident landowners, and federal courts have tended to be more sympathetic to large firms and outside claimants instead of West Virginia residents. Investors have negotiated mineral rights in exchange for surface rights, so many West Virginians signed away access to underground resources in perpetuity. Out-of-state companies have increasingly controlled industry, in small mines at the turn of the twentieth century and large surface and strip mines a century later (J. Williams, *West Virginia* 107–9). As Thomas Shannon writes of the Appalachian economy, "It is hard not to see this economic pattern as one in which outside interests exploited the region" (73). Eventually, this exploitation forced outmigration.

By 1930, sustaining families was increasingly difficult since profits made within the state went to individuals and businesses outside its borders. Like the rest of Appalachia, West Virginia "integrated into the national economy primarily as a producer of cheap fuels, raw materials, and low-wage industrial goods. Indisputably, the bulk of wealth created by the new enterprises left the region in the form of profits for outside owners" (Shannon 73). Between 1930 and 1960, the Appalachian economy continued to shift as transportation and mining practices changed, mill and production work moved overseas, and technologies evolved. Few jobs remained, and this resulted in outmigration causing a loss of nearly three million people from Appalachia, whom Shannon characterizes as "economic refugees" (75). West Virginia was hit especially hard, and these patterns continue to affect us today, since "most of the capital that went into the modernization of Appalachia came from elsewhere and returned to its owners in the form of the lion's share of the profits" (J. Williams, *Appalachia* 229). Products and profits went out. Later, people left, too. There is a clear connection between the role of extractive industry and cultural, social, rhetorical, and ideological norms. Extraction rippled out into culture, leading to isolation and population decline. These effects are echoed in "Country Roads," which speaks directly to outmigration.

In the decades leading up to the song's release, "an estimated three to five million Appalachians left the region in search of work" (Biggers 164). The 1950s and 60s were a period of peak migration for the region (Obermiller, Maloney, and Hansel 242). More specifically, "In the 1950s . . . a fifth of West Virginia and Appalachian Virginia left the mountains in a rural to urban and southern to northern migration" (Bean 57). Outmigration connects directly to economy and extraction, as "nearly seven million Appalachians migrated, impelled by mass unemployment in Kentucky and West Virginia that resulted from industrial automation, the mechanization of coal mining, and the national shift from the use of coal to natural gas as a primary fuel" (Bean 57). Changing industry left residents with no other option but to leave, and with leaving comes longing for home, which, even though temporary, is evidenced by a "stream of return migration" from shuttle migrants who maintain part-time homes in Appalachia (Obermiller, Maloney, and Hansel 258). Outmigration, for West Virginians specifically, contributes to shared homesickness different from but related to hiraeth.

"Country Roads," a text brought in from outside, imbued with homesickness, taps into hiraeth, and speaks to all of these factors. Leaving defines West Virginia.

For the last seventy years, outmigration in West Virginia has continued mostly steadily with only a few years of exception. A 1999 research whitepaper documents census patterns, showing that in 1950, West Virginia "reached its highest mark at 2,006,000." Then, "between 1951 and 1970, there were only three years (1958, 1959 and 1964) in which West Virginia's population did not decline" (Lego 2). "Country Roads" speaks to West Virginians directly because leaving is infused into cultural consciousness. West Virginia's population fell from 2,005,552 in 1950 to 1,860,421 in 1960 in the years prior to the song's release, and losses continued into the next decade. In fact, between 1950 and 2000, despite a small period of prosperity in the 70s, West Virginia lost nearly 800,000 people and continues to lose population in numbers larger than any other state (Rice and Brown). "Country Roads" has remained perennially relevant to West Virginians, who continue to leave, despite efforts to attract and retain homegrown talent. Recent state news reports on census data show that West Virginia is "the fastest-shrinking of any state in the nation, relative to population size" (Crum). For those who left, like my parents in the early 1970s, "Country Roads" captured all the sadness and longing they felt.

Interestingly, in the ten years after "Country Roads" was released, West Virginia prospered. From 1971–81, the state "experienced positive population growth in each year, eventually gaining 184,000 residents, or approximately 80% of the total residents lost between 1951 and 1970. . . . Overall, West Virginia's population increased by 10.4% from 1971 to 1981" (Lego 2). Though the 1980s represented another decline, the 1990s offered a minor resurgence due to increased opportunities in the eastern panhandle and in the university city of Morgantown. More recently, census data show a 3.2 percent loss in state population in the years 2010–20, which equals about sixty thousand people (Mistich, "West Virginia"). As a result, West Virginia has lost another congressional seat, its fourth since 1960; the entire state, which once had six representatives, now has only two. Lack of representation contributes not just to governance, but also to the feeling of invisibility West Virginians already experience, as well as longing from those who have left.

In addition to outmigration, war brought additional and disproportionate loss to West Virginia. The US Army Center for Military History documents 2.3 percent of Congressional Medal of Honor recipients, 1941–76, were West Virginians (J. Williams, *Appalachia* 386). West Virginians died in Vietnam, as well, leading the nation per capita, as "twenty-five West Virginians per 100,000 population had been killed, compared to seventeen per 100,000 nationally" (Branscome 7). Homesickness and longing for home were perpetual. In a place so imbued with loss, longing "impacts the salience of the 'idea' of home for many Appalachians. Those who have had to leave their communities to escape stereotypes or for employment or opportunities elsewhere construct a powerful narrative" (Nardella 3). For West Virginians, "Country Roads" fits neatly within a narrative of displacement, bound with desire to return. When used by West Virginians to recognize place, memorialize loss, and express identity, "Country Roads" serves a similar purpose at local festivals and homecoming events, which can temporarily re-emplace outmigrants, create connections, and foster "compliance and participation" to "restore the rupture" between people who left and those whom they left behind, providing comfort even for those who cannot help but be changed by leaving (Shutika 201).

The song takes a significant place within a genre of songs dedicated to leaving and loss, some of which are homegrown in origin. As Colleen Anderson sings in her song "West Virginia Chose Me":

> Someone's always leaving here
> It's just that kind of place
> It's just that kind of world today
> You learn to live with loss.

Endemic to West Virginian identity, loss, longing, and homesickness are tied to outmigration. In "Country Roads," we find recognition, solace, and positive connection. We see West Virginian history and identity reflected back in the song.

Outmigration also connects to othering experienced by West Virginians and to historical rhetoric traceable to the state's earliest days. Local color writing and missionary work in the 1880s shaped American perceptions of mountain life, establishing a "basis for a regional definition" as a space of need (Shapiro 116). Mountaineers were backward, behind the times, a "peculiar people" and "a problem" (Shapiro 118). At the same time, readers idealized an "authentic Appalachia" as an antidote to economic, historic, and societal troubles. Popular culture exoticized Appalachia as simple, primitive, picturesque (Satterwhite, *Dear* 2–3). This flattening of the region and its people continues, as "Appalachia in the national geographic imaginary, however, has largely remained an essentialist version of the region—white, rural, poor, or working-class mountain people with highly specific cultural traditions that range from quilts and handmade crafts to moonshining and snake handling," making it "a concept as much as a place" (Satterwhite, *Dear* 3). This conceptual Appalachia is pastoral and grounded in both solitude and community, but it is populated with people who are perceived as other. As Rosemary Hathaway explains: "To outsiders, the hillbilly is nasty, poor, and ignorant; to insiders he is friendly, courageous, and noble" (86). Certainly, "Country Roads," with its romantic, pastoral themes, taps into this perception of separateness as well as idealization.

As a singular, predominant representation of place, "Country Roads" expresses a conceptual, romanticized impression of a place with a complicated cultural, economic, and rhetorical history. Real people cannot live within conceptual spaces, but we can use familiar texts, like "Country Roads," to articulate complicated feelings about home. It is an anthem for those who go as well as those who stay, and it helps to orient the state's hills as what bell hooks describes as "locations of possibility" for belonging (55). As Loyal Jones claims, Appalachians are "oriented around places," so songs of mountains often call forth images of belonging and home. Jones calls place "one of the unifying values of mountain people, this attachment to one's place, and it is a great problem to those who urge mountaineers to find their destiny outside the mountains" (7). "Our love of place," Jones argues, "sometimes keeps us in places where there is no hope of maintaining decent lives" (10). So West Virginians are taught they should leave in order to survive, but those who leave face different challenges.

Outmigration comes with distorted perceptions of Appalachians in the places where they relocate. Historically seen as a problem population, outmigrants encounter social, economic, and institutional barriers to success. Carissa Massey, in her work on rhetorics of identity, details perceptions of Appalachian migrants as a "blight" of hillbillies who disrupted the cities into which they moved. Cultural texts like political cartoons depicted urban Appalachian migrants living in squalor, surrounded by farm animals and unkempt, uncontrollable children. "Because of the overabundance of stereotyping," Massey argues, "its variety of media forms, and its resulting symbolic and visual values, images such as these become the most potent force in the production of cultural meaning within mass culture" (47). Amid this influencing imagery, West Virginians were already seen as "other" by mainstream America. These perceptions were evidenced in the years leading up to "Country Roads." Particularly illustrative is this excerpt from a 1959 article in *The Nation,* which distills national sentiments of the day:

> There's nothing wrong with hillbillies—a description which mountain people loathe—that a strong dose of equal opportunity wouldn't cure. Applying every yardstick of social well-being, their Appalachian homeland emerges a sordid blemish on the balance sheet of the wealthiest nation in history. You name it— schools, health services, housing, per capita income—and the

Appalachian South stacks up as an underdeveloped region which produces citizens incapable of realizing their human potential in the complex twentieth century. Their stunted growth not only saps the vitality of the mid-South, but also weakens the nation. (Ernst and Drake 8)

Even today, these beliefs persist, but "Country Roads" presents a counterargument and alternate view, evoking West Virginians' hope of homecoming, but without the actual possibility of return. Even so, the song's popularity shows the power of music to speak to existing cultural narratives.

"Country Roads" directly references longing for return in a way not just characteristic of migrants' lived experiences, but also of common country music tropes, forwarding an already existing story of leaving and loss. "Displacement (real and metaphorical) and anguish are universal; so too are its counterparts of sincerity and simplicity," so that just as in real life, "in blues and country music mobility was often a response to poverty and a necessary escape; travel was accompanied by heartache but rarely by success" (Connell and Gibson 81–82). "Country Roads" exemplifies musical themes that mirror lived experiences of West Virginians specifically. We cannot discuss "Country Roads" without acknowledging the rhetorical visibility of West Virginia in the years leading up to the song's release: Danoff, Nivert, and Denver's portrayal was undoubtedly influenced by cultural conversations of the time.

WEST VIRGINIA IN THE NATIONAL CONVERSATION: "COUNTRY ROADS" AS CULTURAL COMMENTARY

From the earliest missionaries to the Save the Children, New Deal, and homesteading programs in the 1930s, West Virginia has been a focal point for poverty assistance efforts and mass media. In the 1960s the formation of the federal Appalachian Regional Commission (ARC), delineated 410 counties across 13 states; the creation of the region was primarily political (Edwards, Asbury, and Cox). Subsequently, Appalachia was represented in news, politics, economics, labor, environmental issues, and culture; West Virginia, as the only state wholly within the region, became the center of national attention in a number of ways. "Country Roads" entered the conversation after more than a decade of intense focus.

In 1960, both presidential candidates John F. Kennedy and Hubert Humphrey visited West Virginia on the campaign trail. Kennedy, in particular, was drawn to the state to which his success was "indelibly linked" (Kercheval). He reportedly "identified the West Virginia primary as the most important single milestone on his road to the White House" (J. Williams, *West Virginia* 339). West Virginians have remained aware of Kennedy's attention, recalling a line from his speech at the state centennial celebration in 1963: "'The sun does not always shine in West Virginia, but the people always do." This sentiment remains a point of pride and recognition, though not as visibly as "Country Roads." After the election, Kennedy appointed a commission made mostly of West Virginians to make federal recommendations, focusing on highways and road building to bring infrastructure and economic gains. In 1961, Kennedy introduced the Area Redevelopment Act, which allotted funding to fight poverty; West Virginia would receive much of the money, which primarily financed tourism (J. Williams, *West Virginia* 228). In 1965, Lyndon Johnson signed the bill into law establishing the ARC, beginning the War on Poverty. Out of these initiatives came Medicaid, Medicare, Head Start, and Volunteers in Service to America (AmeriCorps VISTA), which fund healthcare, education, and community development. West Virginia was centered in all these initiatives as a model for aid that continued to be in the spotlight nationally throughout the 1960s.

In addition to being at the receiving end of federal efforts to improve economy and infrastructure, West Virginia was also visible due to environmental and labor safety concerns. The environmental movement of the 1960s and '70s noticed the state's acid mine drainage and strip-mining. Kennedy's 1960 campaign speech in Hinton referenced "increasing pollution" that "threatened the beauty and health" of waters and promised federal support to counter "destruction" and support fishing, timberlands, and outdoor recreation (Kennedy). The 1960s brought the Clean Waters Restoration Act, The Clean Air Act, and the National Environmental Policy Act. The first Earth Day was celebrated in 1970. In the reflection of national attention, local groups like West Virginia Highlands Conservancy worked against environmental problems, like strip mining, and toward conservation of natural spaces. It would have been impossible for anyone listening to misunderstand West Virginia's place in the political, economic, and environmental conversation.

Bill Danoff, a Washington, DC, resident, was well aware, and the "dark and dusty" lyrics in "Country Roads" intentionally reference environmental concerns. Danoff told me, "I was conscious of it at the time, the 'stranger to blue water' line. It was specifically about the poison in the rivers and all that stuff. But it kind of goes by, and nobody pays attention to it.... I was thinking of the runoff and stuff like that. Not as a negative, just as a feature." Pollution, to Danoff, was descriptive fact, brought to awareness in discussions of the day. These conversations remain with us: Pollution, chemical hazards, improper waste storage, and stream destruction have continued, despite activism and legislation since the 1960s and '70s. West Virginia was visible nationally due to tragedy in the mining industry, as well. West Virginia's Office of Miners' Health Safety and Training documents more than 150 mining-related victims in the years 1960–70. The worst of these was the 1968 Farmington Mine Disaster, which killed seventy-eight miners, led to the Federal Coal Mine Health and Safety Act of 1969, and again placed West Virginia in the national news through sadness and tragedy. The "miner's lady" in "Country Roads" reflects this rhetorical visibility.

Roads dominated the conversation around Appalachia before "Country Roads," too. In West Virginia, road building has been a focus since the earliest days of white colonialism, representing a taming of the land for industry and for travel. The earliest roads had been built high on ridgetops based on trails made by Indigenous people. Passage through the wilderness was a priority for surveyors even prior to the American Revolution, and West Virginia, a site of extraction, needed roads and bridges, railroads, and ways through hollows, across mountains, over rivers, and into the wild. Major cities, such as Wheeling, Clarksburg, Morgantown, and Parkersburg emerged as ports as early as 1776, part of a network that provided transportation and trade. Road building is key to economic and infrastructural development throughout the state's history, and "the centerpiece of ARC's redevelopment strategy as it emerged during the late sixties was a 3,025-mile system of 'development corridors': modern four-lane highways designed to augment the interstate system" (J. Williams, *Appalachia* 144, 342). Much of this highway work was in West Virginia. Not surprisingly, then, roads were a topic of interest in publications of the time. A 1959 piece in *The Nation* describes West Virginia roads, connected to poverty and industry both:

> Sprawled along the Kelly's Creek Road in West Virginia are dilapidated shacks, rusting oil and gas wells, crumbling coal tipples. The creek winds its way through rotting piles of garbage and old tires. With spring, the hillsides explode into bright colors, providing an ironic background for the misery of Kelley's Creek. Occasionally the winding roads led to islands of industrial prosperity, such as Charleston, where the per capita income is among the highest in the nation. In the river valley dominated by this city, the region's natural resources—including coal, natural gas, salt and water—have blended to create one of the nation's largest and most prosperous complexes of chemical plants. (Ernst and Drake 5)

This portrayal leans heavily on stereotypes of destitution and despair, hillbilly shacks countered by images of riches brought by extraction and industrialization, and exemplifies rhetoric used to describe West Virginia.

Like many social and political initiatives, road building in Appalachia was not supported universally. For example, a 1965 article from *The Reporter* discusses the failure of ARC's federal Appalachia Proposal due to a lack of local resources to supplement connecting roads: "In mountainous areas of West Virginia, for example, Appalachia planners note that it costs $2 million a mile to construct a two-lane paved highway. Moreover, Appalachia needs road money not so much to accommodate existing traffic as to stimulate new traffic" (TerHorst 37). Despite the need for infrastructure, some viewed development money as wasted. This controversy centered roads in the national conversation. Nonetheless, physical building projects funded by federal efforts led to increased accessibility to the interior of West Virginia, throughways to the East Coast, and the historic New River Gorge Bridge, completed in 1977, which simplified interstate travel and now provides access to our country's newest National Park. "The interstate and Appalachian highways built in West Virginia since the 1960s had a unifying impact" on the people who traveled them (J. Williams, *West Virginia* 228). This impact is physical and cultural—and it is rhetorical, audible in cultural texts, like music.

ROAD SONGS, IMAGINED TERRITORY, AND MUSICAL REVIVAL

The rhetoric of West Virginia is filled with road references, before and after the release of "Country Roads." West Virginia is a land of rivers, too, with nearly twenty others crossing through besides the Shenandoah, which borders only part of the eastern panhandle. Roads and rivers feature prominently in conversations about tourism, infrastructure, economics, and politics, and references to travel, trains, and roads were already present in folk and popular culture, including music, long before "Country Roads." The song built upon existing conversations and rhetorical traditions that pervaded the way people talked and wrote about Appalachia. Increased accessibility through roads and rail made transportation possible but represented cultural shift, influencing communication and access to goods and services. This accessibility also provided entry to news and information, including entertainment like music; it provided inspiration for stories and songs, too. Some of this was promoted by industry, like the 1858 Artist's Excursion on the B&O Railroad, a scenic train trip for several prominent writers and artists of the day that had them traveling from Baltimore to Wheeling through much of what would become West Virginia. Early accounts established a pattern of writing about the region as a place apart from the rest of the nation, one that could be visited and left behind.

In folk music, transportation, trains, and roads are a central theme in regional ballads and other songs. John Williams documents the spread of the folk song "John Henry," first collected and published in 1909, as one example. It is "reasonably certain" that the real John Henry worked on the Big Bend Tunnel and perhaps was West Virginian by birth, but the song is about more. "The ballad of John Henry is also an anthem for a society in transition" because at the turn of the century, Appalachia experienced widespread industrial change, so subsistence farming gave way to new occupations (J. Williams, *Appalachia* 216). This created a need for more land travel routes beyond rail. The first federally funded highway, Route 40, began in 1810 in Cumberland, Maryland, and passed through what would become West Virginia. The "National Road," as it was named, made transportation of goods easier and opened connections across the Appalachians, establishing settlement patterns that are still visible, as well as a musical legacy (Ohio Writers'). The Federal Highway Administration celebrated the route in story and song through a Federal Writers' Project book in 1940 to celebrate the road's centennial (Longfellow). Not surprisingly, much of that book employs the same pastoral imagery and nostalgic themes later written into "Country Roads."

Road songs are part of country music tradition, as many hits take up themes of travel, transportation, and home. Roy Acuff's 1936 recording of "Wabash Cannonball" celebrates train travel on the Rock Island line; versions of the song can be traced to the turn of the twentieth century. Hank Williams's famous 1949 recording of Leon Payne's "Lost Highway" uses rambling travel as a metaphor for perdition, as does, to some degree, Roger Miller's 1965 hit "King of the Road." Other country songs that addressed travel and transportation, especially with a sense of missed connection, in the years before "Country Roads," include Dave Dudley's 1963 "Six Days on the Road" and Glen Campbell's 1968 "Wichita Lineman." "Country Roads" differs from these in its nostalgia and longing for home, belonging tied to place rather than to person.

Music aligned with migration patterns, so homesickness forced a market for nostalgic music. Part of the power of "Country Roads" is its capacity to channel the intense sense of loss many outmigrants felt. Jeremy Hill, in his book about the music industry in the 1960s, argues that the Country Music Association adapted to migrant audiences in urban spaces, with working class, "everyday" Americans, rather than with rural listeners. They used the phrase "country comes to town," to describe patterns of rural people moving into cities and looked to provide the genre with a markedly new socio-spatial identity while still preserving the music's rural spirit and deep connection to "ordinary" Americans (Hill 55). Homesick songs fueled a genre within the music industry, one rooted in a "sense of 'lostness' [that] is perhaps most importantly and widely expressed in Appalachian rooted 'country music'" (Bean 83–84). The new Nashville Sound represented a constructed genre, drawing from both traditional country and rock and roll to create a commercially viable, more digestible brand of music. This mainstream sound allowed for more crossover—of which "Country Roads" is an example, even though Denver resisted becoming a country singer for most of his career.

Appalachian outmigrants carried music with them to their new places. This music conveyed romanticized memories, as "music to which Appalachian migrants listened in their new homes and in urban bars and roadside taverns expressed a nostalgia for this way of life that gradually eroded the stinging memories of hardship, replacing them with a sentimental view of country living that belied the manner in which most mountaineers of the mid-twentieth century would live" (J. Williams, *Appalachia* 308). This sentimentality became infused into American popular culture so that music moved not just outward from the region, but inward from outside. John Williams specifically cites Aaron Copeland's 1943 *Appalachian Spring*, which "fixed the mountain region indelibly" in American minds as a "a place apart from the mainstream, with timeless ways of life divorced from hard realities," calling it a "regional anthem ... identifying a place at once haunted and beautiful, a place that will always be—and never was" (J. Williams, *Appalachia* 308). This rhetorical sense of region as an imagined space fused fiction and reality and solidified already existing stereotypes. "Country Roads," as an anthem for those who have left or those who long to visit, is part of an imaginary conception in conversion with popular culture rhetoric of the region.

"Country Roads" was influenced by other musical trends of the time, as well. Bill Danoff cites memories of Wheeling's *Jamboree* radio show (established in 1933) as having shaped his own musical career. However, a revival of Appalachian folk music and culture began in the years leading up to "Country Roads." The folk music movement of the 1950s created a new awareness of traditional music and instrumentation, and the back-to-the-land movement added another layer of interest for outsiders within the region. This led to enthusiasm for old time and bluegrass. Appalachian towns found economic stimulation through tourism in fairs and festivals, as well as arts centers and colonies dedicated to revived musical interests.

West Virginia embraced this pattern: The West Virginia State Folk Festival, the Gardner Winter Music Festival, the Skyline Bluegrass Festival, and others were, and still are, beacons of traditional music. Arts and culture publications were established around this time, too, including *Goldenseal*, a magazine of West Virginia traditional life produced by the Department of Arts, Culture and History. A 1999 book, *Mountains of Music*, written to celebrate *Goldenseal* magazine's twenty-fifth anniversary, profiles West Virginia's traditional musicians and rich musical heritage, showcasing how "from Wheeling radio station WWVA's 'Jamboree USA' to the Augusta Heritage Festival in Elkins, from the weekly international radio broadcasts of 'Mountain Stage' to the annual Appalachian String Band Festival at Clifftop and the state-sponsored Vandalia Gathering, tens of thousands of people each year are drawn through music to the mountains and culture of West Virginia." West Virginia's rurality, even into the 1970s, meant that musical traditions evolved in pockets that served to "reflect the ongoing rediscovery and revival of folk music" (Lilly 2). That revival expanded into music festivals, fiddling contests, weekly jam nights, folk venues, and even punk rock clubs all over the state.

The cultural revival of the 1960s put West Virginia on the map as a kind of music mecca as musicians found "cultural identity" that "live[d] 'below the radar' of contemporary media or popular culture" (Lilly 3). Folk music festivals, according to Robert Cantwell, were not just revivals, but also inventions of culture within a complex system of conditions and curated interactions (190). That undersurface awareness of what was and what was imagined to be bubbled up not just within the state, but also not far from the border in Washington, DC, where the Smithsonian Folklife Festival began in 1967; among the performers in the early years of this festival were West Virginians such as fiddler Clark Kessinger and hammered dulcimer player Russell Fluharty. West Virginia–based bands like Asleep at the Wheel played in clubs in DC, too. Danoff and Nivert, active musicians in the city, were well aware of their presence.

THE RESONANCE OF WEST VIRGINIA AND OF "COUNTRY ROADS"

"Country Roads" spoke not just to West Virginia natives. The region experienced an influx of people looking to serve others and the environment in organizations like Appalachian Volunteers, Save the Children, and VISTA. Many of these folks stayed.

John D. "Jay" Rockefeller, who would become a West Virginia senator, came to the state as a VISTA worker in the 1960s, for example; he later arranged Danoff, Nivert, and Denver's 1980 performance at WVU's Mountaineer Field. As John Williams describes in *West Virginia: A History*, newcomers developed a deep sense of community, creating change in public policy, education, press, culture, and media approaches to West Virginia. This included the development of West Virginia Public Broadcasting, along with its nationally known *Mountain Stage* show, events like the Augusta Festival, outdoor recreation, and a booming tourist industry. Some of these transplants came in service, while others came as part of a new counterculture.

The back-to-the-land movement in the 1960s and 1970s attracted many young, often middle- or upper-class new residents to West Virginia. Jinny Turman-Deal, in her article on the back-to-the-land movement, describes West Virginia as appealing because of the low cost of property, proximity to cities (especially Washington, DC), perceptions of Mountaineers as tolerant of differences, and stereotypes about attitudes of freedom and independence. Others, like Karen and Jamie Zelermyer, describe West Virginia as a place of "magic" for creative thinkers seeking communal living and new ways of being; their podcast, *I Was Never There*, focuses on counterculture in the state in the 1970s and '80s, using Brandi Carlile's version of "Country Roads" as a theme. The West Virginia Danoff and Nivert knew well was one described to them by some of what John Williams refers to as "neonatives," homesteaders who found themselves in West Virginia communes. Nivert told me she and Danoff had a small following of transplants to West Virginia, and one fan wrote them vivid, illustrated letters describing communal life in the state's eastern panhandle; these descriptions inspired the song and surface in a verse that Denver excised from the final version.

In a 2010 performance of "Country Roads" at Georgetown University, Danoff remembers that lost verse, a nod to the West

Virginia transplants who drove to DC for shows: "There used to be this commune of hippies that would come visit us. They would come watch us, and they were from West Virginia. The women all wore these peasant dresses, and the guys all had long hair, and they brought their dog with them, and he'd sit in front all nice.... They made their way into the song." The lyrics of the "lost" verse colorfully describe communal living:

> In the foothills,
> Hidin' from the clouds,
> Pink and purple,
> West Virginia farmhouse,
> Naked ladies,
> Men who look like Christ,
> And a dog named Pancho
> nibbling on the rice

Despite a lack of firsthand knowledge, Bill Danoff told me, West Virginia resonated for a number of reasons and the reference to the state was intentional and "honestly come by." Danoff explained, "We had the first Earth Day that year, everybody was very conscious of it. And I knew a bunch of hippies who were living out in West Virginia, people starting communes. Great band called Asleep at the Wheel started up in Paw Paw.... For myself personally there was an interaction with West Virginians, so maybe that was subconscious in there too." The artists used their existing knowledge—personal in Nivert's case, peripheral in Denver's, and vicarious in Danoff's—as gleaned from friendships and cultural conversations, to construct imagery that captured the magic of place, even for those familiar with it. West Virginians, natives, and transplants felt seen. This made them love the song.

West Virginians were so enamored with "Country Roads" that Denver was invited to perform on the State Capitol steps in Charleston on August 28, 1971. A few days later, a *Charleston*

Daily Mail article discussed the song's popularity, and praised the tune, saying it was an instant anthem:

> The song that prompted John Denver's visit to Charleston Sunday, "Take Me Home, Country Roads," is now No. 2 in the country and apparently destined for the national top spot, he told the massive crowd gathered at the Capitol. The song has received extensive local radio airtime twice this summer—both when "Country Roads" was first released and when it became a national hit. Already it has become a stock number for many youthful folk singing gatherings. ("'Country Roads' Nearing" 8)

The article describes the lyrics as "epitomizing the spirit of homecoming, in 1971 or any other year" and prints them in their entirety, so that all West Virginians can learn "the words to the song memorializing their native hills" in order to better sing along ("'Country Roads' Nearing" 8).

Colleen Anderson, now an established West Virginia writer and musician, came to West Virginia in 1970 as a VISTA volunteer from Michigan and found herself in a connected community that felt like home. Placed with a local craft guild, Anderson was taken in by a motherly group of quilters and remembers an atmosphere that embraced "Country Roads," as well as Hazel Dickens's "West Virginia, My Home," at backyard music sessions as well as community performances. Anderson attended Denver's 1971 concert on the State Capitol steps with her mentor, Stella Monk, president and founding member of Cabin Creek Quilts, who would have been in her fifties at the time. "[Stella] was wild about that song," Anderson told me. It was celebratory and a tribute, but the song was about more than homecoming; it was about longing and loss.

Losses—industrial, environmental, and personal—made West Virginians long for different recognition, something positive. "Country Roads" is an anomalous expression of praise in an otherwise denigrating media environment. Despite its flaws, including lyrics that "evoked a number of hillbilly and coalfield stereotypes that normally provoked an angry or defensive response and, most insulting of all, confused West Virginia geography with that of Virginia," West Virginians chose to overlook the problems (J. Williams, *West Virginia* 188). "Whether or not it said the right things, the song came out at just the right time," as in the context of 1971, "West Virginia was in a newfound, and perhaps unfamiliar, state of hope. Unemployment was approaching the national average, outmigration had slowed, incomes had increased, coal was resurging, and tourism was a burgeoning industry. Adding to this was increased development and well-funded public works programs—the ARC's highway project, a system of highways to replace West Virginia's romantic but dangerous country roads" (J. Williams, *West Virginia* 188–89). "Country Roads" spoke to hope, renewed growth, and prosperity. It fell within a pattern of musical renaissance, as well. In 1970, West Virginia was, without a doubt, in the national spotlight, part of the collective consciousness, represented in the news and in popular culture, in discussions of economics, politics, social concerns, art, and music. Hillbillies and hippies, mountaineers and musicians, found their way into the collective American awareness, and this surely contributed to the generation and subsequent popularity of "Country Roads."

Collective sense of a place both familiar and foreign contributed to the song's reception. The song spoke to a state, nation, and world at the perfect moment, moving beyond the songwriters' intentions. Literacy scholar Deborah Brandt discusses how texts become autonomous from the writer, developing "their own voice, outside of us, referring not to the known world, but to themselves and to each other" (24). This notion that texts transcend the writer, space, and time and become separate from the author is akin to Taffy Nivert's description of the song as a "baby bird that's now got all its feathers, and you put it outside, and it flies away." Influenced by cultural conversation, "Country Roads" was a product of its time, as Nivert explained: "Historically, what is going on with music is an expression being reflected back from the people who make it and who listen to it. . . . And at the time of 'Country Roads' there was a lot of turmoil in the world, in our world anyway. It was 1970, and we were mired in a few political things, all our heroes had been killed. It was a strange and scary time. Just like now." The currency of "Country Roads," however, transcended its reflection of the particular moment; it remains relevant and resonant today.

Let us return again to Jefferson's Rock in Harpers Ferry, West Virginia's easternmost city. Harpers Ferry has long been a "transportation center," which "in every age was celebrated for its beauty" (J. Williams, *West Virginia* 31). And yet, Harpers Ferry is different from the rest of West Virginia. A strange mix of tourist trap, national park, and heritage site, it is hallowed ground, the scene of a bloody insurrection, and also a good place for decent barbeque and craft beer. In fact, as Williams claims, "many of the tourists who visit Harpers Ferry today are unaware that the place is in West Virginia" (*West Virginia* 47). As in "Country Roads," only a glimpse of West Virginia is visible, despite some shared history and culture. As in "Country Roads," West Virginia is merely peripheral for passers through.

Nonetheless, "Country Roads" calls us by name and brings us into awareness, even if peripherally. It makes us just like everyone else, taps into universal love and longing for home: hiraeth. It names West Virginia, but it is not actually about us, as is evidenced by the many variations and interpretations, with still new versions over its fifty years. Still, it exists within a place-rhetoric that includes other texts, as well.

"COUNTRY ROADS" IN CONVERSATION WITH IMAGERY AND ANTHEMS

Texts build understandings and worlds. The world that exists in "Country Roads" persists in imaginary conceptions of West Virginia and does not exist in isolation, but refers to other descriptions of state and region. It also creates new ones, building different versions, variants, and textualities. "Country Roads" exists in conversation with other texts, some of which existed in the years before it was written. These are part of what John Williams describes as "a territory of images" representing "a place that has been invented, not discovered, an 'alternative America' projected onto the mountains and mountain people by reformers whose real purpose is to critique and change things in the nation at large" (*Appalachia* 8–9). Extraction was and is true as much in the culture industry as in coal, timber, and other natural resources. Outsiders writing about a place they do not know, for audiences outside that space, is extraction. West Virginia was already widely used as rhetorical imaginary and metaphorical space prior to "Country Roads." We have discussed how the portrayal of West Virginia as a contradiction—a land of purity and wholesomeness, a source of poverty and shame—only increased throughout the 1960s. This imagery transforms understandings of real places; when depicted through media and music, "place ceases to be a mere geographical space and assumes instead a powerful metaphorical significance that links accepted physical properties of a place with a series of inscribed qualities" that diverge from reality (Bennett 71–72). We may believe that popular music accurately portrays place, but it is by nature designed for a different purpose.

"Country Roads" remains relevant cultural rhetoric. It builds on preexisting stereotypes and cultural conceptions because, "when invoking the nostalgia and freedom of a West Virginia homecoming—no matter how inaccurate the myth is when examined in light of geography or the songwriter's 'authentic' knowledge of Appalachia—it also invokes these rhetorical layers of Appalachian identity as it is articulated through land and stereotype" (C. Massey 130). This rhetoric allows performances of identity. "Country Roads" is adjacent to these performative and appropriative identities: It may be used as a soundtrack for them, or it may be used in other, more complex ways.

It also obscures the voices of West Virginians who speak from within—in West Virginia, of West Virginia, and about West Virginia. In a 2004 article, Richard Ramella discusses a pattern of writers referring to states in which they have never been, addressing West Virginia specifically, "where there is a cabin on the ridge, old folks waiting on the porch, plus the sweetest girls and the purest water, or vice-versa. Many of these songs were written by people who seldom strayed from the coastal entertainment centers" (26). Projecting an imagined sense of place for commercial success is nothing new, but it is different when its impact is more powerful than songs composed from within, by those who are tied to place intimately. "Country Roads," when considered in isolation, creates distortion.

"Country Roads" is always in conversation with other texts about West Virginia, even if those other songs are not sung as loudly or widely. For example, during his travels in the 1960s, Utah Phillips wrote "The Green Rolling Hills of West Virginia," also released in 1971, recorded by The Quinaimes Band. Phillips purportedly traveled through West Virginia, and conversations there inspired him to address outmigration and homesickness, describing West Virginia as "the nearest place to heaven" the speaker knows. When Hazel Dickens and Alice Gerrard recorded "Green Rolling Hills" in 1973, they added a verse referencing return to home to "right the wrongs" and to see an end to troubles.

Despite being covered by artists like Emmylou Harris and West Virginian Kathy Mattea, "Green Rolling Hills" has never gained the popular traction of "Country Roads." Its appeal is more specific to actual place and calls for activism and change. Many songs represent West Virginia from this more complex perspective. Among these are West Virginia's other state anthems.

West Virginia has four state songs. "Country Roads" is best known, despite being adopted most recently. The others have longer histories and interesting origins of their own. "West Virginia, My Home Sweet Home," was officially adopted in 1947. In 1961, unaware of the first anthem, state legislature adopted "The West Virginia Hills," which had been popular since its first publication in 1885. "This Is My West Virginia" was adopted as the official state centennial song in 1963. To rectify confusion, state officials then designated all three songs, "each ranking equally with the others" as anthems by law. "Take Me Home, Country Roads" was added in 2014.

"West Virginia, My Home Sweet Home" was written by Wheeling native and city official Col. Julian Hearne. A decorated World War II veteran, Hearne was protective of his work, and inscribed on the sheet music that the song was not to be "played as country music or in a hillbilly fashion" (Ramella, "Three" 38). This song forwards a narrative common of its time—that West Virginia was abundant in industry, natural resources, freedom, and friendship. Officially adopted during the Cold War, "My Home Sweet Home" is simple, referencing history, family, and patriotism. It spoke to the legislature of its day, who "considered it desirable to have official state songs." Pride of place, where the speaker finds "work" and "play" among deep ancestral roots, is appropriate for official state activities, but has little resonance outside West Virginia. Although well-known West Virginia musician William Matheny sometimes plays it live, it is not often acknowledged popularly.

Iris Bell's 1962 "This Is My West Virginia," voices pride, citing loyalty, landscape, and liberty. A Charleston area jazz musician who performed nationally and recorded several albums, Bell reportedly woke from a dream of the music and lyrics and wrote them down almost fully formed. She took the song to state leaders, and it was selected as the official centennial anthem and designated a state song. Like Hearne's song, Bell's references the state motto, and connections to family, place, and patriotism. It adds work ethic, "honest sweat born of honest toil" as an essential value. A rousing march, "This Is My West Virginia" is ready-made for band performances, parades, and celebrations.

Best known of the original three, "The West Virginia Hills" has perhaps the most complicated story, as there are questions about its authorship. Some sources attribute the lyrics to Ellen Ruddell King, and others to her husband, a poetic gift to his West Virginian wife. Ramella argues that evidence points to Ellen King as the writer due to the song's native perspective. The poem was first published under her name in September 1885 in a Glenville newspaper, so attribution to her husband appears to be rumor, Ramella claims, though other accounts disagree. Henry Everett Engle, a

West Virginia music teacher, set the poem to tune, copyrighting the song in 1886 (Ramella, "Three" 37). Unlike "My Home Sweet Home" and "This Is My West Virginia," King and Engle's song is more similar to "Country Roads," imbued with longing. The final verse of "The West Virginia Hills" actively pines for return to West Virginia; officially adopted as a state anthem in 1961, after years of being used unofficially, it harnessed ongoing pain and patterns of outmigration so profoundly felt in the 1940s and 50s.

Both "Country Roads" and "The West Virginia Hills" employ similar themes including references to heaven, reverent landscapes, and homesickness, as well as a sense of longing. Some articles on the origin of "Country Roads" claim that Taffy Nivert consulted an encyclopedia to learn more about West Virginia; it is worth wondering whether "The West Virginia Hills" was referenced there, either whole or in part. The West Virginia of "Country Roads" is "almost heaven." The West Virginia of the state's first anthem is "like our Prince Immanuel's land," where hills point skyward toward "the Great Almighty." "Country Roads" captures a timelessness in its expression that life in West Virginia is "older than the trees," but "younger than the mountains," where life is still "growing like a breeze." Likewise, "West Virginia Hills" claims "no changes can be noticed," even as the world changes around the speaker.

Most interestingly, both songs look toward home from afar, with the speaker in "Country Roads," longing to be taken "to the place I belong," with an urgency that "I should have been home yesterday." The speaker in "West Virginia Hills" longs too, "still" thinking of a "happy home," a place "ever dream[t] of." A marked difference, though, is that the speaker of "Country Roads" is filled with immediate longing, while the speaker in "West Virginia Hills" hopes to return someday, as life takes place elsewhere, in a "home beyond the mountains," and a return is dependent on fate:

> In the evening time of life
> If my Father only wills
> I shall still behold the vision of those West Virginia hills.

One anticipates a visit, the other prays for final return. Ultimately, "Country Roads" is more hopeful, anticipating an imminent trip home, just a drive away. It is almost heaven, and we can still get there alive.

Ramella discusses "The West Virginia Hills" as having "majesty and thunder" and an "inspired chorus" which prompts a "call and echoed reply." It is prime for singing, and it was sung at family gatherings, "for pleasure," like "Country Roads" is today (Ramella, "Three" 37). It was widely used at state events, at schools, and published for these purposes, even in church hymnals. A 2018 article in *Appalachian Magazine* claims, "Though the song has been largely forgotten by most West Virginians today," it "was published in Appalachian hymnals throughout much of the early 1900s and was once the undisputed anthem of the Mountain State, being sung or played at nearly all official state functions." I found that it is still well-known among state residents. "The West Virginia Hills" is among the anthems acknowledged in my research; in nearly two hundred responses, only one response acknowledged "This Is My West Virginia." About 20 percent of respondents named "The West Virginia Hills" among songs they knew about the state, more than any other besides "Country Roads." Interestingly, many responses indicated that they learned the song as children and held it fondly in their memories. I learned it from my maternal grandmother, a former schoolteacher. She knew "The West Virginia Hills" by heart, and her voice, raspy from years of smoking Salem menthols, was loud and strong. I imagine she sang it with her sixth-grade students at Farmington Elementary, too. I went to my first 4-H meeting already knowing the song because she had taught it to me.

Aside from these official anthems, there exist unofficial songs worth mentioning. "My Home Among the Hills," written in 1961 by E. W. James, is widely used at West Virginia Wesleyan College functions and state and regional events. It plays along with "Country Roads" on hold music rotations on West Virginia University phone systems and is included in 4-H songbooks.

About 12 percent of my survey respondents named "My Home Among the Hills" as a song they recognized and loved for its sentimentality. Though legislation to recognize it officially has been introduced several times, it remains unadopted. Many who grew up in West Virginia will remember Taylor County teacher Pam Spring's "The 55 Counties Song," used in public school curricula, which names state facts, and lists the counties alphabetically. Spring's song, like other pseudo-anthems, is used for teaching and promotional purposes.

In my survey research, many respondents mentioned the 4-H organization as a source of their song-knowledge. One person wrote: "I was in 4H until I was 21. I know all the West Virginia Songs!" Singing is a hallmark of the 4-H program traditionally; it has published songbooks regularly since the 1920s, and each state organization has its own specific songs in addition to national ones. Jason Burnside documents music in West Virginia 4-H camps, and claims that many of participants' favorite songs are ones referencing the state, including "Country Roads" (43). West Virginia 4-H adopts many state-themed songs in addition to the official anthems, including "Rhododendron," "West Virginia Boys and Girls," and even Kathy Mattea's 1986 song "Come Home to West Virginia," which was also used in tourism materials. A tune of the same name as Mattea's, Eugene Landau Murphy's 2016 "Come Home to West Virginia," employs a big band, Sinatraesque vibe. Different from the others, Murphy intentionally wrote "Come Home" as an anthem and tribute, and reportedly offered it, free of charge, to West Virginia's tourism department for promotional purposes (Marks).

These songs all show devotion in ways that cannot resonate beyond place because of their rhetorical purposes: Intended for West Virginians, for learning, promotion, patriotism, and celebration, they are not meant as industry hits. Still, they are heartfelt tributes, no matter how they are performed, heard, or received. In contrast, "Country Roads" has popular appeal. Its generality holds power, evokes hiraeth universally. This is consistent with the songwriters' impressions of the state, too: Nivert gazed over the Ohio toward Wheeling, where she spent time with college friends; Denver's gigs with the Mitchell Trio took him to high-energy clubs and colleges but not into the woods or hollows; Danoff had fantastic stories for reference. These are impressions of fantasy that ring true enough, fueled by cultural conversations, current events, politics, and economics, backlit by the evening news.

Popular music is transactional. When effective, music creates imaginary interconnectedness between listener and artists in "a performance that serves to bring out fully its (inner) meaning and where listeners read this emotional meaning by bringing their personal experience to bear on the performance" (Connell and Gibson 29). A song creates a kind of agreement between performer and audience, and in the case of "Country Roads," meaning is created through that exchange and connected to emplaced being. West Virginians, in individual and institutional ways, are responsible for taking up the song and perpetuating its continued resonance. This is an active transaction. We know it is not of our place, but we believe it anyway. This is evidenced in how so many West Virginian musicians perform and transform "Country Roads."

WEST VIRGINIA *IS* HOME: "COUNTRY ROADS" RECLAIMED BY MOUNTAIN STATE MUSICIANS

A West Virginian hearing "Country Roads" anywhere in the world feels called back to West Virginia specifically. The song, as we have seen, is particularly powerful when heard and experienced by West Virginians who are far from home. Hiraeth manifests in abstract longing, but homesickness is tangible. This feeling is compounded when we look toward home from the place we call home. In other words, we can be in West Virginia, singing "Country Roads," and still feel that deep call, one that cannot be fully realized, since the "almost heaven" of "Country Roads" is exactly that: almost. It almost captures what it means to be West Virginian; we are almost there, almost home—but never truly, because the West Virginia of "Country Roads" simply does not exist. And still, West Virginian artists attempt to reclaim and reframe "Country Roads" to better reflect the homes they know.

"Country Roads" surfaces in many songs written directly about West Virginia. For instance, Jason O'Brien, who became known for his song "Pray for West Virginia," written after 2016 flooding damaged counties all over the state, wrote a tribute called "Almost Heaven," which explicitly references state landmarks and other aspects of life in the Mountain State. Wyatt Turner, in his song "You Remind Me of West Virginia," references "Country Roads" throughout the lyrics. Ohio to West Virginia transplant Joey Adams's song, "Mountain Mama," alludes to themes and words from the song, referring to "roads, moonshine, and almost heaven." West Virginia rap artist 6'6 240, on his 2009 album *Hard Work and Dedication*, collaborated with rockers Shadow of a Martyr on a song called "Almost Heaven," which borrows the chorus verbatim, sandwiched between descriptions of party scenes and women who have a tendency to remove their tops "even in December." Singer-songwriter Aristotle Jones, who labels himself an "Appalachian Soul Man," interweaves "Country Roads" into his version of "The West Virginia Hills." There are many other examples.

Like these artists, for West Virginians displaced or in-place, a renegotiation of identity must occur for us to take up "Country Roads." We must, at the very least, suspend our disbelief and embrace the imaginary place in the song because what we feel is real. West Virginia as a place is real, even though it exists remade in the larger cultural imagination. In his book about returning to Appalachia, *Hollow and Home: A History of Self and Place*, E. Fred Carlisle captures this duality of place, the actual fact of "location, topography, landscape, and buildings" in concert with "psychological, social, and cultural influences at work," describing place as "event." The happenings and shape of the places we inhabit both influence people who inhabit them and structure "how people live" in their environments (Carlisle 12). "Country Roads" does, for many West Virginians, tell us something about ourselves, our culture, and our beliefs. We have already begun to consider West

Virginian identity as it is and is not reflected in "Country Roads": It is one of the stories told about place, rather than a story told *by* the place. The song, performed and adapted, becomes a kind of happening that shapes and is shaped by place through hiraeth, its pastoral sense, and its universal resonance.

Music is a symbol of the self and contexts, "powerful because it brings together both the experience of the intensely subjective and personal with the external, cultural, and collective." Music helps us understand who we are, how we are, and where we are. It belongs to groups and spaces, and it can be rhetorically appropriated to engage meanings. It is mobile, too; a song like "Country Roads" moves across audiences and genres, just as it moves us physically. Music creates affiliations between and among people, and "connects the private experience to the public. It blurs the self and other; the song we listen to expresses our feelings even though we did not write it" (Bloustien, Peters, and Luckman xxiii, xxv). For West Virginians, "Country Roads" declares our place in the world in a way that allows for acceptable recognition. It is *true enough*.

"Country Roads" seems authentic because it feels complimentary in a conversation that for years focused on the negative. Connected to our place, it does not feel imaginary. Its felt sense of honesty resonates. We believe Denver loved us and saw us. While Denver dedicates space in his autobiography (and in his music) elaborating on the theme of home, and while he writes in detail about Colorado, where he lived, as well as other places he toured (China, Russia, Germany, Australia) and visited (Alaska and Hawaii) he never addresses West Virginia as a place. A major theme in his book, *Take Me Home: An Autobiography*, is a sense of homelessness, searching. There is no evidence in Denver's book, however, that the search for home led him to West Virginia. Even if the title references the song, evidence of John Denver's affinity for West Virginia is peripheral.

All tributes to place are like love letters. We see this in "The West Virginia Hills," in "West Virginia, My Home Sweet Home," and in "This Is My West Virginia." We see it in Mattea's "Come

Home," a tribute to love and a lover, warm and well-known. These anthems are specific, capturing the actual place accurately, but lack appeal beyond that place, perhaps *because* of that accuracy. "Country Roads" is like a letter from a brand-new love—surface level and skin-deep. In the warm glow of novelty, filled with potential, "Country Roads" whispers something sweet but not quite accurate. In the blossom of new romance, a compliment like this creates connection, feels like a gift, makes a still-shy lover feel seen, recognized, special. In a moment like this, we accept that declaration as a version of the truth, even if it does not quite align with what we know. The attention feels so good, we believe it anyway. But what we need is long-lasting love, sickness-and-health kind of love, love that sees flaws and takes you as you are. "Country Roads" cannot give us that. It is superficial appreciation and romantic imaginary that allows us to experience hiraeth. "Country Roads" as popular music serves its purpose exceedingly well.

The problem with using "Country Roads" as a definitional text of identity is that doing so fails to seek reality or see the problems, or it highlights the opposite, outside perspective, dismissing West Virginia as wholly unredeemable. The "purely celebratory stance" to looking at Appalachia, Emily Satterwhite tells us, "is that a romantic view often relies on superficial understandings that can be just as reductive as negative stereotypes." This superficiality is "overly celebratory" and can contribute to denial of "full understanding of the complexities of the region's history" and our own lived experiences (Satterwhite, "Intro" 5). This brings us again to rhetorical purpose: The purpose of "Country Roads" was to be a hit song, not to define a region. However, it does both, and in doing so, obscures the voices—and the stories—of people living in West Virginia. As one of my survey responses describes in reference to other West Virginia songs, "'Country Roads' blocked everything else!" But there are songs about West Virginia, written by West Virginians, about, for, and of place, and those songs are worth a listen.

4

A WEST VIRGINIA STATE OF MIND

LIVED AND LIVING STORIES
The West Virginia Music Hall of Fame Exhibits Museum is located on the second floor of the Charleston Town Center, an early 1980s shopping mall, but the organization's offices are situated in a beautiful old house on Lee Street, where Michael Lipton, the director, works. On the day I visit, Michael introduces me to John Ellison, who wrote a song about West Virginia and is a West Virginia Music Hall of Fame inductee. I meet Ellison next door in another old Victorian house, in a rehearsal space full of instruments.

    John Ellison is tall, lanky, and young for his age of almost eighty years. He smiles warmly, takes my hand, sits down with me, picks up a guitar, and immediately plays his original song: "West Virginia State of Mind," full of tangible images that I recognize immediately: gravel roads, coal trucks, porch sitting, blackberry cobbler . . . Despite our differences in age, background, and race, Ellison's song feels like home to me. He tells me his childhood memories of coal towns in McDowell County and the bitterness he felt when he left as a young man in the 1960s. Emphasizing the contradiction, Ellison says, "I love West Virginia, that's why I come back all the time, because I love these hills, but when I left, it was not on a good note." A frequent visitor who performs on *Mountain Stage* and at West Virginia Music Hall of Fame events, Ellison keeps coming back to the place and "beautiful people," some of whom, in his words, "lived in peace and harmony" despite challenges of segregation, displacement, and racism.

Later, I play Ellison's song for my father, who listens with eyes closed. He is moved, too. I try to compare "West Virginia State of Mind" with "Take Me Home, Country Roads," but I am not sure where to begin. These are two different stances completely. The images in "Country Roads" feel dreamlike, idealized. Ellison's depictions feel real. Although both are nostalgic, "West Virginia State of Mind" is solid, bringing me to a place I can touch, hear, see, and smell. Specific, and real, it will likely never have the same kind of global appeal as "Country Roads." I wonder: In the echoes that swirl around "Country Roads," where is there room for John Ellison's voice? Or those of other West Virginians who write about a home they know, rather than one imagined?

West Virginia is a real place that outsiders see as fiction. No wonder we might choose to embrace the simplicity of "Country Roads." The existence of an international music industry within a larger media presence has taken up a beautiful and vivid, but inaccurate, description of our place and flung it out into the world, making it a global anthem, contributing to the way actual place is both visible and invisible at once. When I look for accurate portrayals of West Virginia, I see them in work like Michael Lipton's at the Hall of Fame, hear them in voices like John Ellison's or those of many artists, folks whose words and music offer closer realities but may be silent outside the state.

"Country Roads" is like a glamor shot. In the 1980s, Glamor Shots were a popular national trend in mall photography studios. A person would book an appointment and be greeted by a wardrobe designer, a hair and makeup artist, and a photographer, who would all work together to create an image of the subject, coiffed, poofed, polished. The end result would be several images, airbrushed and touched with highlights, soft glows, dramatic backdrops. These images, created by a team of strangers, reflect a glossy, highly edited, sometimes ridiculous version of the subject, suitable for hanging in the hallway, or gracing a partner's desk at the office. "Country Roads" is a glamor shot we hang in our minds: a created image, polished and airbrushed, suitable for sharing. It is a rhetorical tool: It has purpose, meant for a specific audience, to convey a particular kind of message, a narrative not entirely real.

There are many songs about West Virginia written by West Virginians, but there is evidence that West Virginians do not know them. When I asked survey respondents to name songs they knew about West Virginia, most of them (about 80 percent) said they knew none besides "Country Roads." Most respondents who did know songs about West Virginia named "The West Virginia Hills" (20 percent) or "My Home Among the Hills" (12 percent). Some others mentioned songs used widely at events: "Simple Gifts," "Hail West Virginia," and alma maters. Several noted songs that peripherally reference West Virginia written by popular artists: Alabama, Hank Williams Jr., Gavin DeGraw, George Strait. Others mentioned Tyler Childers, who names West Virginia in some of his songs like "Charleston Girl." A Kentucky native, Childers often played in Charleston. Others mentioned songs that simply reminded them of West Virginia without direct naming: Loretta Lynn's 1970 "Coal Miner's Daughter," the folk song "Mountain Dew," or Merle Travis's 1974 "Sixteen Tons." These songs do not tell the story.

Travis Stimeling's book on contemporary songwriting in West Virginia demonstrates that local artists write music about history, people, events, small towns, and leaving, but they do not generally write the kind of simple homage that "Country Roads" represents. Stories told from within, privy to complications and complexities, cannot provide such a flatly positive, nostalgic view. Awareness of the real story will not allow it. Many West Virginia songs tell nuanced stories of place and help both songwriters and listeners better understand who we are. As Heather Bean argues, narrative is a mode of discourse that communicates values, and "when people tell their own stories, the narratives have multiple dimensions" (36). These self-constructed narratives might develop an image of what happened, without interpretation, as in folk ballads, or they might make a case about what is and how it should be, to move toward action, as in activist music and labor songs. They may also be tied to identity (Bean 37). When people tell their own stories, the stories carry power, are lived and living. Songs about West Virginia, written by West Virginians, take up these purposes, so that constructing a popular hit is secondary to engaging in narrative.

To be clear, it is not John Denver's, or Bill Danoff's, or Taffy Nivert's responsibility to speak a West Virginian truth. It is our responsibility to say and amplify our own truths. As scholar Amanda Hayes writes, "Appalachian rhetorical sovereignty, if one is possible, would require us to name ourselves and our experiences and for others to respect that naming" (37). West Virginians are, and have been, doing that. Music of and from West Virginia is not about abject glory of place. Rather, it wrestles with complexities: leaving and wanting to come home, detailing what we see and love, naming things that tear us apart and destroy us, and showing how we find ways to rebuild. Not typically anthems, these songs still express deep love and connection to place.

In my research, I have found that West Virginia music and songs can be distilled into themes that reveal complexity that "Country Roads" obscures, and while I cannot possibly mention every song (not even every song I love), in this chapter I want to illustrate how music by West Virginians delves into topics that define us, show our complexity, and dwell in identity. The story told by "Country Roads" is limited, and not just by virtue of being written peripherally about but not from and of the state. Denver's "farm-boy" image, with his shaggy blonde hair, and Coke bottle glasses, merges with a narrowed, monolithic conception of what we assume West Virginia is. Songs from West Virginia songwriters reflect it as a place of diverse history, represented with a range of rhetorical perspectives.

SONGS AS EXPLORATION OF A DIVERSE WEST VIRGINIA

Musicologist Andy Bennett discusses the ways in which musicians situate themselves in relation to their homes, a "recourse to local imagery" in an "attempt to resolve a problem of spatial alienation" for them as musicians. Bennett discusses active musicians in lives characterized by placelessness, dominated by touring and other demands of the industry. He claims that musicians "may seek ways to relocate themselves spiritually" at home and that "references to roots, origins, and memories in song, then, may act as a means through which rock and pop musicians attempt to negotiate placelessness associated with itinerant lifestyles and to reassert a sense of place, community and belonging in their lives" (73). Musicians in a place can write about that place to understand it more deeply and to convey that understanding to others. Singing "Country Roads" may be a declaration of West Virginian identity, but writing songs that emplace both singer and listener is an exploration of identity, a testament to reality, and a way of documenting history and its effect on people's lives.

West Virginia music reflects diverse perspectives. Elizabeth Englehardt cites a "hidden background" of a diverse Appalachia, in which "Mountaineers were African-American, Native American, and increasingly in the 1890s, Jewish, Eastern European, and Hispanic," showing that Appalachia's historically assumed "pure whiteness" is a kind of fiction (36–37). Appalachia was an already inhabited space that was colonized by people from across the world, as the coal industry in the 1800s in particular recruited millions, bringing diverse languages, customs, cultures, and bodies into the mountains (Jackson 28). Appalachia has been historically heterogenous, though it has not been recognized as such, even by academics, who have on the contrary perpetuated stereotypes of homogeneity (Jackson 32). Sociological texts, popular culture, and even academic literature, until recently, have presented a whitewashed version of Appalachia, silencing alternate stories, and yet "many things about Appalachia can be true simultaneously" (Catte 52). "Country

Roads" is part of this generalized imagery, but West Virginia musicians have long sung about specific, relevant issues that connect them to home. In his book on country music in West Virginia, Ivan Tribe discusses how musicians historically wrote songs that contained "acute observations" and "social commentary," and that "the harsh nature of the industrialization process in a state with rough terrain and the peculiar characteristics of lumbering, mining, and railroading may have been contributing factors" to songwriters' choices of subject matter (184). West Virginians today write about social and labor issues as well as everyday living.

A lasting example of this is Billy Edd Wheeler. Many of his songs predate "Country Roads" and address, in detail, experiences and spaces of West Virginia, sometimes naming place specifically, sometimes alluding to it. Wheeler's 1960s songs, such as "Coming of the Roads," "They Can't Put It Back," "Red Wing Black Bird," and "Coal Tattoo" are deeper descriptions of place but introduce similar themes as those later taken up in "Country Roads." In "Coming of the Roads," Wheeler sings not about nostalgia for roads that lead home but instead laments on the impacts of industrialization on both places and people, evoking imagery of barrenness, pollution, and smoke. In "Coal Tattoo," the speaker, left jobless by industrial machination and injury in the mines, travels away from home, looking for a dreamland where he can find work in new mines. Wheeler continued to write about Appalachian lived experience with songs such as "My Heart Will Always Be in West Virginia," among others.

Richard Ramella, in a 2004 *Goldenseal* article documenting different West Virginia songs, traces a range of musical compositions, from polkas to rock, from the 1860s forward. "Songs celebrating specific places," Ramella writes, "are of lasting interest to the people of those places" ("State" 26). This internal, personal interest keeps "Country Roads" relevant for West Virginians, but many songs could resonate more truthfully and complexly, if only we were able to hear them. More West Virginia songs and musicians are discussed in Travis Stimeling's *Songwriting in*

Contemporary West Virginia, which collects reflections from musicians, many of whom have written their own songs that "point to the powerful place that West Virginia has in their imaginations." Stimeling limits his text to folk music but includes regional and national artists and claims that "in virtually every community around the state, songwriters are trying to capture the experiences of their everyday lives, to tell the rich histories of the state and the broader Appalachian region, and to reframe its potent folklore for contemporary audiences" (1). This reframing resists the narrative in "Country Roads."

In the next pages, I address a few of many songs and artists who actively work to represent and redefine what it means to sing about West Virginia. My goal is not to simply catalog West Virginia songs; though I have created a playlist to share, and I invite readers to share favorites with me. Many of the songs I document mention West Virginia directly, and a few imply the state without naming it. All are fitting complements and contrasts placed in conversation with "Country Roads." Taken together, these songs present a counternarrative, sloughing away the nostalgic, romanticized, pastoral, and oversimplified visions of West Virginia "Country Roads" represents. In the intention of putting songs in conversation, I offer multiple perspectives and genres but limit my selections here to songs released after 1971, as the existence of "Country Roads," consciously or not, intentionally or not, has affected the way we think and write about West Virginia.

SONGS AND SONGWRITERS EXPRESSING WEST VIRGINIAN IDENTITY

Daniel Johnston's 1980 song "Wild West Virginia" stands in direct contrast with "Country Roads." While Johnston's song expresses a similar desire for return, it is to a deeply flawed place rather than a romantic idyll. Listening to it is like looking at "Country Roads" through a freshly cleaned window. In some ways, Johnston himself stands as a kind of foil to Denver: Raised in West Virginia, Johnston was a prolific songwriter who recorded his first two albums in his basement in the small town of New Cumberland before relocating to Texas. Widely recognized for his artistic genius, profiled in *Rolling Stone*, Johnston, who died in 2019, struggled with mental illness and spoke openly in interviews about how he used creativity to find solace. An influential voice in underground music, Johnston was embraced by punk and alternative musicians such as Kurt Cobain and collaborated with artists such as Lana Del Rey, Tom Waits, and Wilco.

Johnston influenced West Virginia musicians, too. In one article, Morgantown-born one-man band J. Marinelli says of "Wild West Virginia": "It should be associated with the state of West Virginia as much as that damn John Denver song" (qtd. in Mistich, "Hi . . ."). Johnston writes that he will return to West Virginia, a place of rurality, poverty, political corruption, and broken infrastructure but where God "created a pretty picture." An homage to imperfection, "Wild West Virginia" lists problems yet expresses love simultaneously, simply, openly. Songs about place, of place, and from place are more powerfully able to do that: to recognize and still express love in spite of reality.

Many West Virginia artists speak actively within existing conversations. When Morgantown's Aristotle Jones performs his remade version of "The West Virginia Hills," he incorporates "Country Roads" at the end, nodding to "almost heaven" in the final chorus, and closing with "those country roads will always take me home." In doing so, Jones amplifies a silenced perspective. Jones transforms the "West Virginia Hills" not just by singing in his own voice, a Black man's voice, but by modifying the words to the state anthem. Gone are references to leaving; the speaker in this version stays, as do family members, "guided by a mother's skill" and "a miner's will." Jones omits the last verse entirely, since there is no longing for return; Jones himself stays to make a difference. This is about a hidden West Virginian identity, claiming space and uncovering a story that has been obscured. Jones explained to me, "The story I like to tell with my music, and the story I think it's important people hear these days, is of 'the other porches.'" The other porches to which Jones refers include those from Scotts Run, the place from which white miners were removed to populate Arthurdale, and where Black residents were left behind. Reminiscent of bell hooks's description of the "perfect porch," a "place where a soul can rest" and hear "divine voices speak," these are spaces of belonging (152). Voices from these porches tell the histories of Black people in West Virginia, like stories from Jones's grandfather, who had been a miner in Osage, who sang in a gospel group, and who passed along a tradition of music and narrative, unheard outside the small, segregated community. "Essentially there was a whole story that was being told, a whole history that was being passed down from generation to generation of West Virginians, from a whole different set of porches, and the music was different as well," Jones elaborated. In a local TV news interview, Jones tells anchors that he wants to be an ambassador for West Virginia, to celebrate "young people, brave people, and smart people" and to educate others about the state and the "courage, strength and fortitude" of West Virginians. To this end, Jones is doing more than just writing and performing songs. He hosts a weekly radio show and podcast, *Sounds Good to Me*, that features West Virginian artists and hosts festivals and concerts to promote their music. He performs widely, as well.

Jones's "West Virginia Hills" is easy and bluesy, appropriate for a self-described "Appalachian Soul Man" whose credits include several songs about West Virginia life, as well as one about race and growing up Black in the mountain state, "The Talk." For him, "Country Roads" is a beautiful song, but one that glosses over troubling aspects of living in a rural state as a Black man. Literal country roads can be dangerous places of uncertainty rather than the pastoral paths imagined by Danoff, Nivert, and Denver. Jones reiterates, "If I'm on 33 and get pulled over between Elkins and Buckhannon, I don't know how this is going to go. There's nobody out here, there's no lights, there's nothing. It's just me on the side of the road. Nobody's going to stop if they see me pulled over.

Sometimes it's 'Country Roads get me home as fast as I can.' And I'm from this state." He tells me "Country Roads," in his thinking, taps into "a time that almost didn't exist," and is unreflective of lived reality, since what is imagined in the song is "not really what people were doing." Jones's music echoes Bill Withers, another West Virginian who wrote about life as he experienced it; it echoes John Ellison's experience, too.

Like Aristotle Jones's version of "The West Virginia Hills," John Ellison's song "West Virginia State of Mind," names and claims West Virginian identity, providing a counternarrative to "Country Roads." Ellison writes about untold West Virginian experiences. In "West Virginia State of Mind," Ellison actively recalls his childhood. He told me he "wrote that song with this picture in mind: where I grew up," and images of Ellison's memories show vividly: "I see the coal trucks going up and down the mountain. I see the old people sitting in their chairs. You know, I see the dirt, the gravel road." Evocative of the sensory experience of his youth, "State of Mind" describes scenes in detail that may not resonate with someone who lacks specific knowledge of place.

Also like Jones, Ellison is committed to sharing his story as a Black West Virginian. Ellison faced discrimination in West Virginia before leaving in the 1960s. In our interview, he described the pain of being excluded from a songwriting contest because judges could not award a prize to a Person of Color. He recalled the injustice of having his guitar broken and being arrested for playing music in a bus terminal, a public space. He remembered the unfairness of having his most famous song, "Some Kind of Wonderful," misattributed to white musicians because when performed by his band, Soul Brothers Six, it was relegated to Black radio. "When we first recorded it in 1967," Ellison explained, "we were signed with Atlantic Records. Our song went to #2 throughout the U.S. but only on Black radio stations because we were a Black group." When the song was recorded by a white band, they got credit because "white radio stations wouldn't play my song."

As with Ray Charles's and other versions of "Country Roads," the industry looked to profit from all markets.

Ellison explicitly addresses racism in "Wake Up Call (Black Like Me)." This song describes racial violence, citing specific incidents in West Virginia and across the nation, and directly calls for change. Ellison's story is not just one of discrimination, it is also one of outmigration. At seventeen, he boarded a bus to New York on a one-way ticket because "there was no future for me here in terms of recording at the time or excelling in a career that I wanted to be in. So, in order to achieve my goals, I had to leave." Although Ellison's leaving was, and is, complicated by injustice, its effect is vividly demonstrated in "West Virginia State of Mind."

Outmigration Songs: Homesickness, Homecoming, Homegoing

Many West Virginians wrote about leaving contemporaneously with "Country Roads" as well as after. The most famous of these is perhaps Hazel Dickens's "West Virginia, My Home." Richard Ramella characterizes "West Virginia, My Home" as "the lament of the economic exile," which, in the 1960s, "became a musical genre that spoke to the dispossessed" at the height of Appalachian outmigration. These songs are "less about place and more about time—the disappeared, idealized, nurturing West Virginia of youth" ("State" 27). Within this genre, Dickens stands as spokesperson, transforming traditional sounds into songs looking toward home but written from Baltimore, where she moved for work in the 1950s. A pioneer, Dickens, described by Brian Hinton as both "a novelty" and "a threat," stood out as a woman playing bluegrass in the sixties. Her music was widely recognized, as Dickens's collaboration with Alice Gerrard led to Smithsonian recordings and a long discography (Hinton 245–47).

Dickens lived the life "Country Roads" is about; forced to leave home in the mountains to find life elsewhere, she wrote and sang about this explicitly. In a published interview, John Lilly recounts that "Hazel completed the song 'West Virginia, My Home' in about 1972 and first recorded it on an album titled *Hazel & Alice*, with singer Alice Gerrard, released in 1973. Hazel rerecorded the song in 1980, with her own band and with a slower tempo and a more emotive feeling" (Lilly). This song has been covered by country and bluegrass artists, including Ginny Hawker, Kathy Mattea, and others. While not as well known as "Country Roads," one might still hear it played at state events by local musicians. About 5 percent of my survey respondents named "West Virginia, My Home" as known, making it recognized nearly as much or more than some official state songs. It is striking in the way it melds longing for return with regret for having left. Bound in the city, the speaker dreams of home, and, like the speaker in "The West Virginia Hills," return is a homecoming that can happen only at the end of a life of toil.

"West Virginia, My Home" is about displacement. The speaker never finds a sense of place or peace. Dickens told John Lilly that she wrote the song in response to the isolation and homesickness she felt in Baltimore:

> The first verse, I think, came about by the differences between people, you know, the people that you met, which is different than us. People looked down upon us as hillbillies, you know. They just did (laughter). No matter what you did or how much you tried to clean up your act or be like city people, they still looked upon you as hillbillies, and that always bothered me. (Interview)

Beyond nostalgia, Dickens's work is social commentary, "focused on the experiences, needs, and rights" of "Appalachian migrants, who brawled and drank to deal with their alienation" (Bean 103). "West Virginia, My Home," takes up place and relation to place as an outsider in a way that "Country Roads" does not. Adding a layer of regret and sadness, Dickens's speaker is changed through leaving, confined to a life of work in a city, penned in by economic hardship and the pain of being othered. As in "The West Virginia Hills," the speaker in "West Virginia, My Home" visits in dreams, hoping to return to West Virginia in death. A subtext in "West Virginia, My Home," then, is discrimination Appalachians felt away from home consistent with other works addressing outmigration: "The dilemma of staying home and not reaching one's potential versus pursuing opportunity outside the state and losing connection to one's family and traditions represents a major theme" (Creasman 3). This is further complicated, also, by experiences of those like John Ellison, for whom staying was untenable due to racial injustice.

Since the 1950s, Appalachian migrants have struggled to find acceptance and make lives in cities. Industrial declines during the 1980s left many facing the same issues they faced at home, including lack of employment, increasing cost of education, and devaluing of high school diplomas. This made for increased cultural and emotional displacement of an already physically displaced group, one for whom, "despite lack of work in the city, return to Appalachia [was] not an option" (Bean 74). This is a deep homelessness, the opposite of hiraeth—not at home where you are, no home to return to—one that is explicit in other songs, but not so much in "Country Roads."

This sense of displacement may be even further exacerbated, since many Appalachians who have left the region still identify it as home, living there only part of the time. Even those peripherally disconnected from home, as "second or third generation migrants" still think of an ancestral home but are "no longer familiar with Appalachian folkways and are considered urbanites by rural Appalachians" (Bean 90). Neither staying nor returning is an option. Like "West Virginia, My Home," Kathy Mattea's 1986 "Leaving West Virginia" captures loss and pain of leaving but more so for the generation after Hazel Dickens, who were told from childhood that they *must* leave in order to find success. The speaker in Mattea's "Leaving West Virginia" knows it's "her time" to leave, to fulfill her destiny, but she does so at cost. Even so, she can never lose her sense of home or disconnect from West Virginia entirely. In the last verse, she asks philosophically about the meaning of home, settling on the idea that it is kept in the heart as a measure of self and security. This is a song about leaving and never returning, finding a place elsewhere, despite an internalized sense of obligation to stay.

This journey away from home pervades outmigration music and takes on a different relevance today. Benedict Anderson discusses metaphorical pilgrimage in the working world: The modern journey of success (climbing the corporate ladder) is one without return. People are sent from one place to the next, and each move represents new rank so that "the last thing the functionary wants is to return home" because return is regression (55). For many West Virginians, there is no hope of return, and that leads to experiencing life as a kind of unfinished pilgrimage. This incompleteness helps to amplify the shared hiraeth we feel when "Country Roads" plays—like the speaker in the song, we "should have been home yesterday." Yet "Leaving West Virginia" captures this displacement more accurately. The West Virginia Mattea describes, one that sees us as we are and releases us, understanding we can never truly come back, is not the same place depicted in "Country Roads," which sees us as we wish to be and promises belonging.

WEST VIRGINIA CHOSE ME: SONGS OF LOVE, ACTIVISM, HISTORY, AND COMMUNITY

Some West Virginia songs address what it means to come home, to stay home, or to find a home one did not expect. Some explore the taking up of West Virginian identity for transplants—coming in rather than going away. Charleston writer Colleen Anderson, a 1970s transplant, released "West Virginia Chose Me" on a 2006 album, though she had been performing the song long before that. It explores a sense of adopted identity, remembering friends who have left, in contrast to the speaker, who is staying perhaps against her own better judgment, despite her dreams of "higher mountains" and seaside cottages, because "West Virginia won't let go of [her]." This is a song about finding home, as

> It's not we who do the choosing
> We are chosen by the place.

A VISTA volunteer who came and stayed, Anderson describes "West Virginia Chose Me" as "the story of [her] life." Like Iris Bell, Anderson found "West Virginia Chose Me" in a dream. "I actually was sleeping when I began to hear the chorus and grabbed a notepad by the bed," she told me; the song is autobiographical, so it "came together easily" over a couple of days. After she finished, Anderson shared it with Larry Groce, then-host of *Mountain Stage*, and he performed it on the show. "West Virginia Chose Me," Anderson's first West Virginia song, is different from her others, which address social, political, and environmental activism.

Anderson's song "If You Love My West Virginia" was inspired by the state legislature's response to a 2014 chemical spill that contaminated the Elk River in Charleston and subsequently affected water for residents of nine surrounding counties. As she prepared to attend a public hearing, Anderson told me, she took a walk to think about what she would say to legislators. She thought about how the state belongs to its people, and to her as a person committed to making it better—"it's not just this place, it's *my* place"—so loving a place should also translate into action. The song's lyrics express this love directly, grounded in the refrain "if you love my West Virginia," which begins each line: "You will keep her waters clean" and "her mountains green." It also expresses love metaphorically: "You'll respect her like your mother and defend her like your child," and "grieve to see her kneel for the ones who only use her for the riches they can steal." This song is short and powerful—tailored to fit the two-minute time allotment for public comments—and ends in allusion to "The West Virginia Hills," resting on tradition in a way that West Virginians can recognize. When Anderson sang the song, a cappella, during the public comment period, she received a standing ovation. She remembers, "All the people way up in the stands stood up and applauded," while "all the legislators looked away." Looking away—and worse—from those who speak truth to power is a part of West Virginia history, as is a musical tradition that tells the story of that legacy, one that is absent from "Country Roads."

Despite current patterns of West Virginians voting against their better interests, which align with Appalachian studies scholar John Gaventa's sense of quiescence, or apparent consensus with a status quo that does not serve the people, West Virginian musicians have not been "socialized into silence" or "socialized into compliance" (18–19). Music has long been used for organizing, and, as John Williams documents, Appalachian folk music is heavily associated with the labor movement and "struggles for social justice, an identification that persisted throughout the twentieth century" (*Appalachia* 278). For example, Kentucky singer Florence Reece's "Which Side are You On?" is quintessential Appalachian protest music—and women's music. Reece's lyrics express "there are no neutrals" in this music or in this place (Bean 185). Protest songs are complex, fueled by life's complications, written with purpose and urgency—contrasting the simplistic nostalgia of "Country Roads." Many West Virginian musicians write to compel change.

One example is community organizer Elaine Purkey, who spent much of her life as an activist in Lincoln County. Colleen Anderson cites Purkey as an influence, a model for place-specific music, grounded in purpose. Purkey, who died from COVID-19 in 2020, symbolized West Virginian resistance through "her powerful voice and soul stirring songs" (Gartner 16). Best known for her song "One Day More," written in response to the 1985 Pittston Coal Strike and published on Smithsonian Folkways' 2006 record *Classic Labor Songs*, Purkey gained a following as "audiences across the nation have been moved by her mountain singing, which she delivers full throttle, and her heartfelt original songs" (Gartner 16). Purkey found herself moved into activism through need; much of her music addresses issues specific to West Virginia.

Starkly different from nostalgic state songs, Purkey's, like other activist anthems, express immediate need, a call to community and a cry against absentee land ownership, profiteer industrialism, and mountaintop removal. "Keepers of the Mountains," which Purkey wrote at the request of another activist and performed a cappella in her powerful voice, is an essential song of this genre. The first lines set the scene in West Virginia, and the next lines create conflict and urgency by noting "there's something evil happening" and censure those who are causing environmental destruction, threatening them with exposure and justice. "Keepers" depicts environmental spoilage, political corruption, and efforts of everyday West Virginians to protect and preserve place. Purkey is part of a long tradition of real mountain mamas and miner's ladies on picket lines, women who establish community centers, advocate for health care and black lung benefits, and work in local schools to improve the quality of education in West Virginia and across Appalachia.

Stereotypes about West Virginian women narrowly portray possibilities of how to be in the world. Depictions in West Virginia are no different from stereotypes across Appalachia; these are grounded in popular culture and historical traditions of identity. Sally Ward Maggard documents stereotypes of Appalachian women as romanticized or degraded: the woman as the "quiet caretaker" of the family, the wizened crone shooting groundhogs in the garden, or the promiscuous minx in too-short, too tight denim. Stereotypes of mountain women "are counterpoints to the modern world, representing either a simpler rural life or a ridiculous fringe population of deficient, mysterious characters" (Maggard 229). Yet Appalachian women took prominent roles in community organization throughout labor movements of the 1960s and 1970s, fighting to save communities, and this has continued today, as documented by Jessica Wilkerson's scholarship, and as demonstrated by recent teacher leadership, environmental activism, and women's healthcare advocacy. Music is part of that tradition.

In West Virginia music, as well as in social movements, historically women have something to say, but their voices are quiet in "Country Roads." We cannot discount Taffy Nivert's contribution, as she of all three songwriters has perhaps the deepest West Virginia connection. Appalachia still evokes nostalgia for her. Nivert's father worked in a coal mine in bordering western Pennsylvania, and she went to college in Steubenville, Ohio, just across the river from Wheeling, West Virginia, where she spent time during those years. Nivert traveled the highways from her home in Washington, DC, to campus, listening to the hum of the motor and looking out the window. She described the thumping of tires on Pennsylvania concrete roads, and how the sound changed when the car crossed onto West Virginia two-lane blacktop. Nivert remembered her dorm room, where, she told me, "I could look out across the Ohio and see Weirton and Follansbee. And it was beautiful. What I saw was a town, railroad tracks and a road, and then I could see these mountains behind it. It went up, just so pretty, the foothills and then the mountains. I got to stare at that a lot." As much as West Virginia was "peripheral" to her life and experience, the impression remained so that, when she and Danoff began writing "Country Roads" years later, she tapped into memory. She asked herself, "what is it about West Virginia that makes me want to go home?" and she recalled, "well, that's the motherland. So, I admit, and I claim, that I came up with mountain mama." Nivert's "mountain mama" is evocative of home, of hiraeth, but she is conceptual rather than real. She is also complicated because of Nivert's real connection: her own longing for a place of her past.

"Country Roads" evokes stereotypes correlating women and mother figures in place, as it "rhetorically conflates women and land," thus invoking a particular Appalachian identity. In the song's journey, the traveler is "led by a loving woman across majestic land over winding, mountainous roads," reminiscent of many forms of art where man is subject actor and woman is object (C. Massey 132). In "Country Roads" women are peripheral and imaginary, much like landscape and place. Other West Virginian songs center actual experience and person, and one that reminds me of home and of real women there is Mike Morningstar's "West Virginia Girl." Written in the early 1970s, after his return from Vietnam, Morningstar's first West Virginia song describes my own mother, grandmother, friends, and myself—women whom I know may self-identify as "Mountain Mamas." Morningstar's "West Virginia Girl" addresses elements of lived experience, grounded in specific place imagery. Like "Country Roads," it is a love letter, but the similarity ends there. Morningstar's song is of a love that stands the test of time, has weathered hardships, and still endures. A tribute, the speaker names his mother, grandmother, and others, and sings for West Virginian women, including those he does not know. Morningstar names places: Bluefield, Wheeling, Farmington, and conditions that affected people: mine disasters, farming, poverty. The women in "West Virginia Girl" are hardworking and wise, weighed down by time and tragedy. "West Virginia Girl" is appreciation and love, "small comfort though [his] song may bring," Morningstar writes. In contrast with the "mountain mama" of "Country Roads," Morningstar's "West Virginia Girl" is complex and complicated, like the place she inhabits.

In a profile of Morningstar in *Goldenseal*, Charlotte Whipkey writes that he is "honest and forthcoming about who he is and what he stands for. He writes it, and he lives it" (12). Anchored in a sense of commitment to place and people, Morningstar draws inspiration from the world around him. Citing a lack of specificity and interest as a deficit and "what [he] hate[s] about commercial music," Morningstar told Whipkey, "If it doesn't speak to my soul or tell a story or turn a light on—an awareness—I lose interest" (14). "West Virginia Girl" is consistent with his pattern of writing of place, from place, for place. Morningstar aims to "honor" West Virginians and to "help West Virginians be proud of where they come from and who they are" (qtd. in Whipkey, 15). His other West Virginia songs, all of which are made even more compelling when juxtaposed against "Country Roads," include "Mountaineers Are Always Free," a descriptive tribute to preserving place and family legacy, and "Buffalo Creek," which documents a 1972 disaster in which coal slurry flooded a town, killing 125 people. In 2016, Morningstar collaborated with another West Virginia artist, Dustin McCray, on a release, "Almost Heaven," which directly answers "Country Roads" with the question "if this ain't heaven where the hell can it be?" Morningstar writes from love, for a local audience who shares his understanding and finds meaning in specificity, and draws from lived events and experiences.

West Virginian musical voices bring forward historical and cultural legacies in a way that "Country Roads" cannot. These singer-songwriters address history, reality, and labor, as in Kathy Mattea's 2008 album *Coal*, inspired by the 2006 Sago mine disaster, a compilation of others' songs, including Billy Edd Wheeler and Hazel Dickens. A more recent example is Mary Hott's 2021 *Devil in the Hills: Coal Country Reckoning*, a series of vignettes about coal camp and railroad life that addresses history, exploitation, child labor, and other darkness, "hidden in the hills." The song "They Built a Railroad" narrativizes the industrial revolution in West Virginia, describing absentee land ownership, coal baronies, exploitation of women and children, and subsequent mine wars that resulted from worker uprisings. Accompanied by an informational booklet, Hott's album is grounded in documented accounts, academic research, and colored by her own commitment to home. *Devil in the Hills* is infused with traditional themes and traditions in Appalachian women's music: "Aching love ballads, often including a tragic element of separation from the mountains, home, and family [that] clearly focus on issues integral to theodicy, particularly empirical theodicy: the meaning of life, suffering, and love" (Bean 7). Hott's work infuses story with spirituality and legacy. Interestingly, Hott intentionally puts these accounts of history in conversation with "Country Roads," which she includes on the album as a slowed-down, gospel style version. Hott's "Country Roads," like Brandi Carlile's, is mournful rather than celebratory, complementing the tone and texture of her album. Music like this re-creates the past in the present, demonstrating that history is still alive in West Virginia.

Not all songs about West Virginia mention West Virginia explicitly: West Virginian musical practice profoundly connects with story and politics, highlighting values, labor issues, and historical preservation. Travis Stimeling writes that "nearly all the songwriters profiled in [his] collection point to the powerful place that West Virginia has in their imaginations" (1). Many West Virginia songwriters imply or even outright claim that all their songs are about West Virginia anyway. Huntington's Patrick Stanley, for example, told Stimeling "everything [he has] to say—even though it's not directly about the area—is inherently about being from here" (116). Parkersburg musician Todd Burge told me that all his songs are about West Virginia (email communication). West Virginia in songs, even when unnamed, is visible, while the West Virginia of "Country Roads" is obscured.

Many songwriters compose from place without naming it. Larry Groce's lovely "This Is My Home," recorded as a part of a fundraising benefit, names features and fixtures of the Mountain State easily recognizable to West Virginians but flexible enough to appeal to those outside the state, too. Bill Withers' "Lean on Me" (1972) manifests as remembrance of home, the West Virginia of Withers's youth. The song references rurality—the speaker is "right up the road" from neighbors, for example—and captures experiences growing up in tight knit communities like Slab Fork and the more populated Beckley. Though West Virginia is never named in the song, the lyrics essentialize the idea of neighbor helping neighbor, across divides, a feature of Appalachian rhetoric. Likewise, "Grandma's Hands," from Withers's first studio album, describes rural life and captures childhood mischief averted by family love. The child of a maid and a miner, Withers, like John Ellison, sought to escape West Virginia and, according to the West Virginia Music Hall of Fame, a "culture of coal and cycle of poverty." He left the state, making a life in Los Angeles, where he remained until he died in March 2020, but West Virginia never left him. As Withers told Anna Sale in an interview, "wherever you grow up, you can go somewhere else, but you never really leave that place" (Withers and Sale 347). Emplacement exists in the work of so many West Virginia artists. This includes Hazel Dickens, whose 1983 song

"Mama's Hand" also invokes images of rurality and family, but addresses leaving without return, letting go of her mother's hand perhaps for the last time.

Listening to "Mama's Hand" alongside Withers's "Grandma's Hands" evokes lifetimes of authentic nostalgia, from the carefree days of childhood and the protection of family to the deep grief of leaving and loss. "Country Roads" alludes to these themes but does not explore them. "Country Roads" names the place, but from without rather than from within; these songs say the place without naming, harnessing West Virginian identity from an inside perspective.

POPULAR MUSIC AND FICTIONALIZATION OF PLACE

All musical conceptions of place are mediated through artists' experiences, audience reception, and the industry itself. Connection to place is important, nonetheless, and generally music by West Virginians for West Virginians is committed to place and people more than to commercial interest. As John Lilly writes in *Mountains of Music*, which profiles West Virginia traditional musicians, "Faced with an increasingly technological world and the relentless pressures of popular culture, these musicians and the communities they represent rely on folk traditions, especially music, for a large measure of their cultural identity" which "lives 'below the radar' of contemporary media or popular culture" (3). While Nivert, Danoff, and Denver's goal was, ultimately, to write a hit song, this is not necessarily the goal for musicians writing to express identity and connection to place. I wonder whether this makes their conceptualization more authentic.

Musicologist Ian Maxwell puzzles over how to find and represent the sound of a place accurately, asserting that all place-world images are colored by interpretation and imagination. Music about places "can only ever be nostalgic: the re-evocation of a place and time for those who were there, a re-evocation that can be taken up by others as a generic label [serves] subsequently to weave imaginary memories of a place that never *really* existed." Songs about place, even by artists of and from a place, are representations affiliated with the artist's experience and drawn from a "highly mediated and mediatized" imagery (Maxwell 81, 80). Artists create a correlation between two places: one, their actual world, and another conceived world of memory. This creates space, place, and lifeworld as the songwriters imagine it: As in any representation, the author registers the place and makes it real but can never capture it fully. Yet music is critical to how we form and express our identities and "travels effortlessly across various cultural activities and through the various spaces and places that inform our membership of the familial and social networks that make up our myriad experiential communities" (Bloustien, Peters, and Luckman xxii). "Country Roads" connects us to each other, despite its inability to accurately represent the place it names because it is close and resonant enough.

"Country Roads" is about place, despite its flaws; because of its ability to connect us to each other and to a felt sense of home, it feels real. We make it about West Virginia. Music scholar Andy Bennett argues associating music with place is a facet of a modern music industry that attempts to package authenticity: "Part of the process of associating music with place involves a desire to make the music 'real', to give it roots and an everyday, 'lived' context in which to explore its meaning and significance, lyrically, musically and culturally. Even if the reality of contemporary popular music is that it holds little relationship to place in any concrete sense, audiences like to believe that it does" (72). Musicians writing about home may do it for themselves and not for an audience, yet the sense of home they create must resonate with listeners in order for it to be marketable, even when musicians write about their own homes and experiences.

"Country Roads" resonates beyond West Virginia and achieved the goal of marketability through that resonance. Still, the song is written from afar, about every home, which means the West Virginia represented in the song is almost entirely an imagined place. Despite this, the song impacted reality, shaped identity rhetoric within West Virginia. Popular music "provides a mechanism by which the 'cultural baggage' of 'home' can be transported through time and space, and transplanted into a new environment, assisting in the maintenance of culture and identity" (Connell and Gibson 161). "Country Roads," assists in naming and maintaining West Virginian identity through its global visibility; its familiarity creates connection in a way that other, less familiar but more factual songs do not. Still, "Country Roads" is a fictional representation, however real it feels. Part of the magic of "Country Roads" is its power to evoke felt sense of place, of home, of belonging for *everyone*, regardless of their state of origin or affiliation with West Virginia. It is not of the place, but of the sense of the place. Just as it isn't a country song, as Brian Hinton writes, "it's a performance *about* country music [rather] than really *of* it" (27). There is no actual "there" in the song. Like other fictionalizations of Appalachia, it provides a "pastoral provision of escape to a place of refreshment and transformation" and a "distinct sense of place set apart from the so-called world" (Satterwhite, *Dear* 187). This fictionalization of real spaces can prove to be problematic, particularly when the image represented as dominant is more reliant on fiction than fact.

"COUNTRY ROADS" IS THE GLAMOR SHOT IN THE FAMILY ALBUM

A dominant image of place, "Country Roads" brings forward pride in West Virginian identity but also obscures the actuality of who we are. Because "dominant images conceal from us more complex realities," it is important to "recognize representation as a tool for exploitation," distortion, or harmful generalizations, and to analyze depictions both positive and negative, as all representations have effects and consequences (Satterwhite, "Objecting" 69). We must recognize what "Country Roads" represents and see it for what it is: a popular tune that shines a positive light on a place often seen as dark, but one that must be heard and read in conversation with other depictions.

Outside namings affect our relationships with place. Cultural anthropologists Gupta and Ferguson denote a parallel between the way internal-colonialist industry created the company town in mining communities and the way multinational corporations colonized developing nations, fracturing people's sense of place through "loss of territorial roots, of an erosion of the cultural distinctiveness of spaces." Once a place is shaped from the outside, even in popular culture depictions, its meaning shifts, too, both within place and without, so that a definition becomes warped, "for even people remaining in familiar and ancestral places find the nature of their relation to place ineluctably changed, and the illusion of a natural and essential connection between the place and the culture broken." West Virginians' enthusiastic integration of "Country Roads" into the rhetoric of cultural identity affects our memories of place, as "remembered places have often served as symbolic anchors of community for dispersed people," and a sense of home "remains one of the most powerful unifying symbols for mobile and displaced peoples" (Gupta and Ferguson 9–11). "Country Roads" brings us together, but it also keeps us apart from the reality of other depictions of West Virginia.

Generally, we do not want to talk to outsiders about the problems we have in our state—drugs, pollution, poverty, inequity—those are ours to fight, to bitch and moan about, to sometimes surrender to. West Virginia musicians sing about them in songs of protest and anger, at rallies, in bars. These songs are not "Country Roads." They are raw, hopeful or hopeless, sometimes angry. They describe calloused hands, hard work, danger, disaster, tragedy. They are proud visions of who we are, what we can be. They are real, but they are not glossy and positive like "Country Roads," a song many West Virginians love. It is hard to "unlove" something that is so much a part of who you are, that you have grown up with, that surrounds you. We cannot abandon those feelings or those markers of identity. In some ways, "Country Roads" is West Virginia as we want to be seen. It also is influential in our lack of awareness of our own songs, ones written by, for, and about West Virginia. How do we learn to listen to *those* voices? Hear *those* songs? Especially when so many of the messages we hear come from outside our state?

I am not advocating for a dismissal of "Country Roads." As a cultural anthem, artifact, and text, it is important to West Virginian identity and of wider cultural significance. Theresa Burriss and Patricia Gantt, in their book *Appalachia in the Classroom*, describe place as ever changing so that the "distinction between 'insider' and 'outsider' proves challenging" and advocate "a 'both/and' approach . . . since Appalachia comprises insiders and outsiders, rural and urban, Northern, Central, and Southern, Black, white, Hispanic/Latino, and Asian. And again, it is important to emphasize that the Appalachian culture is alive and evolving, continuing to respond to and incorporate local, national, and international influences" (Burriss and Gantt xiv). New music, and new understanding, is being made all the time: Thus, a "both/and" perspective on "Country Roads" seems useful, too. West Virginians, when we face the ugliness of what they say about us, can cue "Country Roads," and suddenly we are recognizable outside the negative stereotypes. We have taken it up as ours, even though it does not tell the whole story, perhaps because the whole story is not entirely suitable for a popular audience.

As we grow and deepen understanding of place, we can choose to leave or love "Country Roads" and also hear the voices of diverse West Virginians who sing about place. As Michael Lipton, director of the West Virginia Music Hall of Fame told me, "The real challenge in places like West Virginia is to make kids understand that there's nothing magic. You know, like there's nothing magic that someone else has that you don't have." Place is central to identity: Knowing who we are helps us make a place in the world. Since 2007, the West Virginia Music Hall of Fame has represented musical voices across our state, having inducted diverse musicians from many genres and perspectives, showcasing talented West Virginians of all backgrounds. Their educational resources include interactive maps, traveling exhibits, and prepared sessions for schools and communities. This is just one of many working to educate by amplifying West Virginia's musical voices and by making visible the complex reality of a unique place.

To extend the glamor shot metaphor discussed earlier, I want to propose that "Country Roads" hangs in public spaces like a gallery portrait. Images like Glamor Shots are effective because they are meant for general viewing and allow a vision of some aspect of ourselves in that viewing, even when we may not know the subject of the photo. The looking is reflective. In contrast, songs written by, for, of, and about West Virginia are more like photographs in the family album: candid images, unposed, exposed, and raw. They capture reunions, separations, love, loss, birthdays, and anniversaries. They feature parents, grandparents, siblings, cousins, friends, lovers, and significant others in unfiltered portrayals of life as it is lived. And, most tellingly in this analogy, family albums are precious to us, though no one outside our families really wants to look at them. We keep them safe and bring them out on select occasions; we use them to tell stories, and we treasure them together. In our metaphorical family album, many West Virginians put "Country Roads" in the first leaf, so we may never make it past that page. West Virginian voices continue to meaningfully express truths: in small local clubs, in large gatherings and festivals, through organizations like the West Virginia Music Hall of Fame, *Mountain Stage*, the West Virginia Humanities Council, and others. All across the state, in all kinds of genres, West Virginians are doing what they can to center voices from here, of here, and about here: keeping the family album. We owe it to each other to look beyond the posed, public-facing shot. How do we know who we really are when the most visible image we have is "Country Roads"? Can we love it and resist its tendency to oversimplify and silence? We must learn to listen carefully, to reclaim and rename, to learn new songs, and to define ourselves.

We must also consider how global context is important. We have already discussed how cultural conversations renewed interest in Appalachia in the 1960s related to poverty, economy, and "saving" the region, often from itself. This played out politically, including interest in West Virginia from President Kennedy, which led to the establishment of the Appalachian Regional Commission and policies to improve infrastructure through road building and other efforts. It played out culturally in TV specials, news features, fiction, and film. It was impossible to ignore West Virginia in the late sixties, but much of the public discourse was related to deficits and deficiency. In a political context where West Virginians were typically portrayed negatively, "Country Roads" spoke, and still speaks; however, the song has reach far beyond this purpose and audience. It is important to acknowledge that its popularity was fueled by a global music industry so that for listeners everywhere, it represents the virtue of "almost heaven" as a place of belonging. This gives it staying power worldwide, in the music industry, commercially, and as a universal sign of hiraeth and home. It is necessary to explore the song's history and other rhetorical uses to fully understand it as its own phenomenon.

5

EVOKING (AND MARKETING) BELONGING AND HOME

CULTURAL RESOURCE AND POPULAR HIT

When I began this research, I assumed that "Take Me Home, Country Roads" was everywhere in West Virginia because of its specific affiliation. It was manifested intentionally by West Virginia University when it adopted the song in 1972. It came to being in the way the state's general public embraced the song so readily, encouraged by media conversations and public and private performances, such as when John Denver performed it on the State Capitol steps as it climbed the pop charts, or when newspapers published the lyrics so that West Virginians could learn the words. I now understand that "Country Roads" is more pervasive. It ripples across the globe. Its shine of hiraeth is pliable, easily applied to any place. "Country Roads" is an artifact that evokes a particular kind of meaning, one that translates across cultures and contexts and can be used to market products, create affinities, and make meaning. It is easily sung and evokes the universal feeling of home and belonging. This chapter focuses on understanding "Country Roads" as a rhetorical text, powerful popular song, and commercial tool, which helps us think critically about its many purposes and audiences.

What defines a powerful, popular song? According to a 1920 interview with prolific American songwriter Irving Berlin, composition of a hit follows nine essential elements or "rules": a melody within range of the average voice of the average singer; a simple title that appears and is repeated in the lyrics; appeal to any listener, regardless of gender; heartfeltness; originality; groundedness in nature and concrete imagery; easily singable lyrics; and simplicity. The ninth quality deals not with the song, but with the songwriter, engaged in the continuous business of songwriting (O'Malley and Berlin 175–76). "Country Roads" embodies all these elements, including the dispositions of Bill Danoff and Taffy Nivert, who were actively working on careers as songwriters and had the explicit goal of writing hit songs. We can see the popular and commercial success of "Country Roads" manifest in a range of uses, meanings, and contexts.

Popular music is integral in contexts in which artifacts, or construable signs, are ascribed with meanings that can be observed, described, and articulated through behavior. These artifacts of culture "draw their meaning from the role they play ... in an ongoing pattern of life." Our emotions are shaped by these signs as "cultural resources" within an "adequate system of public symbols" that constitute a constructed understanding of our feelings. These feelings are shaped by "public images of sentiment that only ritual, myth, and art can provide" (Geertz 17, 51, 82). A powerful song can help us understand events and lived experiences so that we can find our bearings in the world.

So then, a song like "Country Roads" is a cultural resource as well as a popular hit; can sometimes be "fixed" to particular moments, locations, and experiences; and is "at its most basic, sound transmitted from the micro level (in a bedroom, pub, car, between headphones) to the macroscale (through various means, including the global media). Music is also an artifact moving with people, whether as indigenous knowledge, oral traditions, or recordings" (Connell and Gibson 9). Music is transformed through space because it takes on different meanings depending on where it is played, and by whom. This means that the meaning of "Country Roads" shifts within contexts; we can see it used for purposes at both micro and macro levels. As a cultural artifact, "Country Roads," has a significant impact on human experience, emotion, and action. It means something different depending on the speaker, audience, context, purpose, and use. Its uses are wide and diverse but always connected to the hiraeth and sense of belonging the song evokes, foregrounded by genius marketing and worldwide music production. Still, despite its various uses, "Country Roads" is secular pop, a global hit for fifty years. The song brings place into existence for listeners all over the world and taps into a sense of belonging, which the literature of human geography defines as a symbolic space of familiarity, comfort, security, and emotional attachment (Antonsich 646). Yet the "place I belong," is not any real place. It represents the virtue of an idealized nature in its "almost heaven" labeling, calling up pastoral beauty, timelessness, voices of loved ones, belonging, a sense of home. It is about global and universal yearning for imagined home, and it has been since its first release. Tracing this trajectory can tell us more about how it invokes imagined landscapes and place-belonging.

"COUNTRY ROADS" IN A GLOBAL MUSIC INDUSTRY: TRAJECTORY, TRANSLATION, AND TRANSFORMATION

When "Country Roads" was released on April 12, 1971, it was immediately clear that it spoke to listeners. Bill Danoff told me that the song "only got popular because people started calling up and requesting it." He maintains that radio stations in West Virginia (and requests in other states from displaced West Virginians) were instrumental in making the song a hit in the United States.

One story that exemplifies the early popular appeal of "Country Roads" came to me from David Hoyt, a former radio disc jockey who worked at WMOV Radio in Ravenswood, West Virginia. Hoyt described how he broke it on the air: "A listener from Sandyville called one day and said her son was on leave from his service post in Europe, that he bought an album over there that had a pretty song about West Virginia on it. He brought it to the station, I made a copy of 'Country Roads' and started playing it." The song garnered attention, and the station "got more requests for the song than anything before." In addition to listener requests, Hoyt was contacted by other West Virginia radio stations. He "didn't know any better at the time, so [he] made copies for WCAW, WWVA, WVRC and others." The song spread across the state airwaves. RCA noticed.

Soon, Hoyt received a call from Jerry Weintraub, Denver's manager, "wanting to know, and I quote 'Where the hell did you get that? It hasn't even been released in the US.' Guess I could have gotten in trouble for making copies of an 'embargoed' song, but RCA didn't press the issue." In fact, Hoyt claims that in time he received an autographed photo from John Denver himself, on which the singer wrote, "Thanks for breaking 'Country Roads.'" Hoyt immediately understood the song's power, calling it "lightning in a bottle" with "enduring appeal to transplanted West Virginians," and recalls that he expressed to Weintraub that "if they released that album and song in this country, it would sell a million just in West Virginia alone," which ultimately proved true.

However, the song's popularity extended far beyond West Virginia. The single sold a million copies within six months of its US release, climbed to number two on the Billboard charts, and was covered nationally and internationally by artists across genres targeting diverse audiences within five years of its initial debut. As a hit song, "Country Roads" depends on a sense of wide-ranging appeal, exemplifying Berlin's principles for songwriting. Bill Danoff told me that the magical universality of the song, he believes, is "the line 'the place I belong.'" Danoff said, "I think that's the line that resonates. I think if the song went, 'Almost heaven, country roads, take me home to West Virginia,' I think it would alienate everybody." Instead, by emphasizing a more flexible home, the listener can be free to dream of other destinations of longing. Music often taps into a fictionalized sense of place, based on a distorted conception. In this case, West Virginia is a metaphorical "home," even for those who have never been, will never go, and know nothing about the state (see Figure 5).

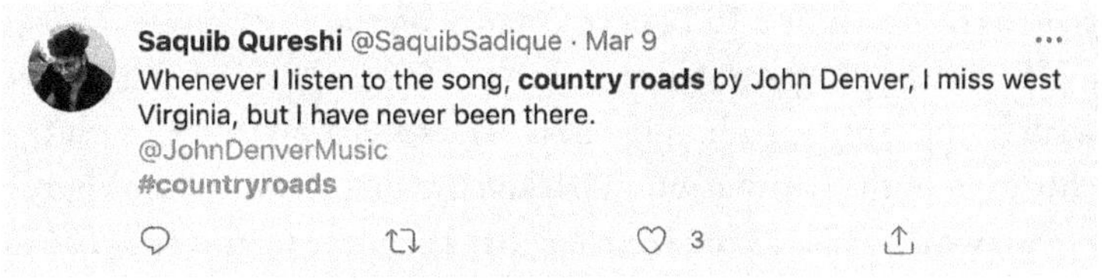

> **Saquib Qureshi** @SaquibSadique · Mar 9
> Whenever I listen to the song, **country roads** by John Denver, I miss west Virginia, but I have never been there.
> @JohnDenverMusic
> #countryroads

FIGURE 5 A tweet references the hiraeth present in "Country Roads"

"Country Roads" had an instant impact not only because of listener demand, but also thanks to the power and reach of commercial distribution and marketing. As Bill Danoff explained to me, "when RCA realized they had a hit record, they went nuts with it, and they wanted to release it worldwide," which led to many recordings—covers, translations, transformations—by other artists who had different audience appeal.

The distribution of "Country Roads" demonstrates vividly the influence of the pre-internet record industry in constructing a popular hit. In the 1970s, before viral video and social media, industry moves, like sharing a song with specific artists or with certain companies for marketing, could ensure a song's popularity in different demographics. RCA moved strategically to share "Country Roads." This resulted in a song that gained global popularity quickly. Famous names like Loretta Lynn, Lynn Anderson, Tennessee Ernie Ford, and the Statler Brothers recorded covers of the song within the first year, but if we examine the song's global impact, three versions stand out: the original folk-country version; Olivia Newton-John's country-pop interpretation; and Ray Charles's R&B cover. From these versions, we can trace variations.

An entirely different flavor from the original, Olivia Newton-John's version, included on her third studio album *Let Me Be There* (1973), reached top 10 in Japan and top 20 in the United Kingdom. There is evidence she was performing the song before that, as is shown by a 1972 performance on the *Reg Varney Review*, a UK variety program. Newton-John's "Country Roads," is peppy, with handclaps and a bouncy beat. The recording begins with the chorus in multi-part harmony, backed by what sounds like a church organ, which fades as the verse begins. Then, the tempo and instrumentation change. Strumming guitar accompanies Newton-John's voice sweetly singing the first few lines, and then plunking bass comes in. More voices build to an energetic chorus. In the second verse, slide guitar and high harmony join additional instrumentation. The bridge is simple, and the final chorus adds clapping and finishes with a full choir. This version feels like sugar-pop gospel, happy and holy.

Newton-John only reached 119 on the Billboard charts in the United States, but her version was embraced by audiences in Europe. Bill Danoff told me a story about a "bizarre moment" in Dubrovnik, Croatia, years after the song was originally released. As Danoff remembered, he and his wife, exhausted after a long flight, arrived at a biergarten where a band played "Country Roads." Surprised, Danoff felt "it was like it was a setup. Except nobody knew where we were—I didn't know where we were. It was like somebody walked in: 'play that song!' But it wasn't that, it was accidental." As coincidence would have it, the band knew only one verse, so Danoff taught them the rest of the song: "two of the people spoke English of the six of them, so I got together with the one guy and I taught him the words, and then they were singing the real words to the rest of it." Danoff enriched the band's knowledge, but he did so anonymously. Then, in a strange exchange at his hotel the next morning, "The guy at the desk said to me, 'Oh, I heard you were popular at such-and-such a place' [and] . . . the next question he asked me was 'Do you know Olivia Newton-John?' And I said 'No, why would I know her?' And he said 'Well, she sang the song.'" As Danoff found, it was Newton-John's version, not Denver's, that was initially more widely recognized in parts of Europe.

Denver's version is prolific now, a perennial favorite at Oktoberfest in Germany, as a *Spotify* article documents: "On September 22, the first day of Oktoberfest 2018, the song was streamed almost 190,000 times in Germany" ("From Mountain Mamas"). Many European artists have covered the song, and though it is hard to trace the first influences of each version, Newton-John's was more popular in parts of Europe than Denver's version, at least at first.

Newton-John's version is popular in Asia as well. In Japan, where it reached number six at its release, Newton-John's "Country Roads" retained its popularity over time partly because it was featured again in the opening scenes of the 1995 anime film *Whisper of the Heart*. Denver's version was influential in Asia, too. Author Jason Jeong writes in *The Atlantic* that "Country Roads" came to popularity during a time of military occupation and "gained massive followings because of the availability of Armed Forces Radio (now called the American Forces Network) over decades in regions with a significant U.S. army presence, such as the Philippines, Viet Nam, and Korea." A 2024 *Switched on Pop* episode on "Country Roads" cites the song's pastoral, bucolic imagery and refrain "I belong" as a uniting feature of the song, as well as sociological research that showed the song's enduring popularity in Asia among listeners of all ages ("How Denver"). In addition, it attributes the song's (and Denver's) popularity in China to post-communist restructuring and opening up to Western culture, the idea of American possibility and beauty during a time of immigration. Author Charles Yu features "Country Roads" as a thematic anthem in his 2020 novel, *Interior Chinatown*, which explores portrayals of Asian immigrants in the United States. For those who stayed in China or immigrated to the United States, "Country Roads" was an anthem of hope, but one that recalled an idealized home. Both Denver's and Newton-John's versions are still listed on the song menu at practically every Karaoke venue in Japan and other Asian nations.

"Country Roads" became more universal as it gained popularity globally, prompting an awareness of West Virginia as a place that perhaps took on mythical qualities. Taffy Nivert believes "everybody brings their own worldview to the song, or places the song within their worldview." This idea of "worldview" speaks to the flexibility of place. To illustrate, Nivert told me a story about her former landlord who moved to Virginia (rather than West Virginia) from Vietnam, who "grew up in a refugee camp, and he said they played it all day long." Although the man could not speak English, the song "made him feel a certain way. And when he came to the United States and learned English enough to know what the words were, he said the words described exactly like he felt the music was trying to tell him." This feeling, connected to place, prompted the man to move to Virginia, in pursuit of "almost heaven," and home.

"Country Roads" was and still is a vehicle for learning English in Asian schools, too, as one of my English 101 students told me, claiming it was part of the eighth-grade curriculum in Japan. Similarly, one of my survey respondents wrote:

> I got my ex's mother, who is from China, enrolled in ESL classes. They had to pick an English song to perform for the class. She chose Country Roads even though she didn't know the words before the assignment. She said she always loved the song because despite him singing about a place she didn't know in a language she didn't understand, she could feel the sense of missing home in it, and it expressed her feelings for China.

These sentiments show an expression of longing for belonging and home, regardless of location; it is specific in its naming of place but ubiquitous in capturing hiraeth, making it ideal for remix and revival from the start. Home, in "Country Roads," is what folklorist Tim Cresswell described as "Place . . . produced by practice that adheres to (ideological) beliefs" and in which these beliefs re-create place and become accepted "in a way that makes them appear natural, self-evident, and commonsense" (Cresswell 16). In the case of "Country Roads," its uses in practice produce a sense of belonging in place, so that the taking up of it produces more uses of the song.

Newton-John's version of "Country Roads," with its longing spoken by a woman's voice, may be more similar to Ray Charles's version than to Denver's in its semi-gospel, multivocal feel. Charles released the song on his 1972 album *A Message from the People*, which contained hymns, protest, and patriotic songs, including both "America the Beautiful" and "Lift Every Voice and Sing." His version is driving, soulful, and upbeat, with a different verse order than the original. Its multitrack recording features Charles's voice in conversation with itself in an elaborate, energetic call and response that borders on the absurd. The song starts out with bass and guitar, and Charles alone sings the first verse. The first chorus begins with a hearty "Come on, y'all," and other voices join in, including laid-over harmonies of Charles and what sounds like a full choir. The bridge, which comes before the second verse in this version, has an orchestral sound, rising, but the second verse is subdued again, as Charles stops the sound, vocalizing "Hold on!" The chorus swells again with voices, and is followed by an electric organ solo. The final chorus adds tambourine and hand claps at Charles's command: "Now put your hands together!" Many voices join together as the song fades away.

This "Country Roads" is conversational and joyful, celebratory, and in moments hilarious, as the singer interjects commentary. At one point, just before the organ comes in, Charles shouts, "Oh, I like that!" and his own voice answers, "Me too!" This version has the feel less of nostalgia and more of reunion, the sense that the trip home is in progress, even finished. It feels more like a revival than it does a longing to arrive. It is also Bill Danoff's favorite cover. Though it received less critical recognition from popular audiences than the original or Newton-John's cover, Charles's version influenced musicians. We can trace this influence directly in the way some artists took up the transposed pattern, with the bridge before the second verse. Toots and the Maytals draw from Charles in their 1974 cover, for example. As Danoff explains:

> Ray Charles being a better musician than me, altered the form, and I kind of like it better. The Toots version, he does a verse and a chorus, then the bridge, and then the second verse and then the chorus. We do the two verses, and then the chorus and the bridge. So that's how I know he did the Ray Charles version. Plus, he does all Ray Charles's licks, like "Oh, yeah," and all that stuff.

Israel Kamakawiwo'ole's version uses Charles's form, too. This Hawaiian interpretation appears on 1993 album *Facing Future*, which also contained a medley of "Somewhere Over the Rainbow" and "Wonderful World," perhaps better known than Kamakawiwo'ole's cover of "Country Roads." Toots and the Maytals' and Kamakawiwo'ole's versions are also two of many that alter the lyrics to reflect other homes, replacing "West Virginia" with "West Jamaica" and "West Mākaha," respectively.

Charles's reimagining of the song influenced others to take up his version. It also represents a targeting of different demographic audiences in a record industry purposely divided by gender and race. The intentional global distribution of "Country Roads" created resonant imagined spaces of home for listeners, regardless of their place in the world. A worldwide music industry, combined with person-to-person sharing, influences "the way in which place, music and audience are positioned through and by global media flows, [which allows] new representations of place [to] emerge that superimpose their own fictional gloss" (Bennett 71). This "fictional gloss," connected to place feeds a sense of longing, and with the words changed to match other places besides West Virginia, "almost heaven" becomes a question that can be answered with any beloved place. "And then people are filling the next line themselves," Bill Danoff explained to me, "so Toots is filling in with Jamaica. Israel Kamakawiwo'ole, the Hawaiian National Treasure, his version is whatever the mountains are in Hawaii wherever he's from. So, I guess it's very easily adoptable." Hiraeth is universal; belonging is interchangeable. The song transforms to fit.

Since the 1970s, "Country Roads" has been taken up and transformed by artists as a tribute to their own homes. Already we have discussed two, but there are many other examples. Versions reveal the universal sense of hiraeth and while it is not possible to consider every variation, a few stand out. One of my favorite interpretations is from The Moipei Quartet, four sisters from Nairobi who have achieved international fame for their close harmonies. Their version of "Country Roads" pays tribute to their home, Kenya, on their 2013 album *In the Land of the Lion*. In it, they sing of the Mara River and evoke imagery of "Maasai maidens" and elephants, pastoral sights specific to the country roads of their own home.

In addition to lyrical adaptations, "Country Roads" is interpreted in new genres, like Indonesian band Kawanlama's banjo-heavy folk cover, or Me First and the Gimme Gimmes' pop-punk version. Australian-based Celtic punk band The Cloverhearts' cover has driving drums and bagpipes, and Norwegian metal musician Leo Moracchioli screams his way through. Harder versions take on an ironic quality: more heavy metal, no less hiraeth. There are dance versions, too: The most famous of these may be Dutch artists Hermes House Band's 2001 cover, which reached the top 10 in the UK and topped the Scottish charts. A more contemporary dance version is a 2017 collaboration between singer Ellena Soule and Atlanta-based electronic creator, Panski. The weirdest might be a 2019 industrial/cyberpunk cover by Italian creators Melodicka Bros. These are just a few examples. There are reggae, a cappella, orchestral, techno, choir, bluegrass, punk, and operatic versions of the song in addition to the expected country and folk versions in English.

Women's voices bend the meaning and intention of the song, as well. Brandi Carlile's slowed-down haunting 2021 version uses minimal instrumentation, in contrast to her 2013 recording with Emmylou Harris or the version she often performs on stage. All-woman folk harmony trio Mountain Man released a gorgeous, dreamy interpretation in 2019. Pop musician Lana Del Rey released a cover in 2023.

It is also translated into other languages. YouTube user Milia Malae created a playlist of thirteen international covers of "Country Roads," among which about ten languages are represented. Some of these are approximate translations. However, others are total reinterpretations, with the lyrics completely changed but the tune, harmonies, and instrumentation preserved; also preserved is a similar pastoral setting and the same felt sense of hiraeth. Nick Brumfield, in an article on "Country Roads" as global phenomenon, compiled a list of international versions, including Bangladeshi, Thai, Romanian, and Slovenian. Brumfield cites specifically "Tapio Heinonen's mournful Finnish cover 'Vanha Tie' (1974)" and explains many non-English versions change setting if not sentiment: "French singer Dick Rivers' 1977 cover ('Faire un Pont') completely changed the song's lyrics, removing all mention of 'country roads' in favor of rustic village imagery. By contrast, in his 1977 cover, Israeli singer Hanan Yovel retained the English words 'West Virginia' and 'country roads' even as he translated the rest of the song into Hebrew." The place in "Country Roads" is every place.

Distinct from translations, new versions of "Country Roads" tap into homesickness for past, places, or people; the same sentiment expressed both in different languages *and* in different words. For example, Daisy Door's 1973 German transformation, "Straße der Vergangenheit" sounds eerily like Olivia Newton-John's version in its arrangement, instrumentation, and singer's voice, but the lyrics are completely changed, so that the song is about the "road of the past," a path that will lead to a lost loved one. This is but one example in which language and lyric are completely altered. This is also true for a Japanese version, featured alongside Newton-John's in the anime film *Whisper of the Heart*, which is about being unable to return home. A few other transformations include Nicola di Bari's song "Libertà," which is about the freedom of childhood, with neither roads nor West Virginia mentioned at all.

Czech artist Pavel Bobek's 1996 version, "Veď Mě Dál, Cesto Má," sounds like Denver's version but is about following one's destiny to the end of life: "Lead me on, my road." Another version worth mentioning is Mocedades's 1992 Spanish "Carretera del Sur," the road that leads south to home; in this interpretation, the speaker is seen as "a stranger" when away from home. Marie Laforêt's 1972 "Mon Pays est Ici" describes the singer's return home to a fishing village so that the mountain scenes of the original are replaced with visions of sand and sounds of the ocean. "Mon Pays est Ici" is considered an unofficial Canadian anthem; it was performed by a children's choir during the country's 150th anniversary celebration in 2017 (Farant, email communication).

Once more, these are only a few examples of many. Each time I talk with people about the song, I gather new versions. We can trace a kind of lineage, fueled partly by marketing and the recording industry, through nearly three hundred recorded versions in English in the last fifty years and variations in more than twenty languages. The song carries its own kind of power, showing that the magic is not only about the lyrics. It is not about a specific place either, it is more about longing, the sense of the known rather than the uncertain, a sense of felt understanding, of belonging.

Nostalgic resonance is generally a feature of much popular music. Connell and Gibson show music allows migrated peoples to maintain a sense of homeplace; while they discuss migrants who bring regional music traditions to their new homes, they also discuss the hybridization of popular music, its transformability, the way it can be made "into something quite new, especially when it is taken up by other minority and migrant groups, without ever losing some link to home, whatever the degree and duration of displacement" (191). We see this repeated use of "Country Roads" as a link to home as it is taken up, transformed, and connected to new homes as well as connected to West Virginia by people who are displaced as well as still living within the state.

In addition to translations and adaptations of the song in its wholeness, we also see examples of transformations, allusions, references and riffs to remake the song through sampling in rap, electronica, and other genres. Apalachee Falls's version, which Appalachian rhetoric scholar Todd Snyder might label "hick hop," is one example that features a slowed down chorus and replaces all the lyrics except "Country roads/Take me home," referencing Georgia and Tennessee but not West Virginia. Electronic musician Pretty Lights remixed "Country Roads" into a hypnotic seven-minute version, which samples the original heavily but mixes in drum, bass, and beats. In this 2011 version, the words "West Virginia" are repeated again and again, but most of the other words are entirely missing. A more recent and more widely known remix is the aforementioned 2016 "Forever Country," a medley of "I Will Always Love You," "On the Road Again," and "Take Me Home, Country Roads."

More peripheral allusions to "Country Roads" appear in other songs, like Baltimore singer-songwriter Jeremiah Lloyd Harmon's 2019 "Almost Heaven," which references West Virginia in its first lines but otherwise diverges from the song entirely. Swiss hair band Gotthard's 1994 song "Mountain Mama," references eyes like coal and a relationship "like heaven." Nashville Country band Restless Road collaborated with country-pop artist Kane Brown on their 2020 release "Take Me Home," which borrows the tune and a partial chorus, but otherwise diverges from the original lyrically; their version addresses going home to loved ones after time away. Restless Road was formed in West Virginia, and one of its remaining members, Colton Pack, is a native of the state. Machine Gun Kelly and Jelly Roll collaborated on a popular remix in 2024. Considering these versions, reimaginings, translations, and transformations, we can see how "Country Roads" has the power to bring imagined home closer.

Observing West Virginia through the narratives of news broadcasts, popular media, letters, dorm room windows, and brief tour visits, Danoff, Nivert, and Denver were, amazingly, able to write about every longed-for home. Those who write about place, folklorist Kent Ryden tells us, must be able "to adopt simultaneously the viewpoints of the loquacious native (or sensitive explorer) and the precise cartographer; he or she must be aware of, and capable of describing, both the invisible and the visible landscape." Like the folklore Ryden describes, "Country Roads" deftly "links these narratives together in a larger structure of meaning, bringing out some unifying theme," creating "simultaneous intimacy and distance" (248–49). That unifying theme—one of belonging—transcends place in a way that speaks to diverse listeners, creating an imagined landscape that nonetheless feels authentic and is ripe for adaptation. We have discussed how the song is about journey and pilgrimage—about coming home, being home, leaving and returning, in physical, spiritual, and metaphorical ways. It exemplifies the idea that "music offers the experience of other realms, imaginary and imagined places" (Connell and Gibson 89). As a construable sign, "Country Roads" is flexible and applicable across cultures and locations for many purposes.

"Country Roads" draws power from its generality. This is consistent with scholarship on John Denver's work; his intention was to capture the universal in the particular, so that places, in his songs, were nonspecific, even when specified. Denver said as much: "I try to take my experiences, and I try to share them in as universal a way as possible.... So even a song like 'Rocky Mountain High,' which is so much about Colorado, can have meaning to somebody someplace else in the world" (Denver, qtd. in Klemt 51–52). We have already seen the way "Country Roads" is applied to many different places and homes, within West Virginia and without. Its flexibility is intentional. Bill Danoff has expressed similar sentiments: "By making something specific, it can be more universal. People can draw from it what they need to. If you write something universal, it doesn't mean anything to anybody" (M. Burnside). As an example of the universal in the particular, "Country Roads" has uses as diverse and varied as listeners themselves.

In addition to being a cultural artifact, a song is also a product of public rhetoric, used in marketing and media and by individuals as an expression of affiliative identity. "Politics, advertising, and entertainment are performances" that can express "the values, sentiments, and desires presumably taken for granted as proof of the worthiness (or the reverse) of particular events, personalities, and products. Rhetorical displays that exhibit demonstrative qualities might very well permeate daily life" in the ways that individuals use texts and symbols to express their identities, positions, and affiliations (Prelli 15). As a text, "Country Roads" is used to make connections for many purposes and audiences, indicating who does (and sometimes who does not) belong. Sometimes "Country Roads" appears seemingly randomly, in television talk or performance shows, which highlights the song's ubiquity, as well as its singability. Sometimes it is used more purposefully. We have already discussed how "Country Roads" is used to promote political positions and candidates. It is also used by individuals and industry, in films and other media, to sell products and services, in protests and rallies, and to market West Virginia University and the state of West Virginia. It is important to consider these rhetorical uses because they demonstrate the song's versatility, and ultimately, they impact understandings of place, home, belonging, and self.

"COUNTRY ROADS" IN MEMES AND MEDIA, MOVIES AND TELEVISION

Everyday people take up "Country Roads" in a range of ways, transforming it for humor, or to declare place, affiliation, and connection. These uses sometimes express identity, but may also, show like or dislike for the song itself. These uses are public rhetoric, allowing us to engage in shared conversation within larger discourse. In our increasingly connected technologies, one of the ways that "Country Roads" comes forward is through memetics. The term *meme* was first coined in the 1970s by Richard Dawkins, an evolutionary biologist, who argued that bits of cultural information could be replicable, like genes, and could reproduce through repetition. Internet memes are visual and textual images, replicated, reposted, and shared on social media. A *New York Times* article defines a meme almost like a technological inside joke: easily shared and modified, replicating with variation, and able to connect digital communities through collective meaning (Benveniste).

"Country Roads" memes are their own genre, capturing lyrics and combining them with images in reference to other texts and as cultural commentary. The website *Know Your Meme* shows eighteen different "Country Roads" images in its gallery, while another website, *Me.Me* (now defunct) crowdsourced a collection of hundreds. A search of the term "Country Roads" on Reddit turns up hundreds more image references to the song. So many examples exist that it is not possible to discuss range and scope of all the variants. Some are peripherally connected to the song, and others are simply offensive, perpetuating derogatory stereotypes. However, a few memetic themes in "Country Roads" memes are worth discussing, including the song's irresistibility, its capacity to evoke hiraeth, and, more recently, its use in other popular media like video games and movies.

Arguably some of the funniest "Country Roads" memes deal with its universal appeal and make the claim, explicit or implicit, that even listeners who do not like country music as a genre are transfixed when they hear "Country Roads." Depicted listeners include children and various animals, including a version of the inhaling seagull and, as seen in the following image, cats (Figure 6).

Also addressing the song's appeal are memes that suggest its irresistibility, depicting the song as bait. In these memes, a speaker sings the first lines of the song, and a listener responds, revealing their hiding place: Characters in these images include medieval soldiers on a battlefield, or my favorite, a bat using "Country Roads" in a pop-culture variation of echolocation (Figure 7).

Other categories of "Country Roads" memes that suggest the song's irresistibility include the "highway drift" image, in which a car careens off a highway exit ramp toward West Virginia, or a spirit rising from an unconscious body upon hearing the song. Another depicts John Denver as an Uber driver who drives all riders to, of course, the place they belong.

FIGURE 6 "Country Roads" cat meme

FIGURE 7 "Country Roads" bat meme

Still others represent parodies and reworkings of the lyrics to address everything from video games, to films, to folklore, as seen in the "Country Gnomes" meme (Figure 8).

Memes suggest what we already know about the song's appeal and public response—part earworm, part anthem, "Country Roads"

country gnomes,

take my bones

to a place,

they don't belong

see shit like this is the reason that it's so hard to turn my back on this website. Where else, pray tell, are you going to find this kind of quality nonsense.

west virginia

FIGURE 8 "Country Gnomes" meme

---

replicates itself in the way it inspires listeners to generate new texts, enmeshing meaning and genre, remixing the song's meaning, suggesting new ways of belonging. Rhetorician Derek Sparby, in his work on memetic rhetoric, asserts that memes and their uses signal belonging in a couple of ways: through identity and in groups, and in spaces online. We see both kinds of use with the "Country Roads" meme: It signals West Virginian identity, and it also signals identity in other groups. When posted as part of an online community, it becomes a kind of "inside joke," signaling belonging in that space.

The song has received newfound attention not just from individual listeners, but also from industry, in reference to West Virginia and otherwise, which in turn generates more memetic replication and return to the song. For example, the *Fallout 76* soundtrack includes a doo-wop re-imagining of "Country Roads" by a group of New York street musicians and includes traditional instrumentation, like fiddle and banjo, but with barbershop harmony and soulful vocals. Released promotionally, the song accumulated thirty million plays within days of its launch and rose to the number one spot on iTunes. One music writer attributes the *Fallout 76* cover as singly responsible for a bump in the song's popularity (Hampp). This is reflected in more crowdsourced popular culture references, as seen in a meme depicting a young person seeing the video and rushing to Google the song (Figure 9).

FIGURE 9 A meme attributing new popularity to "Country Roads" through *Fallout 76*

Today, the official YouTube video for the *Fallout* version has more than forty-three million views, but it is not the only recent example of the song's repetition and remixing.

The video platform TikTok has its share of "Country Roads" references, too. A search of the site reveals more than four hundred thousand videos using the song as a soundtrack for cooking, how-to demonstrations, travel, information, lip-synching, and a variety of others. Some viral videos and memes are remixed allusions inside allusions. For instance, some reference the 2017 film *Kingsman: Golden Circle*, in which a character, Merlin, diverts enemies' attention from his comrades by singing "Country Roads," acting as a decoy. When enemies reach him, Merlin raises the chorus in crescendo and releases his foot from a landmine, saving his teammates while sacrificing himself. Social media videos took on this theme of self-sacrifice connected to "Country Roads" and adapted it, depicting sports events, teenagers triumphing against bullies, speeders avoiding traffic tickets, and all other kinds of victories in which a person might "take one for the team."

Like the *Kingsman: Golden Circle* reference, some new texts created using "Country Roads" are responses not to the song in its original form, but to versions and variations prompted by the song's use in other media, like films, video games, and television. "Country Roads" has been used widely in soundtracks. It was used as early as 1972 in the Goldie Hawn film *Butterflies Are Free*, the 1973 made-for-TV *Sunshine*, and others. It follows logically that films with West Virginia connections would incorporate "Country Roads." The 2019 docu-drama *Dark Waters* tells the story of a legal battle against a chemical company that contaminated water in Parkersburg and uses "Country Roads" in both soundtrack and trailers to signal setting. The 2021 television series *Clarice*, a spin-off of the 1991 *Silence of the Lambs*, uses Brandi Carlile's slowed-down version, giving the trailer for the show a somber tone as it shows the main character traveling to address unsolved murders in her home state. Heist movie *Logan Lucky* (2017) uses "Country Roads" to express love between the main character and his young daughter, and through their relationship, a connection to audience and place.

Other films and shows use "Country Roads" more divergently, without connection to West Virginia, often incorporating it as storyline. In the 1995 Japanese Studio Ghibli film *Whisper of the Heart*, a version of "Country Roads" is used as a plot device as the main character translates and transforms the song. A 2007 episode of animated series *American Dad!* shows undocumented immigrants singing the only American song they know, and, in turn, the show's main characters are moved to protect them from deportation: The song, of course, is "Country Roads." Another example is an episode of the television mockumentary *The Office*, in which characters Andy and Dwight sing "Country Roads" in an effort to impress a new employee, Erin, whom they both see as a love interest; the ploy backfires when the two become so engrossed in their performance that Erin backs out of the room unnoticed. These examples show the song's memetic versatility, hyperbolized power to capture attention, and its many uses: to evoke hiraeth, to express belonging, and to suggest new meanings and other references. Representations of the song are culturally reconstructed as it is borrowed to make new meaning. As an imitated cultural model, "Country Roads" is easily reproduced and remixed as diverse commentary and for different rhetorical effects.

Recently, as in its use in the *Clarice* trailer, we see "Take Me Home, Country Roads" used ironically to evoke darkness. The 2019 film *Alien: Covenant* uses "Country Roads," akin to some memes, as bait, in this case to lure the film's protagonists to a sinister planet. The impact of the song used darkly is unsettling, and, as one critic claims, effective in setting tone: "the voyagers in *Alien: Covenant*, who are en route to establish a colony in a far-flung corner of the universe, should have thought twice before changing course and heading for a previously undetected planet that is broadcasting a crackly rendition of 'Take Me Home, Country Roads'" (Gibley). Instead of drawing the space crew toward belonging, the song draws them toward an inhospitable planet: the opposite of home.

We see darkness in the 2022 television series *The Patient* as well when the show's protagonist, a captive chained in a serial killer's basement, sings "Country Roads" to comfort a fellow victim, who, duct-taped and blindfolded, sings along between sobs. The song reappears in the series to evoke a sense of loss and comfort, but the foreboding remains. These uses show a shadow side to the song, twisting its message to one of lostness and despair. These uses are few, but impactful, diverging from expected meaning, which has often been used in marketing and commerce.

The feeling of hiraeth stirred up by "Country Roads" can be used to suggest affiliative emotions toward products, people, and movements. Marco Antonsich differentiates the geographic literature on belonging into "two major analytical dimensions: belonging as a personal, intimate, feeling of being 'at home' in a place (place-belongingness) and belonging as a discursive resource which constructs, claims, justifies, or resists forms of socio-spatial inclusion/exclusion (politics of belonging)" (645). "Country Roads" is used to tap into *both* dimensions of belonging, bringing forth a feeling of community and connection, and in a declarative way in politics (as we have seen earlier), as well as in protest. Discussing these diverse uses of the song together demonstrates clearly how flexibly "Country Roads" can be used to sell products, positions, and even places.

"COUNTRY ROADS" IN COMMERCIALS: HOMEBOUND, HOMETOWN, HOME COOKED

Modern popular music is always a commercial endeavor. "Country Roads" would never have achieved such reach without the existence and promotion of a global music industry, one that benefits from the use of music for more than just listener entertainment and pleasure. As Connell and Gibson explain, "Music shapes consumer agency, provides an interface between material culture, social action, and subjectivity, and enables retailers to target clientele and brand image, and even to structure the temporal dimensions of retailing" (275). Interfused with consumer rhetoric, music in retail is used widely to associate aspects of culture with products and marketing in both overt and subtle ways. Music scholars Bloustien, Peters, and Luckman assert music can be applied "to appropriate particular songs associated with the original ideologies of rock music—freedom, rebellion, youthful exuberance, anti-materialism—and to re-associate them with commodities from multi-nationals, such as denim jeans, coca cola, and cigarettes" (xxiii). A songwriter's intended purpose can become distorted by a song's use in advertising or popular culture. Even when a song is taken up in seemingly contradictory ways, this is possible because construable signs are flexible. These multiple uses are "only possible because of the arbitrary nature of the sign" so that "the same music is often appropriated by different groups for their own use" despite contradictory meanings (Bloustien, Peters, and Luckman xxiii). We see this in ways "Country Roads" is used to sell goods, services, and ideas, and to create affiliative identities: It is a genius marketing tool, used since the earliest days of its popularity. As such, advertising is an obvious place to look closely at how "Country Roads" is taken up rhetorically.

In terms of specific marketing, researchers document patterns of commercial geography, in which brands use place-narratives and mythologies to create associations with products and services. These associations not only affect what is being sold, but also perceptions of places, so specific goods become connected to regionality and home (Andehn, Hietanen, and Lucarelli 327). This "discursive use of essentializing and romantic narratives of places to expedite commercial aspirations" can have various effects, including market associations of entire nations with a particular product or redefining of places as "destinations" or even as commodities themselves (Andehn, Hietanen, and Lucarelli 328). In addition to shaping places, place-marketing also has the potential to shape people, communicating expectations not just to target audiences but also to current inhabitants, which in turn affects the ways in which people perform place-identity. "Country Roads," when used in marketing, re-creates place in distinct ways. When applied directly to West Virginia, it affects perceptions of the state and of West Virginians, tying to a specific discourse of place-identity. But when applied more universally, as a call to any home, it draws upon hiraeth and belonging to tap into the sense of home more broadly. This flexibility makes it specific and universal at once, and we see this in the way it is used commercially.

"Country Roads" has been used to sell everything from Goodyear tires in the 1970s to more recent food products, beverages, experiences, and technology. In one recent example, a Hillshire Farm ad claims we are "closer to the farm than we think" when our "smoked sausage is crafted with care" while an instrumental version of "Country Roads" plays in the background. Home is home cooking, and we associate farms (and family) with all things country, even though the sausage in question was likely not produced on a small family farm.

Similarly, a 2017 advertisement for Google Home, a suite of smart devices that provide home security, entertainment, light, climate, and electronics and appliance management is soundtracked by a whistled version of "Country Roads" over scenes of social gatherings. The ad ends with a surprise party, complete with a "Welcome Home" cake, as the familiar but remixed tune plays. This is advertising music at its best, writes one entertainment critic:

> Using a song like "Take Me Home, Country Roads" and jinglefying it is smart by Google for two reasons. The first is that people know the song and even though it's been updated, it still feels like something you can remember and automatically bond with. The second is that because people know the song, they could possibly have a memory with the song, they could be more likely to remember the Google Home. It's the brand-new and the familiar, and it's all in one place. Hell, it can even be in your home (Denninger).

This feeling—love for home, your home—is resonant and transfers to products being sold. We see these same images, and feel the same feelings of hiraeth, in ads for grocery stores, hotel booking sites, boots, trucks, beer, and, other products and services. These ads lean on feelings of home and belonging, themes of patriotism and travel.

Bill Danoff told me that the song's use in marketing is just part of the business, and that while he and other rights holders recognized this reality, they worked to retain some control. He explained, "Usually we have been very careful whenever we've been involved, of only approving the song for use for things that would be appropriate.... I wouldn't sell it to an oil company or something, that kind of thing. Tires are OK. We need tires." The songwriters wanted to preserve the feel and integrity of the song, even refusing some contracts. For example, Danoff remembers, "Early on, we could have made a lot of money. Colonel Sanders, Kentucky Fried wanted it. And this was early in the 70s. And we were sitting around thinking, if people just associate the song with licking their fingers, it's going to kill the song, if that was your association. So, we tried to keep the associations clean, simple, things that weren't embarrassing to us."

Taffy Nivert sees commercial uses of music a bit differently, however. She told me that she believed marketing, in some ways, corrupts creativity of artistic expression. She traces this feeling back to the days of "Country Roads," when she believes "we always thought our music was sacred and pure. And I knew that social revolution ... was over the first time I heard Bob Dylan on Muzak in an elevator in New York. And I thought, it's been taken over. And then there was a ketchup ad, and Carly Simon had a song called (singing) 'Anticipation, anticipation.' Anyway, it was for ketchup, and I felt like we had been violated.... I realize that nothing is sacred." Despite the loss of sanctity, the commercial use of "Country Roads" has continued in ways that have added to rather than diminished its appeal, perhaps making it more sacred.

The song's popularity increased its use in marketing, and marketing increased interest in the song so that one use has benefited another. As Danoff explains, "More people know it because more people have heard it, so then more people can like it. But the reason they were hearing it is because it had demonstrated that it had a popularity. People liked it when they heard it." This liking led to commercial uses naturally, so that the marketing industry jumped on the song. According to Bill Danoff, "like everything else people that are into, well outside of creative people who use your work, also there's money people. How can I get to sell more soap, or more cars? . . . They want to make the most money out of the song that they can, which works to my benefit, and to everybody's because people like to hear the song. But that kind of widespread popularity is really business driven and not artistically driven" (personal interview). Recent commercial uses of the song demonstrate that it can be transformed to sell just about anything, as long as it is associated, even loosely, with the feeling of belonging and hiraeth.

A recent Latin-market Corona Extra beer ad demonstrates this well, showing images of people enjoying the beer at sports events, car shows, parties, and beaches. A Spanish language version of "Country Roads" plays as people celebrate together, similar to other ads. In this commercial, however, song and setting are translated altogether, suggesting the global resonance of "Country Roads," its timelessness, and its pliability, like the transformed everyplace versions of the song. This transformation also demonstrates the song's ability to create spaces entirely new. The feeling of hiraeth is present when "Country Roads" is used in commercials, or to name spaces, like businesses, or events, like different festivals, tournaments, or celebrations. In West Virginia alone, we have "Mountain Mama" running races, mountain bike events, and sailing regattas. We have "Country Roads" baseball and pickleball tournaments, 5K races, and other events. Like other popular music, "Country Roads" has proven "an integral part of the process by which spaces are created for social interaction, entertainment, and enjoyment" (Connell and Gibson 15). A created space for sports manifests in interesting and varied ways, both inside and outside West Virginia.

THE HOME TEAM: "COUNTRY ROADS" AND SPORTS

"Country Roads" is popular for sports promotion across the globe. It is used to celebrate wins, advance teams, and announce singular players. Australian football player Charlie Cameron, of the Brisbane Lions, uses "Country Roads" every time he scores. Fans sing along to commemorate the goal—and so does Cameron. As in Cameron's embrace of the song, the Brisbane Lions and many sport associations have nothing to do with West Virginia. The St. Louis Blues hockey team has a tradition of playing "Country Roads" during the third period of each home game, for instance. Begun in 2019, the tradition is "organic and fan driven," says the team's entertainment director, Jason Pippi, who describes the song's use as a "feel good moment," that "draws everyone together" during the game (qtd. in Powers). In Ireland, "Country Roads" plays as part of a soundtrack to the national horse plowing championships (Capplis). "Country Roads" is also used to boost the spirits of England's national cricket team during their warm-ups and games (Stocks). Singing together in support of one's team creates a sense of community and unity. As folklorist Debra Lattanzi Shutika describes in her work on rituals, "social practices that encompass the sense of belonging include initiation rituals and ceremonies that mark rites of passage. Belonging can be expressed through institutional structures" and "includes informal behaviors that are not mandated but nevertheless expected if one is to maintain ties to the people and places" (17). We see this same kind of use when "Country Roads" is employed to unite fans in celebration of their home team: It is ritual tied to group belonging, informally and formally.

This ritual use leads to promotion and ticket sales in interesting ways, too. In one example, an English soccer team's post-pandemic return to live events used "Country Roads," apparently also a fan favorite during games. The Bradford City Bantams' "Take Me Home" campaign uses an orchestral version of "Country Roads" over video of an older gentleman as he journeys from his house to the stadium, encountering other fans on the way. The popular ad was nominated for a marketing award (Bradford City). Similarly, the New York Knicks commissioned rapper Doug E. Fresh's transformation, titled "Take Me Home," as a theme song for a short time.

We see in these examples how music is used to shape space and people's experiences within spaces, for personal and commercial purposes, to "alter human behavior in public spaces through the broadcast of music" as "an emotional and commercial tool" (Connell and Gibson 197). As a West Virginia native, having experienced the song so deeply associated with one particular place, I find it strange to think that "Country Roads" can be as resonant on a sports field in Brisbane or in a hockey rink in Missouri, and yet, these fans feel the call to a home team deeply. Still, nowhere is "Country Roads" as prevalent in sports as it is at West Virginia University.

On a recent football game day, my family went to dinner at Muriale's Italian Kitchen restaurant in Fairmont, West Virginia. WVU was playing Virginia Tech for the Black Diamond Trophy, a symbol of a long-standing rivalry between the two teams. In the restaurant, every employee was wearing game day paraphernalia, and servers and kitchen staff took turns stepping into the room where we were eating to catch glimpses of the game on the big screen. On the field, governor Jim Justice, and his bulldog, Baby Dog, carried out an honorary coin toss to kick off the game, soundtracked by fans chanting "Let's Go, Mountaineers." On the day of this game, the words "Country Roads" were embossed around the back bumper of players' helmets, protecting the base of their skulls. "Country Roads" is an ever-present and anticipated reference on game day: a feature of the pre-game show, played by the Pride of West Virginia marching band. And when WVU eked out a close win, the Mountaineer fired his musket, "Country Roads" played, and the whole stadium joined together in song. In the restaurant, people cheered, and it was not long before the game-day crowd began to trickle in, decked in WVU gear, like the "Take Me Home" signature shirts made for WVU's 150th anniversary in 2017.

"COUNTRY ROADS" AS VISIBLE
IDENTITY RHETORIC

It is difficult to find a local shop in West Virginia that lacks reference to "Almost Heaven" or "Country Roads," especially in tourist towns. The words are carved into wood hangings, embroidered into fabric, made into wall decals and other home decor. From T-shirts and stickers to bags and socks, West Virginia companies like Kin Ship Goods, Loving West Virginia, and Made In West Virginia incorporate the song into designs. The West Virginia Company even references the song in their mission statement, writing "We tried to carry that nostalgia throughout our brand" ("Our Brand"). These companies create wearable rhetoric, signifying pride in place and the power of popular music to help us connect to and recognize one another.

It is natural that we would see WVU students using "Country Roads" references to visually mark identity. The lyrics adorn their laptops and cars and decorate their clothing and accessories. This is true for many West Virginians, WVU affiliated or not. One of my own favorite tees shows a stylized drawing of Blackwater Falls, a state landmark, surrounded by rhododendrons and the words "All My Memories Gather 'Round Her." I know people who always wear West Virginia gear when they travel outside the state, nationally or internationally. Doing so prompts an invitation for West Virginians to find each other in airports and restaurants across the globe. "Country Roads" is part of that recognition. Wearing a T-shirt that references the lyrics is just one example of how we use "Country Roads" to visually declare identity. Wearability goes beyond clothing; some folks inscribe the text on their bodies (as seen in Figure 10). A simple Google search produces thousands of images of "Country Roads" tattoos, some with words alone, or with images, maps of the state or mountains. References to the song adorn forearms, biceps, and in this image, a woman's torso, from hip to underarm, an outline of the shape of West Virginia, the New River Gorge Bridge, mountains, water, and words.

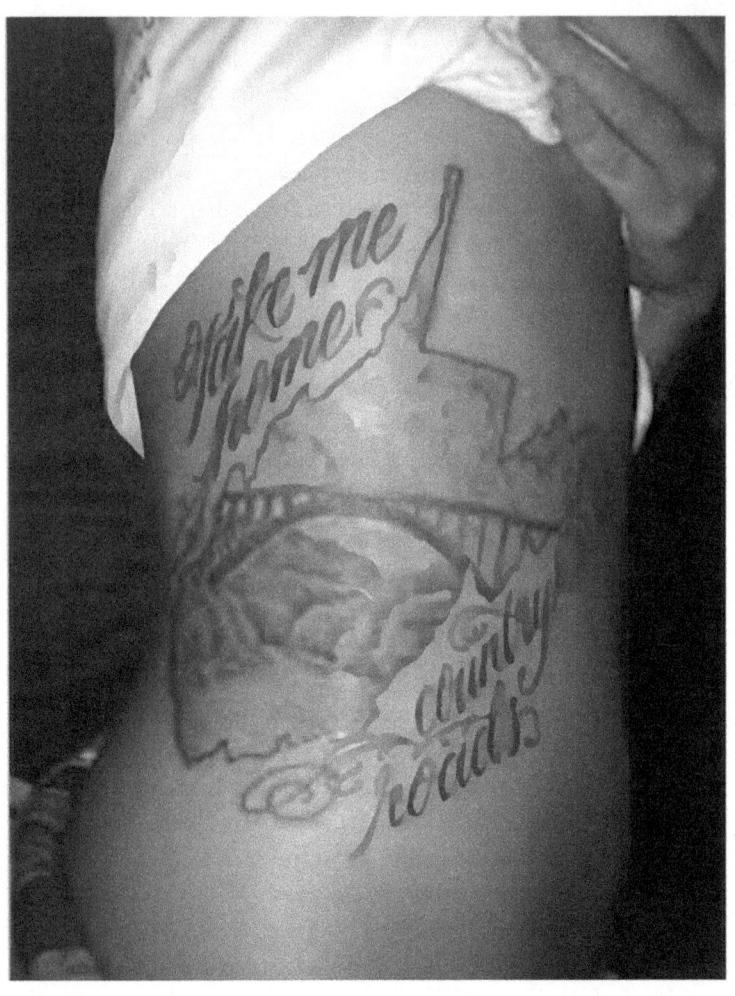

FIGURE 10 A "Country Roads" tattoo

Tattoos mark identity and represent transformation and affiliation (Fenske). Tattooing the lyrics of "Country Roads" on one's body permanently declares an association between embodied self, place, and the text; simultaneously, it transforms the song yet again. A tattoo's permanence is significant here, inscribed on the body as indelibly as the connection to birthplace, family, and home. Importantly, repeated recognition and ritual display of this kind of artifact carries cultural meaning that is taken for granted but also reproduced through continued performance (Butler). If a song is a symbol of the self, social contexts, and culture, we can frame it as something that belongs to groups and spaces, that can be rhetorically applied or appropriated to engage meanings, and that allows us to look in on or back at experience, in critical as well as uncritical ways. It tells us who we can trust, and it creates a sense of belonging not just to place, but to purpose and cause.

PATRIOTISM AND PROTEST: "ALMOST HEAVEN" IS ALL OF AMERICA

"Country Roads" portrays a kind of American anthem, representing the patriotic spirit of the entire nation. Online videos document soldiers singing "Country Roads" on trips home from deployments across the globe; only some are in units returning to West Virginia. In contrast, new American citizens sing "Country Roads" at naturalization ceremonies in West Virginia, a more direct reference to place. The song has been used to awaken astronauts on space missions (Fries), is played on radio stations for Memorial Day and Independence Day, tops lists of best patriotic American songs, and is recommended by the Department of the Interior on their "Ultimate Public Lands Playlist." It was recommended by a *Pop Culture* feature article as being essential to Memorial Day, because "Country Roads" is "patriotic in that Woody Guthrie fashion" and "praises the beauty of the nation, the natural wonders we've grown around and how home is a special place, even if it isn't always in West Virginia." In one viral screen capture, a German social media

FIGURE 11 Screen capture depicting a German social media user mistaking "Country Roads" for the American national anthem

user purportedly admits mistaking the song for the American national anthem (Figure 11).

Whether authentic or contrived, this internet sentiment extends beyond the awareness of one person since on the online petition site Change.org, at least six separate pages entreat various political figures to make "Country Roads" an official national anthem. Collectively, these petitions, generated by users from Kansas, Texas, New York, Ohio, Illinois, and other states, have more than three hundred supporters, representing a small but serious number of Denver-devoted patriots, most of whom do not report to be from West Virginia.

In these uses, West Virginia becomes a proxy home for all Americans, representing the pastoral simplicity of an imagined nation, a return to values of place that never existed to begin with. Folklorist James Abrams discusses the notion of *heritage discourse* in representing place as malleable and flexible so that desired traits can be widely taken up by people, lending a powerful and even distorted sense to what is ours (25). Abrams also discusses a "media of nostalgia" represented through "mediascapes" and tourist structures that create a past that is not remembered but represented and referenced anyway as it becomes interpreted as part of the historical and cultural discourse of place (27). As a kind of heritage discourse of both specific place and mediascape anyplace, "Country Roads" is relevant not just to West Virginians, but also to a much wider audience as it functions as a kind of national and international anthem that can be used to orient to home in commercial, political, and cultural representations.

As an ersatz national anthem, "Country Roads" speaks to a constructed notion of society, and as Connell and Gibson remind us, "Anthems are musical texts, historical documents, and a means through which a sense of the contemporary nation is created and contested" (128). As a representative text that expresses nostalgic homegoing, it makes sense that "Country Roads" carries a sense of place more broadly. This sense of hiraeth in general is complicated by the fact that West Virginia is a real place, albeit one often fictionalized or associated more with stereotypes than reality. As in the travel writing of the nineteenth and the novels of the twentieth centuries, which portray Appalachia as a nostalgic place apart from the rest of the United States, "Country Roads" evokes homesickness for a kind of constructed reality disconnected from tangible geography and cultural influence. In her book, *Dear Appalachia*, Emily Satterwhite discusses this, specifically addressing the ways texts compel a reader to imagine "returning to a place they had known in their past or that their forebears had known," an ancestral home "where the people and culture were distinctly different from mainstream America," characterized by "wholesomeness" and rurality (193). Akin to the regional fiction that is Satterwhite's focus, "Country Roads" serves much the same function, allowing readers to "[access] national heritage" and "[comprehend] their own personal roots" (Satterwhite, *Dear* 193). The result is an idyllic, whitewashed, nonexistent place. The fictionalization of real places allows readers to "consume an Appalachia imagined as simple white America, an alternative to mass consumerism and rootlessness and the foundation for national identity and missions of uplift" that allows them to preserve ambiguous American values (Satterwhite, *Dear* 128). The Appalachia of popular fiction represents a fabricated authenticity that readers accept as real, and "Country Roads" does the same, constructing truths listeners can apply to their lives and longings. In some settings, "Country Roads" becomes a rhetorical unifier and is used to declare an argument. This is evident in its use at nationalistic events, protests, rallies, and ceremonies connected and unconnected to West Virginia.

Used in protest, "Country Roads" declares a position on issues across social and political spectra. For instance, one *Washington Post* article associates the song with a "Freedom Convoy" of truckers that circled the capital in March 2022, protesting a range of policies and causes. Gathered outside the Capital Beltway, "the group was celebratory and proud. Truckers blared the song 'Take Me Home, Country Roads'" (Silverman, Davies, Thompson, and Duncan). In this particular use, the song references literal roads on which the truckers drove. In another example, anecdotal accounts claim "Country Roads" was sung by Tiananmen Square protesters in 1989 during the demonstrations that resulted in the massacre of hundreds of Peking University students. Several online videos have been crafted to show footage of the events soundtracked by an amateur rendition of the song; however, I have not been able to find clear documentation of its use by protesters there.

"Country Roads" has been associated with climate and environmental action as well. A 2019 climate change sit-in at the annual Harvard-Yale football game used "Country Roads" as a catalyst for protesters as they rushed onto the field (O'Daly). In that moment, the song "enlivened students on both sides of the field, if not in solidarity for the cause then at least in appreciation for the music and its cultural relevance—and as such, it enabled protestors, however unintentionally, to overcome the collective action problem as a critical mass of students gathered to prolong the sit-in" (Shand 7). Already in the spirit of the moment, the song compelled protesters to act more fully. In 2010, the Rainforest Action Network gathered at the Environmental Protection Agency headquarters in DC to call attention to the widespread practice of mountaintop removal (MTR) mining. As they sat, activists "locked themselves together with metal 'lock boxes,' and began to play West Virginia's adopted state song, John Denver's 'Take me Home, Country Roads,' mixed with intermittent sounds of Appalachia's mountains being blown apart by MTR explosives" (Global Energy Monitor). In this instance, the song references landscape directly. Different from more general uses, protests intimately related to West Virginian issues remake "Country Roads" as an anthem of place and preservation.

Protesters sing "Country Roads" for a range of reasons in West Virginia, from adopting a rhetoric of identity to showing solidarity. West Virginians use it to demonstrate against mine sites, chemical facilities, and entities likely to cause environmental impact. "Country Roads" became a kind of anthem against Rockwool, a Danish insulation company that built a facility in the state's eastern panhandle; demonstrators used the song at the build site, at city and county government agencies, as well as at the national capitol. In one account, "Capitol Police arrested 11 people for 'unlawfully demonstrating' outside of [West Virginia senator] Manchin's office, while the demonstrators sang 'Country Roads.' They were charged with D.C. Code 22-1307, Crowding, Obstructing, or Incommoding" (Tully-McManus). At least one activist claims that being arrested while singing "Country Roads" is quintessential West Virginian experience—"peak Appalachian" (@dewmouth)—used to express community, affiliation, and freedom.

Tying to place is evident when West Virginians transform "Country Roads" in protest, using the words or just the tune, as in a 2015 movement against a Dollar General store in Morgan County. Activists composed words related to promoting local businesses rather than the coming corporate store; this version echoes the sentiment West Virginians have for Denver's song but conveys a cause-specific message. Likewise, "Country Roads" was used in West Virginian activism by students at Huntington High School during a walkout for religious freedom and by students at other walkouts for various causes. In local and national news coverage, West Virginia's 2018 teacher's strike showed teachers converging on the State Capitol in Charleston, singing "Country Roads" outside meeting rooms where legislators deliberated. As part of the #55Strong movement, teachers sang it on picket lines, both in solidarity and in celebration when a compromise was reached. These varied examples show the range of activist rhetorical uses: for identity or to show pride of place, conviction to a cause, or a tie to home.

In West Virginia, "Country Roads" in protest is part of a tradition of Appalachian activism, one that includes passive as well as active resistance. In his work on grassroots involvement, Stephen Fisher shows how Appalachian movements tend to be small, local, and immediate because "regional culture informs the construction of class consciousness, race and gender relations, regional identity, and community life" in complex ways ("Grass" 208). Unlike more traditional protest anthems—hymns like "We Shall Overcome," or "We Shall Not Be Moved," or songs written specifically in protest, like Woody Guthrie's "This Land Is Your Land," or Bob Dylan's "Blowin' in the Wind"—"Country Roads" is regionally relevant in its representation of place-identity. In Appalachia, identities of place and resistance are connected since activism originates from geographically specific causes, like environmental issues and landholder rights. Identity, place, and resistance are intertwined because "location is not just important. In situations where the landscape itself is affected, it becomes the center from which the community is based" (Nardella 3). Expressions of resistance, rooted in community, are naturally tied to place. When regional identity is tied to activism, and when an expression of place is so prevalent as in "Country Roads," it follows that local movements would leverage the anthem.

The American and West Virginian embrace of "Country Roads" as a kind of common protest anthem may serve to "recast the past" as Roger Abrahams describes with folkloric preservations so that it exists as a kind of de-historicized tribute to a place or places that never existed anyway. This is part and parcel of American culture, however, as Abrahams argues, because "American society not only constantly reinvents the past to engender nostalgia but also, under present media conditions and the ever-mounting value placed on entertainment services," keeps adding to the collection of representations of place (83). While Abrahams is primarily concerned with folklore and cultural preservation, we can see how "Country Roads" becomes an emblem of reinvented space and time, particularly in commercial and political uses. "Country Roads" describes everyplace worth fighting for, but meaning changes in West Virginia.

The romanticized version of West Virginia portrayed in "Country Roads" lends itself to expressions of resistance because it suggests physical and spiritual connection to place, giving movements more resonance, despite the song's inaccuracies and reliance on stereotypes, which become undone in the practice of West Virginians taking up the song. This is related to Castells's concept of *resistance identity*, created through shared bonds tied to place, which may cause people to embrace stereotypes to dismantle them. As a highly recognizable cultural text, "Country Roads" marks regional identity for West Virginians. "Regional identities are strong because they are often linked to these shared bonds and cultures that exist within communities," and rhetorics of identity tie us more closely together, since "romanticized notion[s] surrounding a region (or a reaction to a negative stereotype)" can place "people into further connections with each other" (Castells 8). "Country Roads" is an artifact of connections, part of the rhetoric of American and West Virginian identity and place-belonging, factoring not just into activist rhetoric, but into tourist rhetoric, too.

MARKETING A RE-CREATED WEST VIRGINIA: "TAKE ME HOME" TOURISM

One Saturday afternoon, I play "Country Roads" on the jukebox in a neighborhood bar. My friends and I are eating wings and drinking beers. Some people have already had too much to drink: This space is small, a little greasy, and loud. The first strains of the song are unmistakable. Plucked out on the guitar, the music is a short riff, three notes, pensive, then four more, until the other instruments and vocals come in: immediately recognizable. A momentary hush falls, and then the whole bar, friends and strangers, sings along. It is reverent, offkey, and a little absurd. No one is crying as far as I notice, but we are in Morgantown. If we were in another state, West Virginians at a dive bar far from home, "Country Roads" on the jukebox, we probably would.

What is clear here is the way the song creates a kind of instant community among West Virginians. Connections among people within a nation are imagined, not material or real. Nations are limited by finite borders, bounded in clear, specific, but imagined ways. States, too, are sovereign, bound together in similar ways, in a community imagined through "deep, horizontal comradeship" (B. Anderson 7). West Virginians find each other in other states, in other countries; they home in on one another, someone else who "gets it." We recognize accents in shops, say something, connect.

This connection is facilitated through "Country Roads" as a construable sign. We feel connected to place, even when we are absent from that place. This use of the song shows how cultural identity, and relationships of belonging, work interdependently with cultural artifacts to create and re-create meanings, a "contextualized narrative inscribed around certain objects." Through articulation of shared stories in place, we develop a sense of belonging to that place and community, identifying with others. Furthermore, through ritual performances of place-identity, "spaces are re-membered, with participants reinscribing themselves into the space, evoking corporeal memories of previous enactment" and creating new spaces of belonging (Leach 127, 130).

The stories we tell through performances of identity, like singing "Country Roads" in both formal and informal contexts, call upon past performances and create new spaces so that singing together in a situation like this is more than an event, it is a new third space, momentarily conjured through ritual. "Country Roads" has been prompting this kind of ritual reaction and re-creation in West Virginians since 1971, but its use for state purposes was a long time coming. Despite its early adoption by WVU, it was not until 2014 that "Country Roads" was legally made a state anthem, the namesake relationship official.

The connection between song and state extends to the songwriters, too. We have already discussed that Denver, Danoff, and Nivert's individual relationships to West Virginia were largely peripheral. Yet the song's widespread popularity has created an affectionate, familial feeling toward the artists. This is evidenced by the multiple times they have been invited to perform at events: for the opening of Mountaineer Field, during a telethon to support recovery efforts after the devastating 1985 floods, or when the West Virginia House of Representatives forwarded an official resolution to acknowledge Denver's death.

Nivert feels a deep connection based on the song's reception among West Virginians. She told me that the affinity is "like we're cousins but twice removed or something," and that she, Danoff, and Denver were officially recognized at state events as a result of the song. Nivert remembered, "We were made one of those honorifics that doesn't really mean anything, just warm ephemera. We were made honorary West Virginians twice. Once by Arch Moore, and once by Jay Rockefeller." Despite the "warm ephemera," West Virginians feel recognized by the songwriters and the song, and that recognition is acknowledged in a range of ways, officially and unofficially, publicly and privately, at occasions joyful and somber.

In shared moments, at a local bar or sports event, at a wedding or memorial, "Country Roads" creates togetherness, shared experience, and, in the instance of this kind of anthem—one that names a specific place—community. This is more than emotional: We experience music in embodied ways. We feel the pulse of drums, the vibration of guitars, the tension of close harmony, and corporeality in space, engaged together, creating place. As scholar Ian Maxwell explains, "Sound penetrates, or perhaps better, resonates with, in and around bodies in a material corporeal way, registering somatically with the listener in a manner far less susceptible to the logics of separation and distance than the visual. Sound moves us, literally, as well as figuratively." Movement together, singing together, is connected deeply to the way we take up space because we physically experience music, as "the way to make sense of the relationship between popular music and place: to move our own bodies close to and with the bodies for whom those particular musics are sensible. And, in doing so, we find ourselves coming back to places" (Maxwell 87). "Country Roads" renders human experience, moment, and place, even if the song is not of or from the place. It brings us back to the place as remembered, as imagined.

Music has long been associated with place-making, and in our modern era, the affordances of technology and global culture allow that "musicalized narrativizations of place may not simply occur within particular places, but can also be imposed from without" (Bennett 70). "Country Roads" came to West Virginia from the outside, and yet, it has become defining language of state identity, despite its imaginary qualities. Within West Virginia, the tellable narrative of "Country Roads" is a story that shines, sets a positive tone, and projects a sense of belonging, connected to a state that is often portrayed as less than positive. In this way, it takes up a kind of constructed authenticity, one used to market the state as a place to visit or as a place to live.

Over time, "Country Roads" has undergone a transformation in its usefulness and meaningfulness. As a now essential part of the place it names, "Country Roads" speaks to Ryden's sense of imaginary landscape in folklore. The song acts like local lore in West Virginia: It is used in traditional, almost formulaic ways; it transmits intimate insider knowledge in the ways that we use it specifically within West Virginia; and it provides a sense of identity connected to group belonging and grounded in place (Ryden 64–65). *Folklore of place* connects self to space and feeling, "anchored firmly to the facts of geography, history, and identity, [it] is a final stratum of emotion, a level of feeling which is inseparable from place, which intensifies local knowledge of that place, and which probably contributes most to separating the perspective of the insider from that of the outsider. For those who know the local folk traditions, a map or a tourist snapshot is only the most cursory of starting points" (Ryden 67). What is interesting about "Country Roads" is that it was, once, a cursory starting point, the "briefest of allusions," and yet it has become intrinsically linked to the story of place now. First used as a cursory description from the outside looking in, the song is now used from within to self-describe and to invite the listener to experience place as destination.

Today, "Country Roads" is an essential part of the rhetoric of place, despite its flaws, as "music is a cultural resource bound up in how places are perceived, and how they are promoted. It is one means by which places can be represented in wider mediascapes, shaping local or regional identities and, by design or default, music influences the images that attract tourists" (Connell and Gibson 221). Tourism was slow to take up "Country Roads," but the song now represents and markets an entire state, in the hope that lyrical descriptions match up with travelers' experiences once they arrive. It took forty-seven years, but West Virginia came full circle when the state went from being named by the song to incorporating the song to market the state, re-creating and naming itself with the song.

Although the legislature made it an official anthem in 2014, it was not until 2017 that West Virginia purchased rights to use "Country Roads" for tourism, paying almost $100,000 to Denver's estate for the master recording (Lawrence). Tourism commissioner Chelsea Ruby justified the purchase by describing not using the song as "a black hole" in marketing, explaining, "When there's a song that millions of people already love and associate with your state, it's an obvious way to promote the tourism industry. . . .

We are Almost Heaven, and this lets the world know" (qtd. in Lawrence). The purchase was made only after West Virginia's tourism office conducted market research to determine the effectiveness of using "Country Roads" played over images of scenic mountain views and other state destinations in a thirty-second television advertisement. Shown in a test market that included six major cities, the research found that "100 percent of those who viewed the ad campaign said it made them more likely to visit West Virginia" (Kabler).

After many years of being applied to remember and describe, the song was now being used as an argument to encourage outsiders to come in. This is consistent with Kent Ryden's work on place, which argues that, "in the absence of hard experiential information about the landscapes and culture of a place, people rely on positive and negative stereotypes of the kind found in movies, television, newspapers, advertisements, popular music, and books. People thus can and do attach meaning to places they've never been" (Ryden 55). Harnessed to showcase the positive, and combined with vivid imagery, "Country Roads" is persuasive and lends itself well as an argument for those looking to escape and travel. Tourist campaigns using "Country Roads" create new meaning and impressions of West Virginia.

"Country Roads" marketing in state tourism has spread to include participatory elements, including the "Place I Belong" campaign, which borrows a lyrical reference and includes coloring pages and media content. Hashtag marketing invites participants to contribute by sharing social media content labeled #placeIbelongwv and #AlmostHeaven. State officials report "reach throughout the campaign topped out at over 21 million" and received high social sentiment ratings from participants. In 2021, the "Place I Belong" campaign won a National State Tourism Directors Mercury Award for best community-building effort and was recognized by judges for its capacity to "provide stimulating social media content to destination partners throughout the state" including "innovative, engaging, and relevant" content that allowed for easy public and business participation (National State Tourism Directors). General public and local businesses took up the campaign visibly, as is evidenced by numbers of posts using the hashtags on sites like Instagram and Facebook.

Further, in 2022, nine "Almost Heaven" swings, produced by students at a Nicholas County technical school, were placed strategically around the state, in parks, cities, and overlooks. Official photos for the announcement of this campaign show Governor Jim Justice's dog, Baby Dog, perched happily on the swing installed in view of the gold-domed State Capitol building in Charleston (Young). Visitors are encouraged to pose on the swings for sharable photo opportunities, and the state continues to add new swings in scenic spots. Tourist materials and efforts including the song have continued on the official tourism page, in advertising, and on social media. The lyrics are used across these efforts, on state websites, and in publications, with a specially designed and licensed "Almost Heaven" script and possibilities for brand marketing partnerships. Successful applicants pay a royalty fee to the state, signaling ownership of the song, at least partially, has come home (West Virginia Tourism). The song has moved from naming the place, to representing the place, to being owned by and used by the place to name itself, rhetorically re-created to promote recreation.

"Country Roads" has become part of the production of place, shaping perceptions of listeners who may only know *of* West Virginia, impressions of those who visit, and identities of those who are *from and of* West Virginia. Public participation in this naming and description is especially relevant as the song has become more than a song. Like regional fiction, which "produced Appalachia as a commodity" not just for literature, but also for tourism and popular culture, music also influences American perception of place. "When pitched in the right way to the right audiences," Appalachia is "a profitable commodity produced, marketed, sold, bought, and circulated" (Satterwhite, *Dear* 228). "Country Roads" commodifies the feeling of home and transfers that feeling to West Virginia itself.

"Country Roads" shapes visitor expectations, as tourists are drawn to the descriptions of mountain views, pastoral settings, and flowing water, images made all the more powerful when coupled with photographs and videos of West Virginia. These representations create an experience, as "tourists often base their expectations of particular destinations around mediatized images of those destinations, so music has become another primary means by which individuals think about and visualize space" (Bennett 70). Music shapes internal perceptions, too. By sharing the song from within, West Virginia becomes "implicated in the continued circulation of romantic stereotypes about the region" (Satterwhite, *Dear* 209). West Virginia is more than "Country Roads," but we love the song anyway, and we hope people who visit will too. It is a product of rhetoric that represents as much as it obscures, a kind of performance of identity: constructed, imagined, and concealed complexity.

In this chapter, we have discussed how "Country Roads," as a product of a global music industry, has been taken up and used as a construable sign connected to many places and every home. The song has the power to reach wide audiences for varied purposes within a larger consumer culture. When used strategically, hiraeth can encourage nostalgia for more than place so that "Country Roads" can sell products, ideas, and ideologies grounded in the sense of togetherness and home, both in and out of West Virginia. Its uses are diverse, varied, and sometimes surprising. As commercial rhetoric, "Country Roads" sells tires and real estate, sausage and sports, and sundry other goods and services. It sells political positions and creates affiliations to cause. More pervasive, though, is the way it sells an impression, an image, however fractured, of what it means to be from a place: to be West Virginian. It is important to understand what it is about "Country Roads" that prompts West Virginians to embrace it, and it is important that we dismantle the anthem in order to better name ourselves. Doing so can help West Virginians "become aware of our own invisible landscapes," to move beyond them, "to see and believe that other people live in invisible landscapes of their own, imaginative vistas built upon the actual physical landscape, and [they] will then be less inclined to do either of those landscapes harm" (Ryden 293). In this book's final chapter, I argue that our embrace of "Country Roads" may be attributable to a gap in our literacy identity, and filling that gap begins with teaching and learning about place for the good of place: others' places as well as our own.

6

THE WINDOW, THE MIRROR, AND THE LENS: PEDAGOGICAL IMPLICATIONS

AN ANTHEM AS AN ANSWER
Throughout this book, I have discussed "Take Me Home, Country Roads" as emblem of identity, call to home, cultural artifact, marketing device, paean of protest, and place-based rhetoric. I have considered how it amplifies some voices and obscures others, how it simplifies and glosses over complexity. I have approached this topic as a West Virginian and researcher, but I am first and always a teacher. And that is where this inquiry originates: This project began with a pedagogical dilemma, and I want to conclude with pedagogical implications.

In first-year composition my students, like many, struggle with understanding rhetoric. They confuse analysis with summary, misinterpret purpose and audience, and substitute opinion for evidence. I tried with varying success to teach critical reading with a variety of popular and more traditional texts, using advertisements, music videos, short literary works, essays, and articles, finally realizing I needed to model the process using a text resonant enough to sustain student engagement. Then, one spring afternoon, I noticed a gathering crowd in front of the Mountainlair student union at West Virginia University (WVU), where a speaking area creates a standing-room amphitheater

FIGURE 12 Tweet describing WVU students singing "Country Roads" in response to a street preacher

---

for public demonstrations. Standing on the wall was a preacher holding a divisive sign conveying a fire-and-brimstone message. His mouth was open, his face passionate as he shouted, and he was waving a Bible in the other hand. He was yelling, but students gathered in front of him were singing. From across the street, all I heard was a chorus of voices drowning him out with "Country Roads." In this context, the anthem was an answer, resisting an unwelcome message. I was not the only one who noticed (see Figure 12).

Hearing "Country Roads" transformed in this way called attention to the song yet again, and I knew that I had found my teaching text. "Country Roads" is medium and message, conveying ideas not just about identity and home but also about values connected to place. What was interesting to me then, and now, is the way students take up a text commonly used for prescribed purposes and make it into something new. They apply the familiar in an unfamiliar way, generating new meanings connected to past and future purposes, audiences, and contexts. This transformative use of "Country Roads" as rhetoric is something students do often and organically. This use is not limited to students, as I have demonstrated throughout this book. As we have seen, West Virginians take up "Country Roads," as do musicians, markets, protesters, and politicians, locally and globally. Amid these purposes the song provokes questions not just about rhetoric and interpretations of place, but also about classroom uses and implications for pedagogy. What can we learn from this? How can we use "Country Roads" to deepen thinking and learning?

UP THERE IN MORGANTOWN: "COUNTRY ROADS" AT WEST VIRGINIA UNIVERSITY

A starting point for understanding "Country Roads" as a teaching text means understanding it in the context in which I teach. "Country Roads" has a range of rhetorical uses at West Virginia University, and it is clear that the administration and brand management recognized the potential from the moment the song hit the charts. "Country Roads" was released in 1971, became a hit later that year, and WVU, in a moment of genius marketing, gained usage rights in 1972. Since then, "the song has become associated with WVU, in part because of the Pride of West Virginia marching band's rendition of it, arranged by James Miltenberger, a professor of music" (M. Burnside). It is played at nearly every event, is referenced on parephenalia and publicity materials, rings out from bell towers, and is used for hold music on campus phone systems. WVU's football uniforms and much of WVU's trademarked apparel, both for teams and the public, reference the song. WVU's official licensing information specifies that both use of the words from "Country Roads" and the song itself are protected brand elements held by the University's trademark office. The tradition itself, in which "Country Roads" is "played after every home win and fans are encouraged to stay in the stands and join in singing" is part of WVU's portfolio of *indicia*, or distinguishing marks. As mentioned before, John Denver, Taffy Nivert, and Bill Danoff even performed "Country Roads" at the opening of Mountaineer Field in 1980, famously flown in by a helicopter provided by the then governor Jay Rockefeller.

"Country Roads" is used for recruitment, as well. William Brustein, former Vice President for Global Strategies and

International Affairs at WVU, told me he regularly used it as a point of connection with international students looking to study abroad. On campus, "Country Roads" is all around us. University-sanctioned uses are ubiquitous, but to be part of singing it—at games, or graduation ceremonies, or other events—is moving nonetheless. Part of the community rhetoric at West Virginia University, it is sung during rites of passage. These rituals evoke a sense of togetherness across time and space, similar to patriotic or nationalistic rituals that depend upon faith in a mutually moving community and require "complete confidence" in others' "steady, anonymous, simultaneous activity" (Anderson 25–26). These activities tie us to each other culturally because we assume others are participating with us, feeling the same emotions, moving through the same rituals. "Country Roads" is a manifestation of this notion of community through synchronous, shared understanding in action, though community uses may vary.

WVU students take up "Country Roads" to participate in school-sanctioned rituals all the time. They wear it on their clothes, tattoo it on their bodies, and use it in social media. But they also transform it in unexpected, unsanctioned ways that sometimes resist WVU's message and marketing. It is not only a sign of school pride, but also an emblem of party culture, a persistent point of conflict between students and the administration. Students sing it spontaneously at illicit parties, for example. An Instagram video from entertainment site *dartywvu*, posted March 12, 2021, shows a crowd at an unsanctioned block party in Sunnyside, a student housing area. Hundreds of people, cups raised, shout the chorus of "Country Roads" a cappella. The street, porches, and rooftops are entirely filled with bodies as partiers sing their hearts out, eyes closed. In another instance, a different purpose but a similar scene: Our student population lost one of their own in a death by suicide in Spring 2021. In an off-campus public memorial, outside the reach of the administration, who had received criticism for a lackluster response, mourners sang "Country Roads" at sunset between the buildings of the apartment complex where the student lived. Again: same song, different sentiment, in public use divergent from official indica.

Students make "Country Roads" their own, and adapt it as rhetoric, official message be damned. Rosemary Hathaway, in her book *Mountaineers Are Always Free*, documents a similar disruption of sanctioned narrative in images of the school mascot, writing: "The administration recognized that there was something potentially productive in an event that celebrates 'Mountaineer' identity—but they wanted to be the ones who defined that identity" (102). WVU has long worked to cultivate an image of the school and students from the top down, but what is compelling is the way students appropriate and transform construable signs for their own purposes and audiences. From the "Take Me Home" campaign in T-shirts and marketing materials, to the song as part of WVU's official indica, to students singing "Country Roads" at unsanctioned parties or to protest hate speech on campus, we see fluid meaning and interpretive use based on how the song translates into students' lived experiences, and how they apply it, as well as how it marks them as part of a discourse community.

COME HERE, FROM HERE: OUT-OF-STATE AND IN-STATE STUDENTS

Community at WVU is different for students who come to West Virginia as opposed to those who are from West Virginia. Out-of-state students comprise more than half the population in this land-grant university: In Fall 2023, 54 percent of students came from other places. For them, "Country Roads" is a unifier that signifies the University experience. Every decision season, students and parents post social media of themselves with the slogan "Take Me Home, Country Roads" to announce public decisions to attend WVU. The song is a gold and blue thread that ties students to place and each other, but for most out-of-state students, that identity is emplaced for only a few years and centralized on campus.

As a rhetorical text, "Country Roads," suggests membership in a group within a cultural space and discourse community of belonging. As with any school symbol, an anthem is a marker of identity and affiliation. The song "is powerful because it brings together both the experience of the intensely subjective and personal with the external, cultural, and collective" (Bloustien, Peters, and Luckman xxiii). It helps students see a window into possible lives, community, and identity in place with similar others.

We can again reference the notion of imagined community, since "Country Roads" is a "cultural product" that fosters attachment to Mountaineer nation and identity through shared vocabulary of kinship and home (B. Anderson 143). For example, my student Aubrey recalled that when she traveled to Ireland in high school, all of her Irish cousins knew "Country Roads" and were always singing it. She had never consciously heard the song before and learned it there from people she loved: "We were all singing it everywhere: in pubs, hiking the sides of mountains, in the streets. . . . I don't know any other place that is so proud as West Virginia of being from a state. I thought: I want to go there." Aubrey told me that when she later began to explore her options for college, these memories of singing "Country Roads" affected her choice. For Aubrey, an out-of-state student, the song became a window through which to view a possible future, one deeply emplaced in a space of belonging. And, prior to this experience, remember, she had never heard the song before; in contrast, students from West Virginia grow up with "Country Roads" as being part of the soundtrack of their lives.

West Virginian children learn "Country Roads" in school, at home, and in other spaces. Their parents post videos of them on social media when they learn to sing it as toddlers and buy copies of the 2005 Christopher Canyon illustrated children's story for them. To illustrate, in March 2022, West Virginia governor Jim Justice filmed a read-aloud of that book for Read Across America Day (Jeff Morris). Justice explained that the book choice was meant to help children "always remember home and just remember how great this state is." For West Virginians, "Country Roads" is first about home, and then, perhaps, about college. It is about staying, noticing what is good and true, and trying to make a difference. This is complicated by the notion that to succeed, we are told, we must leave the state.

My student Rebecca told me a similar story to Aubrey's about hearing "Country Roads" while traveling in London during her senior year of high school. An in-state student, Rebecca felt transported, called back, and able to see "home" from a different perspective, one of longing. Rebecca wrote about her experience:

> My mom and I were walking from the Trinity College Campus to a restaurant when I heard a familiar tune. We spotted a street performer singing Denver's song while playing the guitar. I was stunned to hear the words of West Virginia being sung overseas while I was wearing a WVU string backpack. I looked around at the people observing the indie singer and was amazed as I watched them sing along. They knew the words just as well as I did. Did they wonder what West Virginia was like? Could they imagine the beauty of the hills while singing about the country roads?

Prior to this moment, Rebecca reflected, "In my mind, my home wasn't that appealing." She noted this dissonance: She had been excited to leave West Virginia, but seeing this version of her home changed this perception and ultimately resulted in her decision to attend WVU.

The decision to stay and attend WVU has different implications for West Virginian students than attending does for those of out-of-staters who find themselves in West Virginia; to be educated as a West Virginian is to simultaneously prepare to leave. As Rosemary Hathaway claims, one role of WVU is representing and preparing students as citizens who can function "outside" Appalachia. As the flagship university, WVU "symbolizes the state's connection and conduit to the larger culture outside its borders and represents the state's literal investment in providing the education and experience to prepare its citizens to enter the larger and, some might say, more elite sphere" (Hathaway 67). For many, committing to becoming educated is equivalent to committing to a future elsewhere. "Country Roads" then becomes an outmigration anthem for those who become educated and cannot stay. It symbolizes an unfulfillable commitment, a divided identity.

Scholars who study first-generation education address the divide students experience when they find themselves on the outside looking back on their families and communities. As Erica Locklear explains in her work on Appalachian women's literacy, the identity shift first-generation students experience can cause a fracture between them and their community. It can fracture their conception of self, too, since setting out into the world shows us our difference to the world, including markers of rurality, dialect, mannerisms. This was certainly true for me as a first-generation West Virginian college student when I left home. I fielded questions about my home state and stereotypes; I represented a place people knew little about. I felt disconnected from others and also from home, and when I was fortunate enough to return, I was grateful, but changed. "Country Roads" evoked all manner of emotions at different points on my journey: homesickness, resentment at its misrepresentation, and pride in recognition.

So West Virginia University's in-state student population experiences college, and "Country Roads," differently from out-of-state students. Todd Snyder, from Webster County, West Virginia, studied transitions first-generation West Virginian college students make when they pursue higher education and attributes the prevalence of extraction industries to the struggles that West Virginian students, in particular, face when they are the first in their families to leave. Cultural rhetoric that praises industry (in West Virginia, predominantly coal) and that values a pioneering spirit pulls Appalachians toward home (Snyder, "Transition"). Attending college is a primary step on the way to leaving, but first-generation Appalachian college students report staying or returning home is a specific, measurable goal. Nearly all of Snyder's participants planned to live in their home state after receiving a degree and felt an "internalized obligation to remain" (*Rhetoric* 203). For many West Virginians, "to leave the community is to abandon all that the family has made for you. To leave the community, even if it's to attend college, is to leave the rest of the family behind," and "family-based rhetoric keeps Appalachian kids in their respective communities," without opportunity (Snyder, *Rhetoric* 81). This sense of home is a cyclical and generational construct, tied to work, life, death, family, worship, and states of mind (Snyder, *Rhetoric* 70). "Country Roads" is a living artifact of that rhetoric. Ironically, for many Appalachian college students, especially those from rural areas, a college degree prompts a kind of exile, even though "we want to find a college and a career that will allow us to stay" connected to "legacies, family histories, and our standing in the communities" (Snyder, *Rhetoric* 128). Staying feels impossible in a state where, historically, opportunities are decreasing, population is declining, and demographics are shifting. For those of us who want to remain but must leave, "Country Roads" is colored with grief.

This grief is compounded in places where becoming more educated creates division, as it does for many first-generation learners. Factors influencing a sense of school belonging and the association between belonging and achievement may be different for rural youth. In Appalachia specifically, "lower high school completion rates, and thus college attendance rates, were related to perceived irrelevance of educational attainment to economic circumstance" (Chenoweth and Galliher 3). If first-generation college students experience disconnection at school because of their differences in an unfamiliar community and at home because of their educational gains, they may find themselves without a place to belong. "Country Roads" speaks to this deep loneliness, again tapping into hiraeth. The physical home we know is not the home we long for, spiritually and emotionally, and becoming more educated separates us further.

For many residents, West Virginia is potholed roads, mine reclaims, broken barns, deserted communities: not growth and opportunity. It is not the West Virginia of "Country Roads," the romanticized, idealized space. When we leave, we are changed. When we return, that change is amplified. We may still belong, but the fit is not the same. "Country Roads" represents impossible return and evokes existential longing for imagined space. This is consistent with the message across the region, as bell hooks describes, "The insistence that the best and the brightest ... need to move elsewhere to become fully self-realized comes with no insistence that this elite group should return to their homeplace" (67). This leads to loss of human resources and commitment to place beyond visit and memory, much like what is suggested in "Country Roads": nostalgia without covenant.

This is hiraeth: "literally 'longing,' 'nostalgia,' or sometimes plain 'grief.' It has come to signify, however, something even less exact: longing, yes, but for nothing definite; nostalgia, but for an indeterminate past; grief without cause or explanation" (Jan Morris). "Country Roads" triggers hiraeth, except the place where we want to belong no longer belongs to us; it has been swept away by the sense of "Country Roads" as a vision of home. Unlike out-of-state students, who associate "Country Roads" with college, West Virginian students' associations are bound in complicated notions of home, homesickness. Rather than "where I went to college," it is "where I lived, and where I left," or "where I fought to stay," or even "where I hope to return." Often that return is impossible, making West Virginia "the place I [no longer] belong." This makes the song a powerful symbol, one used by West Virginians in all kinds of ways. As an anthem, for West Virginia University students and for West Virginia residents more widely, those who are still in state, and those who have left, "Country Roads" presents identity, unites community, and even divides. Understanding that rhetorical meaning within a critical pedagogical context, incorporating a place-based teaching approach, adds another layer of meaning.

PLACE-BASED PEDAGOGY IN APPALACHIA

Place itself is a kind of happening, visible when analyzed rhetorically: for example, when we sing "Country Roads" to express joy, as at a wedding, or to memorialize, as at a funeral. In these cases, "Country Roads" makes an implicit argument about uniqueness and exceptionality of shared place, the pull of homesickness, hiraeth, and place-identity. When intentionality and critical reflection are added, and when we approach the world with an awareness of place, we become centered in something greater than ourselves. Place becomes more than just the mention of "Blue Ridge Mountains, Shenandoah River." Place becomes an experience, a personal and shared resonance, that shapes how we process historical, personal, and educational events. Where events occur shapes our perceptions as much as how and when; all our experiences are emplaced. Phenomenologist Edward Casey elaborates that "place becomes an event, a happening not only in space but in time and history as well. To the role of place as facilitative and locator we need to add the role of place as eventamental" (xxv). When we learn to look carefully at context as part of identity development, we are better able to discern our own vantage points. We are better able to critically question the ways place is represented, to recognize oversimplification, and to read with complexity. As bell hooks explains, "since the culture produced in mass media often uses existing stereotypes and biases for raw material," what we know about people different from ourselves—and in this case about ourselves as portrayed in popular media—is flawed. Still, hooks tells us, we have a choice to engage with texts and cultural materials about people we don't know, and doing so "opens up the possibility that positive curiosity will be awakened and lead to positive contact" (57). Reading for place with cultural texts helps us better read the world as a setting imbued with diverse values, perceptions, and conceptions.

Perceptions of place are shaped by our positionality, time, and history, as well as artifacts, like texts. Scholars of place-based education argue for the approach across the curriculum because it allows students to better understand communities and communal needs (Sobel; Jacobs; Brooke). Working with place as a framework for pedagogy allows us to move beyond personal responses and consider contexts, uncovering components that create place, including human relationships, historical events, and artifacts. Suellen Campbell, on the complexity of place, writes that "personal responses can make us feel that our understanding of any given place, any landscape, is complete, when of course it never is. For all places are endlessly complex—intricately composed of not only the immediate and personal, but also of what other people can see, know, and remember; what is present but invisible" (84). These invisible elements include history and geography, but also remembrances and rhetorics we use to talk about place and identity. These elements of place-making build realities that are reflected, framed, and magnified in stories like those told by and with "Country Roads." These narratives unfold in ordinary space, which geographer Doreen Massey describes as "the space and places through which, in the negotiation of relations within multiplicity, the social is constructed" (40). Like Campbell, Massey recognizes that multiple stories happen simultaneously, all over the world, but we are pulled toward the universal. Embedding our stories in place allows narratives to be connected by emotions and lived experience and can help explain why a charismatic text like "Country Roads" resonates so widely and timelessly: It has special meaning for those who live within the specific place it names, but it taps into universal longing in ordinary space as well. Interrogating how and why it is used reveals something about communities who take it up and how they exist in the world.

Engaging deeply with artifacts of place allows us to unpack the power of representation over reality so that we can see a text like "Country Roads" as both a fixed image that freezes time and space, and also as a living image that itself changes over time and in context. An excellent example of this is a GIS mapping project created by West Virginia University students in Barbara McLennan's World Regions Geography class in 2018. Together, undergraduate students identified fifty-five versions (one to represent each West

Virginia county) of "Country Roads," analyzed them, and nominated them for placement on a digital artifact they labeled "the world's largest crowd-sourced map of John Denver's most famous song." Based on the concept of "Deep Mapping," MacLennan's interactive project directs viewers to diverse global interpretations and transformations of the song to name other homes like Kenya, Jamaica, and more; performances in a range of languages, including American Sign Language, Japanese, Spanish, Hindi, and Navajo; and many genres and instrumentations, including classical, symphonic, harmonica, accordion, ukulele, Taiko drum, a professional whistler, and even a Sri Lankan wedding party band. Through this project, MacLennan hoped to create community and investment in a large lecture of about three hundred students, in which personalization and engagement are difficult. When she introduced "Country Roads" as a familiar text, a lens through which to apply geographic concepts, her students gained more than just course skills and outcomes. They saw shifting contextual and cultural representations, with "Country Roads" as a central image, both familiar and new, a catalyst for more conversation in and out of the classroom.

This deep map affected more than students' conceptual understanding; it created a shared sense of place and community, becoming its own resonant text. As students found and aggregated versions, analyzed their effects, and placed them on the map, they were doing more than cataloging. As they carefully chose video clips, MacLennan told me, they were in essence "designing" a "sense of place," tied to spatial reality. They asked questions about where versions originated and drew conclusions about where the song was taken up and where it was not. Students identified patterns of popularity in mountainous regions, which required analysis not just of topography, but also of felt sense. Students engaged in a relevant and living "microcosm of geography." Many of them, MacLennan told me, shared the map with family and friends; they continue to tell her how it changed their thinking. This place-based work prompts students to reconsider a text that is personal and translate it into the universal through languages, genres, and meanings. This approach is especially impactful for classrooms and individuals in Appalachia, where imagined realities collide with human experience. Familiar texts like "Country Roads" are an entryway to critical analysis.

Appalachia is a place where reality can fracture from perception, and in this space, learners may struggle with academic challenges in different ways. When cultural assumptions impact learners' self-perceptions, as seen in Chenoweth and Galliher's study on college aspirations in West Virginian students, stereotypes may influence success, as when West Virginians, "are often stereotyped as 'hillbillies,' destined to be undereducated and often unemployed" (3). When cultural expectations predict failure, families and communities may experience isolation that "perpetuates the cycle of economic and educational deprivation, exacerbated by this self-fulfilling prophecy" (Chenoweth and Galliher 4). Rural college students face additional challenges related to self-perceptions and identity. First-generation students may face culture shock, social anxiety, homesickness, and dissonance inseparable from the rhetoric of home colored by an "Appalachian pull" and pressure to return (Snyder, "Transition" 94). Snyder claims that rural families and communities employ a kind of pioneer rhetoric about college, stepping into the unknown both metaphorically and literally, as students move into new physical spaces (often larger cities) and new mental spaces in the classroom. Learning about place—the place of their origin and the place where they study—can help make territory recognizable and transition smoother. Critical engagement with familiar texts, like "Country Roads," can deepen understanding of rhetoric about the region in more academic ways.

Place-based learning, grounded in identity, is one way to counter warped images and empower students to define themselves and their communities. In Appalachia, place-based approaches specifically address challenges unique to the region and allow students to develop clearer understandings of identity and dismantle stereotypes. For example, teacher-educator Sharon Teets advocates that place-based learning, "if used faithfully and over time, has the real potential to empower the youngest citizens of the Appalachian region to become increasingly decisive about how their lives will be held," disrupting debilitating patterns and forwarding positive change (135). Education connected to spaces inhabited by learners fosters agency and deepens community rather than exacerbating disconnect and displacement.

Representation in cultural rhetoric is an especially important aspect of place-based learning, as is critical analysis of that rhetoric. Scholar Anne Shelby claims that Appalachians "live in a real place that other people see as a symbol. And in the wide gap between the reality and the symbol—we have to live there, too." Living in the gap is difficult because "being Appalachian means being presented throughout one's life with images of Appalachia that bear little to no resemblance to one's own experience. The difference between the image and the reality creates dissonance, a contradiction to be resolved" (Shelby 154).

When we critically assess this imagery, seeing ourselves and communities in academic ways, we may see different available paths to success and resolve contradictions. For Appalachian studies scholar Stephen Fisher's students, "learning about the region was empowering—like discovering a missing part of themselves"; the work of academic engagement with regional rhetoric, "deconstructing outside definitions" and reclaiming place narratives, "helped them take power over their own images" ("Claiming" 59). Students "came to see a deliberative claiming of identity as a conscious act of resistance, as a way of fighting back. Claiming Appalachia gave them . . . a place, a people, a sense of who they are and want to become" (Fisher, "Claiming" 59). Like Fisher and his students, I found space for myself when I began learning about West Virginia as a complex, dynamic place. I had been taught to see myself as West Virginian, but I felt distinctly different from general and familiar rhetoric like "Country Roads." I did not know that there were writers, scholars, and others who cultivated in their work a sense of place, one of inquiry and depth. I found a complex West Virginian identity when I saw there were others like me.

Many Appalachians, myself included, face identity issues as we become educated. We discover part of ourselves when we learn about Appalachia. We learn that place and identity are inextricably linked and bind us to families, ethics, the land, and ourselves. Meredith McCarroll, in her essay "On and On: Appalachian Accent and Academic Power," expresses that she "came to understand" her identity in a college Appalachian studies class, one that led her to deepen a sense of complex and complicated identity. McCarroll documents the intentional loss of her accent in order to combat others' preconceptions and stereotypes as she navigated the academic landscape. For students in West Virginia, where distorted perceptions create a real sense of displacement, thinking critically about place is vital. It helps us see complexity rather than simply rejecting or believing stereotypes, and it helps us maintain a sense of identity without losing our roots. This kind of learning can help students from marginalized places, less represented in scholarly discourse, to see themselves as participants in academic conversations.

Place-work can counter cultural, experiential, and geographic isolation. It also addresses fragmented culture and what we may perceive as a necessary loss; in order to find futures, we must turn our backs on our homes, lose our accents, and leave. Linda Tate teaches at Shepherd University, in West Virginia's eastern panhandle, about an hour from Washington, DC, and not far from Harpers Ferry. Many of Tate's students "do not perceive the value of remaining connected to the past or to the place that has been home, and the faculty who teach them face the key challenge of showing these students that being Appalachian is not a limitation, as many outside the region would have them believe, but a real source of groundedness in a rapidly changing world" (97). Cultivating a nuanced sense of place-identity within West Virginia and Appalachia counters shame and dispels the myth that to leave is to succeed. It also allows interrogation of beloved conceptions of place, which can flatten complexity despite positivity.

PLACE-BASED PEDAGOGY IN WEST VIRGINIA

Elizabeth Catte, in *What You're Getting Wrong About Appalachia*, claims the region serves as scapegoat and symbol of regional poverty and despair, allowing America to both confront and distance itself from these issues, "a mirror that reflects something troubling but recognizable back to the nation" (9). This reflection reveals a concentration of persistent problems throughout the United States, at the same time allowing blame to fall on Appalachian people. Consistent with historical portrayals, these images exclude more than include and represent a flattened caricature. This amounts to an erasure of people, communities, or groups who do not fit neatly within stereotypes. And no person, community, or group fits neatly within stereotypes. "Country Roads" is part of a collection of mirror images, and while mostly positive, it reflects a West Virginia that is distorted and oversimplified.

"Country Roads" is also part of the rhetoric that makes stereotypes and challenges present in the Appalachian experience more acute for West Virginians. As discussed in earlier chapters, negative conceptions are everywhere and have been so historically: from local color writing of the late nineteenth century to offensive T-shirts, *The Beverly Hillbillies* to *Buckwild*, Jesco White to Oxyana. As Boyd Creasman asserts in his book about West Virginia literature, "West Virginians often find themselves cast in the role of 'the Other,' outside of mainstream American culture, and the targets of negative stereotypes" so that "in many ways, West Virginians face a steadier barrage of negativity than do residents from the other states in the region" (3). We are both visible and invisible, caricatured and ignored.

When not plied with negative imagery, West Virginians may experience cultural and academic invisibility. Erica Abrams Locklear, in her book on Appalachian literacy, references writer Denise Giardina as having believed that there were no writers from West

Virginia. Giardina struggled to write about her state because of "damaging media portrayals of ignorant hillbillies[;] the literature Giardina read while growing up also taught her that ... seemingly no one wrote about Appalachia" (Locklear 143). This is true to my own experience. I did not know writers in or literature about West Virginia existed until I took Appalachian fiction in college, despite having attended West Virginian schools my entire life. My students tell me the same. West Virginians may feel absence or erasure, lacking depictions of themselves—with the exception of "Country Roads"—throughout their learning lives.

If West Virginian students do see themselves portrayed in their schooling, it may be to their detriment rather than for their benefit. For example, sometimes taught in high schools, Jeanette Walls's memoir *The Glass Castle* is critically acclaimed but nonetheless describes West Virginia with violence, incest, prostitution, and poverty. Barbara Kingsolver's more recent *Demon Copperhead*, which won a Pulitzer Prize, beautifully addresses the opioid epidemic but barely mentions West Virginia, where the issue centers. More problematic is the trend of schools adopting J. D. Vance's *Hillbilly Elegy*, which has been widely criticized for reinforcing stereotypes and categorical descriptions, generalizing the region as a whole. While texts like these may accurately portray authors' life experiences or contemporary issues, when they are taught as unequivocal truths about the region, they perpetuate invisibility and despair. They also leave students whose experiences are different without a sense of place connection. Left unexamined, texts like these can do harm; careful, critical reading can empower students to join a larger conversation, one that can make them visible and provide a counternarrative.

One complicated facet of teaching in West Virginia is the limited way in which learners are exposed to stories, told from within, that do more than gloss over or buy into stereotypes. Positive imagery must be critically examined, too. I did not learn about the complications of heritage and history while I was a public-school student despite West Virginia studies being a curricular requirement.

In my class, we prepared for the Golden Horseshoe test, learning "facts": geography, dates, people, places, like all West Virginian eighth graders have since 1931. We might have learned official state songs; "Country Roads" was not one yet. In the spring, we took the standardized test that determined membership as "knights" and "ladies" of the Golden Horseshoe Society.

A middle-school teacher friend who has helped students prepare for the Golden Horseshoe test describes the current version as a geography exam mostly, one that requires memorization of places, counties, county seats, dates of establishment. Similarly, West Virginia writer Jeff Mann, in an essay about teaching Appalachian literature, recalls the test as a knowledge bank lacking the critical engagement students need to understand social, political, and economic patterns. Mann remembers, "I did not know enough to realize I had never heard of Matewan or the Paint Creek/Cabin Creek strikes, Sid Hatfield's assassination, the battle of Blair Mountain, the ruinous environmental effects of mining, the War on Poverty, or the economic consequences of absentee land ownership" (84). Granted, the preparation leading up to the test does not usually reinforce negative stereotypes. Instead, it lacks the complexity of a counternarrative. It offers the kind of state story that "emphasizes facts and themes that bring personal satisfaction to people who were born in or who otherwise identify with that state" (J. Williams, *West Virginia* 207). This is the kind of history that shines light, but not necessarily into darkness.

The Golden Horseshoe Award is presented to a couple hundred eighth graders each year, and its "primary goal . . . is to promote pride in our state, develop intellectual and participatory skills, as well as foster attitudes that are necessary for students to participate as effective, involved, and responsible citizens" (WVDE). Although goals of responsible citizenry and state pride are worthwhile, I wonder how they can be fostered or measured through a multiple-choice test. Learning like this teaches students "to memorize the West Virginia locations of such items as the world's largest clothespin factory, the world's largest ashtray, and the world's oldest plant, and to make an inordinate fuss about West Virginia natives who have become prominent nationally" (J. Williams, *West Virginia* 304–5). Learning decontextualized "facts" without critical engagement may prime us to accept "Country Roads" as a singular artifact of identity, despite other rich texts describing a more nuanced and interesting West Virginia.

Critical literacy through place-based education empowers learners and builds on existing tradition in West Virginia, where roots are traceable back to Elsie Clapp's work in the Arthurdale school in the 1930s. There, "local culture, skills, and language" made up "a place-centered curriculum, the goal of which was to bolster a sense of regional self-sufficiency," of which "rhetorical and linguistic traditions" were a part (Hayes 169). We perhaps have not carried on Clapp's legacy well, especially if we have limited our teaching to names and dates disconnected from lives and learners' experiences. As rhetorician Todd Snyder explains, "Thinking and writing about the rhetoric that most directly influenced my life allowed me the opportunity to more fully understand my family's place within these hierarchical systems of cyclical Appalachian poverty" (*Rhetoric* 177). Critically considering rhetorics of place allowed Snyder, as a West Virginian looking at his home, to see himself and the people in his life within systems affecting the region.

Learning like this is important for students who are from West Virginia. It is also important for students who are in West Virginia from other places. People who move to Appalachia to attend school are part of the wider community, yet they may not understand how they impact the environment, economy, and culture. Turning their attention toward the interrelationship between students, campus, and community can help them see their influence and develop advocacy. Nathan Shepley, discussing pedagogies of place, writes, "for non-Appalachian-identifying students studying in Appalachia, invitations to identify with multiple locations can make Appalachian identity building and regional maintenance the work of *those who take certain actions*, as opposed to those who come from a certain location" (140). Shepley highlights the importance of identity within Appalachian contexts, arguing that place-based approaches are not just for students who are from here, but also for those who come here—to help them think more critically and advocate more actively in other settings, as well.

In my classes at West Virginia University, we use "Country Roads" as a window, a mirror, and a lens into critical thinking about what it means to be in a place, of a place, and from a place. When I introduce first-year composition students to "Country Roads" as a rhetorical text, one that carries emplaced meaning, they learn something about campus, about each other, and about themselves. Students at West Virginia University already use "Country Roads" for many purposes: to enact school pride, to show solidarity, to resist power. Students already participate in transformations and engagements with the song, but these occurrences, whether planned or spontaneous, may happen without conscious decision. Adding a layer of critical analysis changes the way students view the text in action and reveals hidden meanings.

In composition courses specifically, place-based pedagogy helps students find real world relevance. It shows how research is everywhere through social issues, community planning, environmental observations, and agentive change. It makes place personal, so student inquiry can arise from their own sense of connection and wonder about spaces they inhabit. In introductory courses to research, like the ones I teach, a place-based approach helps connect us to the world so we can see through the lenses of lived experiences and join inquiry with emplaced lived experience. In classrooms and out, responses to texts occur within shared social realities and constructed contextual meaning. Writing instruction that incorporates place can help writers "see a text not as a fixed artifact but the public social reality in which reading and writing unfold" (Brandt 39). "Country Roads" is a frame for talking explicitly about social contexts, identities, and ideas. We interrogate ways the song's meaning shifts depending on who is listening, who is singing, and where the song occurs, and then we add more West Virginian voices to the conversation. It becomes a window into meaning.

"Country Roads" as a text has changed over time, crossing thresholds, but it also has changed through space—crossing borders—which makes more interpretations possible, as we see when artists transform it to depict their own homes. The song impacts place as well, as it is used both at West Virginia University and widely in West Virginia. Viewed as a vehicle for meaning across time and space, "Country Roads" helps us understand the interactions among audience, speaker, context, and purpose, packaged in a familiar way. Just as we have in this book, when my students and I listen to, analyze, and respond to different versions—or the same version in different contexts—we do so within shared place and meaning. When we put "Country Roads" in conversation with other West Virginia songs, our analysis broadens. Our understandings vary based on the identities we bring to the conversation.

When we ask students to consider texts and topics of and from home, we ask them to "write to explore issues and experiences to which their very identities [are] tied," and in doing so, to "consider multiple perspectives in order to present that writing to a reader for a clear purpose: to affect a greater conversation in the world beyond the classroom" (Ritchie 128–29). We may ask students to take up different facets of their identities in order to write to potential audiences or stakeholders and to examine what happens when they do. "Country Roads" is a window that provides a glimpse into a limited and potentially reductive picture of West Virginia. It is a mirror that reflects students' perceptions of home and allows them to start to see those perceptions differently. And it is a lens through which students can pose meaningful research questions and engage in academic inquiry. Taking a close, critical look at this familiar text as rhetoric helps us discern what is important and real and know ourselves and our places in more intimate and actionable ways.

"COUNTRY ROADS" IS A WINDOW

"Country Roads" represents an uncomplicated representation, a glimpse through the windshield as one passes through. We have seen this in previous parts of this book, as when my student Aubrey felt called to attend WVU because she heard "Country Roads" on a trip with her cousins and wanted to go to school in a "place like that." Rebecca saw her home in West Virginia in a new way while listening to a street performer in London. Similarly, one survey respondent, a West Virginian who was studying out of state, wrote about the homesickness and simple imagery the song evokes: "I am literally counting down the days until I get to move back (I'm away for school). Images that come up are its natural beauty—the fog rolling down the mountains on a hazy morning, the winding roads, iconic bridges..." These moments of resonance are a portal into a nostalgic, pastoral space, one that, seen from outside, recalls hiraeth. In these moments, "Country Roads" is a window looking in on belonging, but within imaginary dreamscapes.

For West Virginians and WVU students, "Country Roads" may be the only positive public narrative; 60 percent of my survey respondents and nearly all of my students could name no other songs about West Virginia. My students, like Emily Satterwhite's, "arrive with unexamined assumptions about the region—predominantly negative stereotypes, but also romantic views of Appalachia as a simpler, more wholesome place that is homogenous in landscape and culture" ("Intro" 4). Like the survey respondent quoted previously, students from the region have "learned, by way of self-defense, to talk about it in glowingly positive terms not unlike the romantic stereotypes held by metropolitan 'outsiders'" (Satterwhite, "Intro" 4). "Country Roads" is too-pleasant rhetoric, in which simplistic and romanticized representations are windows that offer but a glimpse of an actual place. They neglect complexity and suppress agency because "a purely celebratory stance... often relies on superficial understandings that can be just as reductive as negative stereotypes," which may "rob students of a full understanding of the complexities of the region's history and their own experiences of the region" (Satterwhite, "Intro" 5). The window view simplifies and divides, even as it celebrates.

Simplification begins to crack when we invite critical examination and multiple perspectives. When I first used "Country Roads" with my English 101 students, it was at the release of *Fallout 76*. We listened to the soundtrack version by New York City doo-wop group Spank. Comprised of four African American men, Spank cover songs such as "Lean on Me," another tune with West Virginia resonance. Their version of "Country Roads" features traditional country instrumentation blended with rich R&B harmonies. One of my students, an African American West Virginian, said, incredulously, "You would never hear a Black man singing 'Country Roads' in Huntington." Her perspective opened conversation that allowed us to interrogate how "Country Roads" fails to give voice to some communities and populations. Considering "Country Roads" in different voices and contexts leads us to a discussion of creation, naming, and ownership of ideas specifically connected to place and identity and reflects back new meaning. As Higgs and Manning remind us, "A mirror for Appalachia is needed, which will help Appalachians become 'aware of who we are and why, and be at ease with this knowledge.' The record of the past suggests that Appalachians cannot expect others to provide that mirror. It must be a mirror of our own making" (448). "Country Roads," as a rhetorical text that invites critical examination, allows us to interrogate not just the way the song provides a frame both for belonging and exclusion, but also how it helps us see, claim, and name our identities. It is a mirror reflecting back the West Virginia and the West Virginia University we may want to see, but it still invites reflection.

"COUNTRY ROADS" IS A MIRROR

In West Virginia and at West Virginia University, we see "Country Roads" everywhere, reflected back at us, intentionally and without critique. This is especially clear in sports, when "Country Roads" expresses celebration in victory or solidarity when facing a loss. But there are limits to who can be reflected in that mirror, as exemplified in an incident from February 2012, when Marquette basketball coach Buzz Williams danced to "Country Roads" on his way to the press table after his team defeated the Mountaineers. WVU students had to be held back by security to prevent mob violence. In that moment, students used preexisting narratives of identity to shape their own stories of self, to negotiate cultural scripts reflected back. Buzz Williams enacted an identity that (in context) did not belong to him, resulting in volatile outrage as WVU students asserted ownership. The identity performance Williams reflected, dissonant from accepted performances, caused active conflict and outrage. As Neil Leach explains in his work on place identity, "mirrorings occur not only in the engagement between the self and the environment, but also between that engagement and memories of previous engagements" (132). Williams acted out of place and pattern, distorting reflection under the gaze of those who actively use the song as a rhetorical performance and narrative of belonging.

Let us return to Sara Webb-Sunderhaus's application of tellable narrative in considering "Country Roads" as identity discourse in West Virginia and at WVU. Webb-Sunderhaus applies the framework of tellability and its alignment with performative identity to Appalachian student writing in composition courses. In educational environments, "issues surrounding identity, narrative, and tellability may be of particular interest and importance when teaching certain genres of writing, but they are important in all interactions with students, both inside and outside the classroom. Tellable narratives of identity matter because they shape our perceptions of, and our relationships with, our students" (Webb-Sunderhaus 30). In addition, tellable narratives shape our interactions with the world around us because, through them, we understand how we are seen. Transcending them can help us better see who we actually are. Loving "Country Roads" and leveraging it as a symbol of West Virginian identity rhetoric forwards a tellable narrative. Questioning its scope and origin, wondering whether it actually does what listeners across the state report it does through their embrace of it—captures the "untellable."

When I teach using "Country Roads," I want my students to consider multiple perspectives in relation to a familiar text, one that we all know, but one that takes on different resonances for different purposes and audiences, with direct implications in our wider context. Students at West Virginia University represent a range of stakeholders, with layered relationships and identities that respond in various ways to this common text. Out-of-state students who have no prior connection to West Virginia see "Country Roads" simply as a school anthem, connected to sports, events, Mountaineer pride. Unless they look closely, they see only a student identity mirrored back.

Students from West Virginia, on the other hand, respond differently. Again, recall Rebecca's experience of hearing "Country Roads" while traveling in Europe. Hearing it from afar, Rebecca felt transported, called back, and able to see "home" from a different perspective, one of longing rather than one of disconnect or shame. In an end-of-course reflection, Rebecca wrote that prior to that moment in London, "In my mind, my home wasn't that appealing." She acknowledged this dissonance, noting that she had been excited to leave, but seeing a new version of home changed her mind. The imagery in the song, heard in a new context, affected Rebecca's sense of identity and perception of place: "While listening to the performer, I missed driving down the spiraling roads to the New River. I missed hiking up mountains and exploring abandoned mining towns. I missed homemade sweet tea, and fishing trips with dad. I really missed my small town of fifteen hundred people living within a valley of two mountains hidden from the rest of the world." Like a magic mirror, the song reflected previously unnoticed depth and complexity.

Rebecca experienced home viewed through reflections outside herself. Her inside knowledge added layered meaning to the voices of the street performer and listeners, filtered through the words of Danoff, Nivert, and Denver, at once connected to and disconnected from an actual place, West Virginia. These fractured conceptions of place, coming together in a moment in space, time, and sound, merged, allowing Rebecca to see West Virginia in a new way: a mirror reflecting a collaboratively constructed image, authentic and conceived at once, tinged with hiraeth. This takes up but moves beyond the "tellable" version of West Virginia "Country Roads" conveys.

Theresa Burriss writes about how impressions of Appalachian identity are often constructed from outside, and like Higgs and Manning, she references Jim Wayne Miller and Loyal Jones in calling for expressions of identity that come from within, that "mirror of our own making" (214–15). When students look closely, they see reflected back an identity but recognize that it is perhaps not one that reflects reality, not one from within. This is where we start to use "Country Roads" as a lens.

"COUNTRY ROADS" IS A LENS

Remember: This book's origin and conclusion are ultimately pedagogically driven. I am first a teacher-researcher "oriented to the world in a pedagogic way," toward interactions with learners as deeply connected to the experience of research (van Manen 151). When I teach inquiry, I model inquiry. I position myself as a writer and researcher in the room with others who are practicing and developing as writers and researchers, with shared textual analysis applied as a framework for thinking about self, place, and identity. I make my own process visible. This approach moves students into their own inquiry projects. By grounding my work in place-based questions, I allow my students to do that, too, and it makes them more aware of the world on campus and beyond.

Literacy development is contextual, connected to self, space, and communities of constructed meaning, and it "flourishes only in local forms" (Brandt 7). In my class, as we have in this book, we use "Country Roads" rhetorically to talk explicitly about the social contexts, identities, questions, and ideas it conveys. We interrogate how its meaning shifts depending on who is listening, who is singing, and where the song occurs, and we put it in conversation with other West Virginia songs written by West Virginians. This helps us understand interactions among audience, speaker, context, and purpose. We make the familiar strange, stepping back to step closer, and do so within a shared context, place, and purpose, our understandings of which vary based on the identities we bring to the conversation. The questions we ask *are research questions*, with a lens on this familiar text.

Students can use this shifting understanding of shared meaning as a model to help them develop their own research inquiries. For example, in an end-of-course reflection, one undergraduate writer explained: "I've always known 'Take Me Home, Country Roads' by John Denver was a popular song and especially known by the people of West Virginia. When Dr. Morris told us in class that she was doing research on the song and people's experiences with it, I was very intrigued. Learning that something I am very personal with could be academically researched was eye-opening." The student continued, revealing that discussions about "Country Roads," expanded collective understanding of research: "It was clear the significant impact many [classmates] felt from it. Then it made sense to me why someone would research this phenomenon. For the first time, I saw how personal research could be. I was able to pick out so many more topics I could research that related to me that never crossed my mind before. Plus, those research topics probably resonate with many more people than I would have thought." This student's own research project investigated the popularity of dirt track racing in her hometown—something her father did, her family loved, and that she wanted to better understand. In her work, she uncovered ideas related to economy, family, entertainment, culture, and gender, as well as place.

When we ask students to consider texts and topics close to home, we ask them to explore their own identities and ethos, to consider multiple perspectives, and to write for a clear purpose: to affect a greater conversation with audiences they envision as real readers.

When I take a place-based approach, using "Country Roads" as a window, mirror, and lens, students see profound connections. Topics for research that have arisen from this model, from students across majors and from in and out of state, reveal questions connected to place and authentic inquiry. Through this approach, my first and second-year composition students have explored research related to

- China's one-child policy
- The psychology behind sports fandom
- The impact of local farmers' markets
- Human ecology in Morgantown city planning
- Big box stores' impacts on small communities
- Reality television depictions of stereotypes in *Jersey Shore*
- An investigation of dilapidating towns

Not all of these topics seem connected to emplaced identity, but they are deeply tied to student understandings of place. The writer who wondered about China's one-child policy was adopted as a result of it, and the writer who questioned sports fandom wondered why WVU football is important to family members who never attended college. When we look together at commonplace texts, we cocreate meaning and develop community understanding, multifaceted and complex, like our identities as writers (and Mountaineers). As John Ackerman argues, a "georhetorical method" for teaching and learning composition involves a naming of place, a relocation of the self within that place, and thus produces a "literature of place" that is "imaginative, interpretive, and critical as it speaks in emboldened and embodied ways about places lost, found, lived, and loved and where the spirit and mind are inextricably linked to habitat" (114). When inquiry is emplaced, it has a different sense of purpose and identity—one that is tied to space in ways that can be subversive, intertwined with experiences, grounded in questions, and conceptual as well as real. These methods are also interdisciplinary, imbued with rhetorical purpose for a range of audiences, and infused with writerly ethos in a physical landscape or a conceptual one. This makes our writing workshop a space in which students can "reclaim experiences" and "redefine social relationships" (Ritchie 122). A critical, place-based perspective allows deeper looking and opens resistance against tellable narratives and shallow definitions, leading students to find meaningful questions, lenses for their own research.

CONCLUSION: "COUNTRY ROADS" FOR CRITICAL LITERACY

I want to return to the story that began this chapter, as I see it differently now. At first, when I saw students using "Country Roads" in protest, I observed a spontaneous expression of a familiar marker of identity transformed in a new way. And that is accurate. But using the song as a tool of protest is also an act of resistance we can intentionally help students cultivate through critical literacy. As students gain agency over their voices in the classroom, they can forge agency outside the classroom; they can create and claim their own spaces. This leads to what Satterwhite calls "project identity," which allows multiple perspectives and is critically self-reflective, inclusive, and committed to change. It illuminates marginalized identity to expose conflicts and complexities and to foster resistance. "Country Roads," as a place-text and lens, examined critically for rhetorical meaning and identity resonance, becomes a soundtrack by which we can develop advocacy.

Student-driven inquiry, like the "Country Roads" mapping project or my students' research, aligns with Nedra Reynolds's assertion that we deepen critical inquiry when we consider how place representations shape reality. Place imagery stands in for materiality, so images become entwined with understanding of place. These images are "tangible, physical, and reproducible; they can be bought and sold, copied and distributed, enlarged or reproduced, or sharpened—all of which has a huge influence on people's experiences with or responses to place" (Reynolds 252–53). Spaces have both physical reality and symbolic reality, so these images tell us how to be, what to expect, and how to act. "Country Roads," for example, is inseparable from and synonymous with place, activity, people. It is identity rhetoric, marketed within cultural systems. "Identity" is "made subject to a capitalist epistemology that increasingly ascribes frames of possibility and desirability, but it is inescapably linked to its situatedness in geographical knowledge, which is simultaneously being discursively made to abide by market logics" (Andehn, Hietanen, and Lucarelli 335). "Country Roads" is so ingrained into West Virginian perceptions of place, that we cannot be without it in West Virginia. This capitalization of place is akin to the ways in which West Virginia has been owned from outside and dominated by outside interests in land rights, industry, and investments. We must navigate cultural and physical landscapes, including rhetorical artifacts like "Country Roads," in our daily lives; this navigation relevantly translates into academic learning.

Communication is not placeless, and texts like "Country Roads" tie our understanding of ourselves in place. Place study is beneficial within academic programs as a whole and within rhetoric and writing classes in particular. Like communication, composition is not placeless. Grounding in place allows writers to "connect their literacy to the world around them—to the places, people, and interests that make their world personally meaningful" (Bangert and Brooke 23). Part of talking about being in or from Appalachia means recognizing and reconciling the cognitive and emotional dissonance West Virginian and Appalachian students feel. Whether that world is home or the University, writing from place can help accommodate differences and ease transitions. Critical pedagogy emphasizes reevaluating our place within dominant social hierarchies, and critical pedagogy of place specific to Appalachia can allow us to respond to economic and social injustice.

A place approach has benefits for our students, no matter their home state or nation. As Nathan Shepley asserts, developing "Appalachian adjacent" identities allows students who are not from Appalachia to better understand and advocate for themselves and others in places they inhabit, even temporarily. I agree with Shepley that "identifying oneself as Appalachian or as allied with Appalachian people becomes a rhetorical move accessible to countless potential supporters of the region, a step toward identification building practices that scholars today support for the purposes of avoiding rural exploitation" (140). As students research and write about place, they are more able to engage in community conversations, understand stakeholder perspectives, and navigate the complexity of a changing world. Writers better understand themselves and others, as well as regional issues because "opening up how we identify gives Appalachia more supporters as it adapts to changes in literacies, technology, ethnicities, and livelihoods" (Shepley 153). Students who understand the power of place are better positioned to become active advocates rather than passive observers, to name themselves beyond existing namings. Educating students and encouraging their inquiries about place deepens their commitment to bettering any places where they learn and live and to which they may want to return. When we ground courses that focus on development of language, writing, and rhetorical skill in place, we help student writers gain ethos and agency and to speak from where they are and who they are. "Local literacy environments . . . invite writers to . . . contribute to rhetoric about the region" so students can "write and use others' writing to challenge non-existent or otherwise damaging representations of Appalachia" (Shepley 153). An artifact of local literacy with global reach, "Country Roads" is prime for transformation but demands closer reading, particularly for students in and from West Virginia.

When we engage with "Country Roads," students move from being consumers of the song to understanding the complexity of it as identity rhetoric that reflects back an image of home that reduces rather than defines. Home, true home, as bell hooks helps us understand, is a place where we feel a "culture of belonging," where we feel "a landscape of memory, thought, and imagination" (221). It is more than momentary, and more than just notion. Engaging beyond "Country Roads" helps students who feel they must leave consider the intimate relationship of return and the recognition that our place needs us, cultivating a "vital sense of covenant and commitment" for a new future (hooks 65). They also begin to think about text as event, itself a place in which meaning happens, where "writer and reader are together, in that they are, at any moment, at the same 'place' in a text, a right-here, right-now social reality of their mutual making. As a text unfolds, this joint history of shared place forms the context for what is to follow. Textual language finds meaning within this common lived experience, this developing history of the 'we who are involved here'" (Brandt 30–31). Literacy education then becomes a deepening rather than a severing of identity. "Country Roads" is place and identity rhetoric that invites critical questions. Listeners who learn to ask these questions can decide for themselves whether to reject the song, embrace it, or both.

REFERENCES

Abrahams, Roger. "Powerful Promises of Regeneration or Living Well with History." *Conserving Culture: A New Discourse on Heritage*, edited by Mary Hufford. University of Illinois Press, 1994, pp. 79–93.

Abrams, James. "Lost Frames of Reference: Sightings of History and Memory in Pennsylvania's Documentary Landscape." *Conserving Culture: A New Discourse on Heritage*, edited by Mary Hufford. University of Illinois Press, 1994, pp. 24–28.

Ackerman, John. "Teaching the Capital City." *The Locations of Composition*, edited by Christopher Keller and Christian Weisser. SUNY Press, 2007, pp. 109–30.

Acuff, Roy. "Wabash Cannonball." *The Essential Roy Acuff, 1936–1949*. Sony Legacy, 1992.

Adams, Joey. "Mountain Mama." *My Home*. 678030 Records DK2, 2021.

"Alien: Covenant | 'Take Me Home' TV Commercial | 20th Century FOX." *YouTube*, uploaded by Alien Anthology, 3 Apr. 2017. https://youtu.be/dcfSnaCRoKE. Accessed 24 Nov. 2024.

"American Dream Factory." *American Dad!* Dirs. Rodney Clouden, Ron Hughart, and Anthony Lioi. By Seth MacFarlane, Mike Barker, and Matt Weitzman. Season 2, Episode 11. 20th Century Fox Television, 28 Jan. 2007. https://www.imdb.com/title/tt0954362/. Accessed 24 Nov. 2024.

Andehn, Mikael, Joel Hietanen, and Andrea Lucarelli. "Performing Place Promotion—On Implaced Identity in Marketized Geographies." *Marketing Theory* vol. 20 no. 3, 2020, pp. 321–42.

Anderson, Benedict. *Imagined Communities: Reflections on the Origin and Spread of Nationalism*. Verso, 2006.

Anderson, Colleen. Personal interview. 2 Apr. 2021.

———. "If You Love My West Virginia." *Trail Through the Trees*. Colleen Anderson, 2020.

———. "West Virginia Chose Me." *Fabulous Realities*. EDNA Records, 2006.

Antoine, Jonathan. "Country Roads (A Music Video for Our Time)." *YouTube*, uploaded by Jonathan Antione, 21 April 2020. https://youtu.be/lImjP8q2uS4. Accessed 24 Nov. 2024.

Antonsich, Marco. "Searching for Belonging—An Analytical Framework." *Geography Compass* vol. 4 no. 6, 2010, pp. 644–59. https://doi.org/10.1111/j.1749-8198.2009.00317.x.

Apalachee Falls. "Country Roads—Apalachee Falls (Take Me Home) John Denver Cover." *YouTube*, uploaded by ExodusKlan, 20 Sep. 2014. https://youtu.be/AltjBNZOjek. Accessed 24 Nov. 2024.

Appalachian Magazine. "West Virginia's Original State Song That's Even Better Than 'Country Roads.'" 16 Oct. 2018. http://appalachianmagazine.com/2018/10/16/west-virginias-original-state-song-thats-even-better-than-country-roads/. Accessed 24 Nov. 2024.

"Aristotle Jones West Virginia Hills 2019 Live Performance in Studio 3." *YouTube*, uploaded by Aristotle Jones, 16 Dec. 2019. https://youtu.be/HE5_4BTrR-w. Accessed 22 Nov. 2024.

Ballard, Sandra. "Where Did Hillbillies Come From? Tracing Sources of the Comic Hillbilly Fool in Literature." *Back Talk from Appalachia: Confronting Stereotypes*, edited by Dwight Billings, Gurney Norman, and Katherine Ledford. University Press of Kentucky, 1999, pp. 138–49.

Bangert, Sandy with Robert Brooke. "Inviting Children into Community: Growing Readers and Writers in Elementary School." *Rural Voices: Place-Conscious Education and the Teaching of Writing*, edited by Robert Brooke. Teachers College Press, 2003.

"Bats locate their food using sound . . ." *iFunny*, 20 Aug. 2021. https://ifunny.co/picture/bats-locate-their-food-using-sound-country-roads-take-me-MgkjrHGr8. Accessed 24 Nov. 2024.

Bean, Heather Ann Ackley. *Women, Music, and Faith in Central Appalachia*. Edwin Mellen Press, 2001.

Bell, Iris. "This Is My West Virginia." *Official West Virginia State Songs*, MH3WV, 2022. https://mh3wv.org/music.

Bennett, Andy. "Popular Music, Media and the Narrativization of Place." *Sonic Synergies: Music, Technology, Community, Identity*, edited by Gerry Bloustien, Margaret Peters, and Susan Luckman. Routledge, 2016, pp. 69–78.

Benveniste, Alexis. "The Meaning and History of Memes." *New York Times*, 26 Jan. 2022. https://www.nytimes.com/2022/01/26/crosswords/what-is-a-meme.html?smid=url-share.

"Best 'Country Roads, Take Me Home' TikToks." *YouTube*, uploaded by Chiron, 30 Ap. 2020. https://youtu.be/rBfQNPkRAR0. Accessed 30 Oct. 2019.

@bettemidler. "What @JoeManchin, who represents a population . . ." *Twitter*, 20 Dec. 2021, 10:41 a.m. https://x.com/BetteMidler/status/1472955243935711236. Accessed 3 Jan. 2022.

Bigart, Homer. "'Wild, Wonderful West Virginia,' Shocked by Exodus of People, Seeks to Woo Industry and Hold Young." *New York Times*, 3 Aug. 1970. https://www.nytimes.com/1970/08/03/archives/wild-wonderful-west-virginia-shocked-by-exodus-of-people-seeks-to.html. Accessed 30 Oct. 2019.

Biggers, Jeff. *The United States of Appalachia: How Southern Mountaineers Brought Independence, Culture, and Enlightenment to America*. Counterpoint, 2007.

Billings, Dwight. "Introduction." *Back Talk from Appalachia: Confronting Stereotypes*, edited by Dwight Billings, Gurney Norman, and Katherine Ledford. University Press of Kentucky, 1999, pp. 3–20.

Bloustien, Gerry. "Introduction: 'Be Not Afeard; the Isle Is Full of Noises': Reflections on the Synergies of Music in the Creative Knowledge Economy." *Sonic Synergies: Music, Technology, Community, Identity*, edited by Gerry Bloustien, Margaret Peters, and Susan Luckman. Routledge, 2016, pp. xxi–xxviii.

Bobek, Pavel. "Veď Mě Dál, Cesto Má (Take Me Home, Country Roads)." *Veď Mě Dál, Cesto Má*. Panton, 1975.

"Booking.com TV Spot, 'Tyler's Resolution' Song by John Denver." iSpot TV, 22 Dec. 2019. https://www.ispot.tv/ad/ZSVD/booking-com-tylers-resolution-song-by-john-denver. Accessed 24 Nov. 2024.

"Boot Barn TV Spot, 'Where Will Your Boots Take You.'" iSpot.tv, 8 Apr. 2018. https://www.ispot.tv/ad/wvRu/boot-barn-where-will-your-boots-take-you. Accessed 24 Nov. 2024.

Bradford City Club News. "'Take Me Home' Nominated for Football Business Award." Bradford City AFC, 30 Mar. 2022. https://www.bradfordcityafc.com/news/2022/march/take-me-home-nominated-for-football-business-award/. Accessed 24 Nov. 2024.

Brandt, Deborah. *Literacy as Involvement: The Acts of Writers, Readers, and Texts*. Southern Illinois University Press, 1990.

Branscome, James. *Annihilating the Hillbilly: The Appalachians' Struggle with America's Institutions*. Appalachian Movement Press, 1971.

Brooke, Robert E. *Writing and Sense of Self: Identity Negotiation in Writing Workshops*. National Council of Teachers of English, 1991.

Brumfield, Nick. "'Country Roads:' How John Denver's Hit Became the World's Most Popular Song." Expatalachians, March 5, 2019. http://expatalachians.com/country-roads-how-john-denvers-hit-became-the-worlds-most-popular-song. Accessed 24 Nov. 2024.

Brustein, William. Personal interview. 24 Feb. 2020.

Burge, Todd. "Re: Interview Request." Received by Sarah Morris, 23 Mar. 2021.

Burnside, Jason A. *West Virginia 4-H Songs and Music Traditions*. Master's Thesis, West Virginia University, 2011. https://researchrepository.wvu.edu/cgi/viewcontent.cgi?article=1466&context=etd. Accessed 24 Nov. 2024.

Burnside, Mary Wade. "'Take Me Home. Country Roads': The Song, The State, The Story." *Corridor Magazine*, June/July 2013. http://mwburnside.com/magazine/take-me-home-country-roads/. Accessed 24 Nov. 2024.

Burriss, Theresa. "From Harlem Home to Appalachia: Teaching the Literary Journey." *Appalachia in the Classroom: Teaching the Region*, edited by Theresa Burriss, and Patricia Gantt. Ohio University Press, 2013, pp. 214–31.

Burriss, Theresa, and Patricia Gantt. "Introduction." *Appalachia in the Classroom: Teaching the Region*, edited by Theresa Burriss, and Patricia Gantt. Ohio University Press, 2013, pp. xxiii–xxi.

Butler, Judith. *Gender Trouble: Feminism and the Subversion of Identity*. Routledge, 1990.

Butterflies Are Free. Directed by Milton Katselas, written by Leonard Gershe. Columbia Pictures, 1972.

Campbell, Glen. "Wichita Lineman." *Wichita Lineman*. Capitol, 1968.

Campbell, Sueellen. "The Complexity of Places." *Teaching About Place: Learning from the Land*, edited by Laird Christensen and Hal Crimmel. University of Nevada Press, 2008, pp. 83–97.

Cantwell, Robert. "Conjuring Culture: Ideology and Magic in the Festival of American Folklife." *Conserving Culture: A New Discourse on Heritage*, edited by Mary Hufford. University of Illinois Press, 1994, pp. 167–83.

Canyon, Christopher. *John Denver's Take Me Home, Country Roads*. Dawn Publications, 2005.

Capplis, Conor. "Furrowed Brows Relax as Ploughing Finally Makes a Welcome Return." *Irish Examiner*, 20 Sep. 2022. https://www.irishexaminer.com/news/arid-40965854.html. Accessed 24 Nov. 2024.

Carlile, Brandi. "Take Me Home, Country Roads." *YouTube*, 7 Feb. 2021. https://youtu.be/0NAmdXjDmks. Accessed 24 Nov. 2024.

Carlisle, E. Fred. *Hollow and Home: A History of Self and Place*. West Virginia University Press, 2017.

Casey, Edward. *Getting Back into Place: Toward a Renewed Understanding of the Place-World*, 2nd ed. Indiana University Press, 2009.

Castells, Manuel. *The Power of Identity*. Wiley, 2010.

Catte, Elizabeth. *What You Are Getting Wrong About Appalachia*. Belt, 2018.

Charles, Ray. "Take Me Home, Country Roads." *A Message From the People*. Tangerine Records, 1972.

Chenoweth, Erica, and Renee Galliher. "Factors Influencing College Aspirations of Rural West Virginia High School Students." *Journal of Research in Rural Education*, vol. 19, no. 2, 2004, pp. 1–14. https://jrre.psu.edu/sites/default/files/2020-06/19%282%29.pdf.

"Clarice (CBS) Trailer HD—Silence of the Lambs Spinoff." *YouTube*, uploaded by TV Promos, 10 Jan. 2021. https://youtu.be/vsjoRzezy4I. Accessed 24 Nov. 2024.

Clayton, Martin. "What Is Entrainment? Definition and Applications in Musical Research." *Empirical Musicology Review*, vol. 7, no. 1-2, 2012, pp. 49–56. https://kb.osu.edu/bitstream/handle/1811/52979/EMR000137a-Clayton.pdf. Accessed 24 Nov. 2024.

Clinton, Hillary. *What Happened*. Simon and Schuster, 2017.

The Cloverhearts. "Country Roads." Bandcamp. https://thecloverhearts.bandcamp.com/track/country-roads. Accessed 24 Nov. 2024.

Collis, John. *John Denver: Mother Nature's Son*. Mainstream Publishing, 1999.

"Company." *The Patient*, created by Joel Fields and Joe Weisberg, season 1, episode 5, FX on Hulu, 13 Sep. 2022. https://www.fxnetworks.com/shows/the-patient. Accessed 16 Sep. 2022.

Connell, John, and Chris Gibson. *Sound Tracks: Popular Music, Identity and Place*. Routledge, 2003.

"Corona Extra: Heritage Anthem 60." *iSpotTV*, 28 Mar. 2022. https://www.ispot.tv/ad/bqrc/corona-extra-heritage-anthem-spanish. Accessed 20 Nov. 2024.

"Country Gnomes . . ." *imgflip*, 13 Feb. 2020. https://imgflip.com/m/MS_memer_group/tag/country+gnomes. Accessed 24 Nov. 2024.

Country Music Association. "Forever Country: Artists of Then, Now, and Forever." *YouTube*, uploaded by CMA, 20 Sep. 2016. https://www.youtube.com/watch?v=E2pAslx5az8. Accessed 24 Nov. 2024.

"Country Roads—Life's Reflections Vault Applique." Wilbert Funeral Services, Inc, 2022. https://www.wilbert.com/country-roads-life-s-reflections-vault-appliqu/. Accessed 24 Nov. 2024.

"'Country Roads' Nearing No. 1" *Charleston Daily Mail*, 31 Aug. 1971, 8.

Creasman, Boyd. *Writing West Virginia: Place, People, and Poverty in Contemporary Literature from the Mountain State*. University of Tennessee Press, 2016.

Cresswell, Tim. *In Place/Out of Place: Geography, Ideology, and Transgression*. NED-New edition. University of Minnesota Press, 1996.

Crum, Travis. "Census Shows Some Growth in WV, but State's Population Is Shrinking." *Charleston Gazette-Mail*, 19 Apr. 2019. https://www.wvgazettemail.com/news/census-shows-some-growth-in-wv-but-state-s-population/article_115f9944-f505-5dfa-ba45-83295283d5d0.html. Accessed 24 Nov. 2024.

Daisy Door. "Strasse der Vergangenheit." *Straße Der Vergangenheit / Für Dich*. Ariola, 1973.

Danoff, Bill. Personal interview. 24 Sept. 2020.

———. *Bill Danoff*. http://billdanoff.com. Accessed 26 Sep. 2019.

Danoff, Bill, Taffy Nivert, and John Denver. "Take Me Home, Country Roads." *Poems, Prayers, and Promises*. RCA, 1971.

Dark Waters. Directed by Todd Haynes, written by Mario Correa and Matthew Michael Carnahan. Focus Features, 2019.

Dartywvu. "Miss This Shit" (video). Instagram, 13 Mar. 2021. https://www.instagram.com/p/CMVUIPFjMbx/?igshid=1nwqycok0tows. Accessed 29 Oct. 2021.

Denninger, Lindsay. "The Google Home Commercial Song Sounds Familiar." *Bustle*, 5 Feb. 2017. https://www.bustle.com/p/the-song-in-the-google-home-commercial-makes-everyone-feel-at-home-35712. Accessed 28 Sep. 2021.

Department of the Interior. "The Ultimate Public Lands Playlist." *US Department of the Interior Blog*, 19 Aug. 2020. https://www.doi.gov/blog/ultimate-public-lands-playlist. Accessed 20 Aug. 2020.

Denver, John, and Arthur Tobier. *Take Me Home: An Autobiography*. Harmony Books, 1994.

@dewmouth. "Getting arrested while singing country roads is peak appalachian, yall." *Twitter*, 23 May 2022. https://twitter.com/dew_mouth/status/1528779983602204680?s=20&t=zHp3MkBYj1Q3qS68ftz0pw. Accessed 15 June 2023.

Di Bari, Nicola. "Libertà (Take Me Home, Country Roads)." *Mi Historia*. BMG Chile, 2002.

Dickens, Hazel. "Mama's Hand." *By the Sweat of My Brow*. Rounder, 1983.

———. "West Virginia, My Home." *Hard Hitting Songs for Hard Hit People*. Rounder, 1980.

———. "West Virginia, My Home: A Visit with Hazel Dickens Interview by John Lilly." Interview by John Lilly. Native Ground Books and Music, no date. https://nativeground.com/west-virginia-my-home-a-visit-with-hazel-dickens-interview-by-john-lilly/. Accessed 6 Feb. 2021.

Dickens, Hazel and Alice Gerrard. "The Green Rolling Hills of West Virginia." *Hazel and Alice*. Rounder, 1973.

Doge. "Cowboy Cat Take Me Home to West Virginia." *DogeMuchWow*, 16 Feb. 2021. https://dogemuchwow.com/country-roads-take-me-home-to-west-virginia/. Accessed 28 Sep. 2021.

Donehower, Kim. "How to Reread Appalachian Literacy Research." *Rereading Appalachia: Literacy, Place, and Cultural Resistance*, edited by Sara Webb-Sunderhaus and Kim Donehower. University Press of Kentucky, 2015, pp. 13–31.

Dudley, Dave. "Six Days on the Road." Single, Golden Wing, 1963.

Ebuyer. "A Shortlist of the Best 'Country Roads' Fallout 76 Memes We've Seen This Year." MediaHub, 15 Nov. 2018. https://www.ebuyer.com/blog/2018/11/a-shortlist-of-the-best-country-roads-fallout-76-memes-weve-seen-this-year/. Accessed 24 Nov. 2024.

Edwards, Grace Toney, JoAnn Aust Asbury, and Ricky L. Cox, editors. *A Handbook to Appalachia: An Introduction to the Region*. University of Tennessee Press, 2006.

"Elaine Purkey Sings 'Keepers of the Mountains.'" *YouTube*, uploaded by West Virginia Folklife, 15 Aug. 2017. https://youtu.be/2OgFaHVw7ac?si=iqxjHT1H-DA8Iywr. Accessed 24 Nov. 2024.

Ellison, John. Personal interview. 7 June 2021.

———. "Wake-Up Call (Black Like Me)." *Wake-Up Call (Black Like Me)*. PopMi, 2020.

———. "West Virginia State of Mind." *West Virginia State of Mind*. Jamie Record Co, 2021.

Englehardt, Elizabeth. "Listening to Black Appalachian Laundrywomen: Teaching with Photographs, Letters, Diaries, and Lost Voices." *Appalachia in the Classroom: Teaching the Region*, edited by Theresa Burriss and Patricia Gantt, Ohio University Press, 2013, pp. 33–49.

Ernst, Henry W., and Charles H. Drake. "The Lost Appalachians." *Appalachia in the Sixties: Decade of Reawakening*, edited by David S. Walls and John B. Stephenson. University Press of Kentucky, 1972, pp. 3–10.

Fallout76. Bethesda Games, 2022. https://fallout.bethesda.net/. Accessed 8 Apr. 2023.

Farant, Michel. "Re: Country Road." Received by Sarah Morris, 27 Dec. 2021.

"15 Songs for a Memorable Memorial Day Celebration." *PopCulture.com*, 29 May 2022. https://popculture.com/country-music/news/15-patriotic-songs-memorial-day-2022/#8. Accessed 30 May 2022.

Finan, Eileen. "The Story Behind Country Music's Epic Mash-Up! Plus: Hear Blake, Carrie, Miranda and 36 Other Stars Sing 'Forever Country.'" *People*,

16 Sept. 2016. https://people.com/country/forever-country-the-story-behind-the-epic-50th-anniversary-cma-mash-up/. Accessed 24 Nov. 2024.

Fisher, Evie. "Image: Coronavirus Apparently Fears..." Facebook, 14 Mar. 2020, 8:06 a.m. https://www.facebook.com/evie.hudgeons/posts/pfbid027emCeu6KDyFDVM6ETjmjzhMcK9TbtX69sLjiiRDdR24UGmYfwP9z34jw3wHwiakWl. Accessed 8 Apr. 2020.

Fisher, Stephen. "Claiming Appalachia—And the Questions That Go with It," in "Appalachian Identity: A Roundtable Discussion." *Appalachian Journal* vol. 38, no. 1, Fall 2010, pp. 58–61.

———. "The Grass Roots Speak Back." *Back Talk from Appalachia: Confronting Stereotypes*, edited by Dwight Billings, Gurney Norman, and Katherine Ledford. University Press of Kentucky, 1999, pp. 203–14.

Fisher, Stephen and Barbara Ellen Smith. "Conclusion." *Transforming Places: Lessons from Appalachia*, edited by Stephen L. Fisher, and Barbara Ellen Smith, University of Illinois Press, 2012, pp. 267–291.

Fitzwater, Joe. "WV Kid Sings and Plays Amazing Grace at WV Legislature." *WOWK 13 News*, 16 Jun. 2017. https://www.wowktv.com/archives/wv-kid-sings-and-plays-amazing-grace-at-wv-legislature/amp/. Accessed 24 Nov. 2024.

Fenske, Mindy. *Tattoos in American Visual Culture*. Palgrave Macmillan US, 2007.

Fries, Colin. "Chronology of Wakeup Calls." National Aeronautics and Space Administration, 26 Oct. 2010. https://history.nasa.gov/wakeup.htm. Accessed 24 Nov. 2024.

"From Mountain Mamas to Munich: John Denver's 'Country Roads' Winds Through Oktoberfest." *For the Record*. Spotify, 23 Oct. 2018. https://newsroom.spotify.com/2018-10-23/from-mountain-mamas-to-munich-john-denvers-country-roads-winds-through-oktoberfest/. Accessed 24 Nov. 2024.

Gartner, Paul. "'One Day More': Activist Songwriter Elaine Purkey." *Goldenseal* vol. 32, no. 2, Summer 2006, pp. 14–19.

Gaventa, John. *Power and Powerlessness: Quiescence and Rebellion in an Appalachian Valley*. University of Illinois Press, 1982.

Geertz, Clifford. *The Interpretation of Cultures: Selected Essays*. Basic Books, 1973.

"Georgetown University GEMA Rocks 2010—Bill Danoff—Take Me Home, Country Roads." YouTube, uploaded by GEMA Rocks, 28 Dec. 2011. https://youtu.be/jBN3PSNCr1Q. Accessed 24 Nov. 2024.

Gilbey, Ryan. "More Than Its Monsters." *New Statesman*, 11 May 2017. https://www.newstatesman.com/culture/film/2017/05/more-its-monsters. Accessed 24 Nov. 2024.

Global Energy Monitor Wiki. "Nonviolent Direct Actions Against Coal, 2010." 30 Apr. 2021. https://www.gem.wiki/Nonviolent_direct_actions_against_coal:_2010#cite_ref-24. Accessed 24 Nov. 2024.

"Google's Super Bowl Ad." *YouTube*, uploaded by WOOD TV8, 30 Jan. 2020. https://youtu.be/Z9v6bLABU5Q. Accessed 24 Nov. 2024.

Gotthard. "Mountain Mama." *I'm on My Way*. Ariola, 1994.

Groce, Larry. "This Is My Home." *Take Me Home: A Concert for West Virginia, Vol. 1*. Low Heat Records, 2016.

Gupta, Akhil, and James Ferguson. "Beyond 'Culture:' Space, Identity, and the Politics of Difference." *Cultural Anthropology,* vol. 7, no. 1, Feb. 1992, pp. 6–23.

Hampp, Andrew. "Songs for Screens: How a John Denver Classic Resurfaced Thanks to 'Fallout 76.'" *Variety*, 31 July 2018. https://variety.com/2018/music/news/songs-for-screens-how-a-john-denver-classic-resurfaced-thanks-to-fallout-76-1202891172/. Accessed 24 Nov. 2024.

Harkins, Anthony. *Hillbilly: A Cultural History of an American Icon*. Oxford University Press, 2005.

Harmon, Jeremiah Lloyd. "Almost Heaven." *Namesake*. Joyful Noise Recordings, 2020.

Harris, Emmylou and Brandi Carlile. "Take Me Home, Country Roads." *The Music Is You: A Tribute to John Denver*. ATO Records, 2013.

Hathaway, Rosemary. *Mountaineers are Always Free: Heritage, Dissent, and a West Virginia Icon*. West Virginia University Press, 2020.

Hayes, Amanda. *The Politics of Appalachian Rhetoric*. West Virginia University Press, 2018.

Hearne, Julian. "West Virginia, My Home Sweet Home." *Official West Virginia State Songs*, MH3WV, 2022. https://mh3wv.org/music. Accessed 24 Nov. 2024.

Hermes House Band. "Country Roads." *L'Album*. Zeitgeist, 2002.

Higgs, Robert, and Ambrose Manning, eds. *Voices from the Hills: Selected Readings of Southern Appalachia*, 2nd ed. Kendall-Hunt, 1996.

Higgs, Robert, Ambrose Manning, and Jim Wayne Miller. "Introduction." *Appalachia Inside Out: A Sequel to Voices from the Hills. Volume 2: Culture and Custom*, edited by Robert J. Higgs, Ambrose N. Manning, and Jim Wayne Miller. University of Tennessee Press, 1995, pp. 349–50.

Hill, Jeremy. "'Country Comes to Town': A New Urban Identity for Country Music in the 1960s." *Country Comes to Town: The Music Industry and the Transformation of Nashville*. University of Massachusetts Press, 2016, pp. 31–55.

"Hillshire Farm Country Roads AD." *YouTube*, uploaded by Steve, 20 Feb. 2018. https://youtu.be/HowLhoQITNU. Accessed 24 Nov. 2024.

Hinton, Brian. *Country Roads: How Country Came to Nashville*. Sanctuary Publishing Limited, 2000.

hooks, bell. *Belonging: A Culture of Place*. Taylor and Francis, 2009.

Hott, Mary, with the Carpenter Ants. *Devil in the Hills: Coal Country Reckoning*. CD Baby, 2021.

House, Silas. "In My Own Country." *Talking Appalachian: Voice, Identity, and Community*, edited by Amy Clark and Nancy Hayward. University Press of Kentucky, 2013, pp. 193–204.

"How John Denver Got Huge in Asia: The Globalization of 'Country Roads.'" *Switched on Pop*, created by Nate Sloan and Charlie Harding, episode 304. Rock Ridge Productions, 7 March 2024. https://switchedonpop.com/episodes/john-denver-country-roads-asia-ian-fitchuk-jason-jeung. Accessed 24 Nov. 2024.

Hoyt, David. "Re: Take Me Home." Received by Sarah Morris, 26 Dec. 2021.

Inscoe, John. "The Southern Highlands According to Hollywood: Teaching Appalachian History through Film." *Appalachia in the Classroom: Teaching the Region*, edited by Theresa Burriss and Patricia Gantt. Ohio University Press, 2013, pp. 50–65.

Jackson, Stevan R. "Peoples of Appalachia: Cultural Diversity within the Mountain Region." *A Handbook to Appalachia: An Introduction to the Region*, edited by Grace Toney Edwards, JoAnn Aust Asbury, and Ricky L. Cox. University of Tennessee Press, 2006, pp. 27–49.

Jacobs, Eliot. "Re(Place) Your Typical Writing Assignment: An Argument for Place-Based Writing." *English Journal*, vol. 100, no. 3, January 2011, pp. 49–54.

James, E. W. "My Home Among the Hills." *West Virginia Music and Dance*, MH3WV, 2022. https://mh3wv.org/music. Accessed 24 Nov. 2024.

Jefferson, Thomas. *Notes on the State of Virginia*. Omohundro Institute and University of North Carolina Press, 2006. *EBSCOhost*, discovery.ebsco.com/linkprocessor/plink?id=7aa7ba7b-8488-300f-8d12-b14e5b59cae9. Accessed 24 Nov. 2024.

Jeong, Jason. "The Song That Sold America to a Generation of Asian Immigrants." *Atlantic*, 4 May 2021. https://www.theatlantic.com/culture/archive/2021/05/what-john-denver-means-some-asian-immigrants/618784/. Accessed 20 Nov. 2024.

John Denver Facebook Page. "In response to the comments and calls . . ." *Facebook*, 6 May 2016, 6:50 p.m. https://www.facebook.com/JohnDenver/posts/in-response-to-the-comments-and-calls-received-since-donald-trumps-campaign-play/10153683578868691/. Accessed 14 May 2019.

"John Denver Sings 'Take Me Home, Country Roads' in Charleston, WV." WCHS Eyewitness News, Facebook, 18 April 2019, 4:00 p.m. https://www.facebook.com/watch/?v=418550728718099. Accessed 15 Aug. 2020.

Johnston, Daniel. "Wild West Virginia." *Songs of Pain*. Eternal Yip Eye Music, 1980.

Jones, Aristotle. "Aristotle Jones West Virginia Hills 2019 Live Performance in Studio 3."

YouTube, uploaded by Aristotle Jones (Appalachian Soul Man), 16 Dec. 2019, https://youtu.be/HE5_4BTrR-w?si=5kQycUQEG2u7PUkk. Accessed 24 Nov. 2024.

———. Personal interview. 26 May 2021.

———. "The Talk." *The Go 1st Mixtape, Vol. 1*. Go 1st Records, 2021.

———. "The West Virginia Hills." *Appalachian Soul Man*. Aristotle Jones Music, 2019.

Jones, Loyal. *Appalachian Values* (pamphlet). Berea College Appalachian Center, no date listed. From WVU's Appalachian Collection. Reprint from *Voices from the Hills*, edited by Higgs and Manning. Edward Unger Publishing, 1975.

Kabler, Phil. "Musical marketing." *Charleston Gazette-Mail (WV)*, 12 Apr. 2018, sec. News, P1C. *NewsBank: Access World News.* infoweb.newsbank.com/apps/news/document-view?p=AWNB&docref=news/16B3F1422B282438. Accessed 10 Oct. 2022.

Kamakawiwo'ole, Israel. "Take Me Home, Country Road." *Facing Future.* Island Heritage Music, 1993.

KAWANLAMA. "Fallout 76 COUNTRY ROAD—John Denver (Cover by KAWANLAMA)." *YouTube*, uploaded by KAWANLAMA, 10 Feb. 2017. https://youtu.be/pZ3OFX4uTRY?si=OhFdbWJcqscm6Lur. Accessed 23 Nov. 2024.

Kennedy, John F. "Remarks of Senator John F. Kennedy at Hinton, West Virginia April 27, 1960." John F. Kennedy Presidential Library and Museum, 2022. https://www.jfklibrary.org/archives/other-resources/john-f-kennedy-speeches/hinton-wv-19600427. Accessed 24 Nov. 2024.

Kercheval, Hoppy. "Remembering John F. Kennedy and West Virginia's Birthday." Hoppy's Commentary. West Virginia Metro News, 20 Jun. 2018. https://wvmetronews.com/2018/06/20/remembering-john-kennedy-and-west-virginias-birthday/. Accessed 24 Nov. 2024.

Kielar, Samantha. "Hiraeth." *Word of the Week: Unique, Interesting, Rarely Used Vocabulary.* Penn State. 2 April 2016. https://sites.psu.edu/kielarpassionblog2/2016/04/02/hiraeth/. Accessed 13 July 2020.

King, Ellen Ruddell, and Henry Everett Engle. "The West Virginia Hills." *Official West Virginia State Songs*, MH3WV, 2022. https://mh3wv.org/music. Accessed 24 Nov. 2024.

Kingsman: The Golden Circle. Directed by Matthew Vaughn, by Jane Goldman, Matthew Vaughn, and Mark Millar. 20th Century Studios, 2019.

Klemt, Barbara. *John Denver's Autograph: His Lyrics as a Cultural and Literary Record.* Diss., Middle Tennessee State University, 1994.

Koppe22. "Marquette Coach Buzz Williams decides to dance to John Denver . . . nearly is murdered." YouTube, 25 Feb. 2012. https://youtu.be/t8ILUBm-65I. Accessed 23 Nov. 2024.

Kurlinkus, Will, and Krista Kurlinkus. "'Coal Keeps the Lights On': Rhetorics of Nostalgia for and in Appalachia." *College English*, vol. 81, no. 2, 2018, pp. 87–109.

Laforêt, Marie. "Mon Pays est Ici." *Marie Laforêt.* Polydor Records, 1972.

Lanier, R. Parks, Jr. "Appalachian Poetry: A Field Guide for Teachers." *Appalachia in the Classroom: Teaching the Region*, edited by Theresa Burriss and Patricia Gantt. Ohio University Press, 2013, pp. 189–212.

Lawrence, Chris. "Tourism Commissioner Believes Country Roads Rights Fee Was a Strong Investment." WV Metro News, 3 Nov. 2017. https://wvmetronews.com/2017/11/03/tourism-commissioner-believes-country-roads-rights-fee-was-a-strong-investment/. Accessed 24 Nov. 2024.

Leach, Neil. "Belonging: Towards a Theory of Identification with Place." *Perspecta* vol. 33, 2002, pp. 126–33.

Lego, Brian. "West Virginia: A 20th Century Perspective on Population Change." WVU Research Corporation (whitepaper), Dec. 1999. https://researchrepository.wvu.edu/cgi/viewcontent.cgi?article=1265&context=bureau_be. Accessed 24 Nov. 2024.

Leonard, George. *The Silent Pulse: A Search for the Perfect Rhythm That Exists in Each of Us*. Gibbs Smith, 2006.

Lilly, John, ed. *Mountains of Music: West Virginia Traditional Music from Goldenseal*. University of Illinois Press, 1999.

Lipton, Michael. Personal interview. 21 July 2021.

Locklear, Erica Abrams. *Negotiating a Perilous Empowerment: Appalachian Women's Literacies*, 1st ed. Ohio University Press, 2011.

Loersch, Chris, and Nathan L Arbuckle. "Unraveling the Mystery of Music: Music as an Evolved Group Process." *Journal of Personality and Social Psychology* vol. 105, no. 5, 2013, pp. 777–98. doi:10.1037/a0033691.

Logan Lucky. Directed by Stephen Soderbergh, by Rebecca Blunt. Bleecker Street, 2017.

Longfellow, Rickie. "Back in Time: The National Road." *Highway History*, US Department of Transportation Federal Highway Administration, 27 Jun. 2017. https://www.fhwa.dot.gov/infrastructure/back0103.cfm. Accessed 24 Nov. 2024.

MacLennan, Barbara. Personal interview. 10 Sep. 2021.

Maggard, Sally Ward. "Coalfield Women Making History." *Back Talk from Appalachia: Confronting Stereotypes*, edited by Dwight Billings, Gurney Norman, and Katherine Ledford. University Press of Kentucky, 1999, pp. 228–50.

Mann, Jeff. "The Feast Hall, the Arsenal, and the Mirror: Teaching Literature to Students at Risk." *Appalachia in the Classroom: Teaching the Region*, edited by Theresa Burriss and Patricia Gantt. Ohio University Press, 2013, pp. 82–94.

Marks, Rusty. "Landau Murphy Pens Swingin' Mountain State Tribute." *The State Journal* (WV), 23 Jun. 2016. https://www.wvnews.com/landau-murphy-pens-swingin-mountain-state-tribute/article_2eb10285-28de-5ab1-8609-c38aa72f34aa.html. Accessed 24 Nov. 2024.

Massey, Carissa A. *The Responsibility of Forms: Social and Visual Rhetorics of Appalachian Identity*. Ohio University, 2009.

Massey, Doreen. *For Space*. Sage, 2005.

Mattea, Kathy. *Coal*. Captain Potato Records, 2008.

———. "Come Home to West Virginia." *Walk the Way the Wind Blows/Come Home to West Virginia* (Single). Mercury, 1986.

———. "Leaving West Virginia." *Walk the Way the Wind Blows*. Mercury, 1986.

@mattkellyradio (Matt Kelly). "God Bless WV." Twitter, 18 Sept. 2018, 2:31 p.m., https://x.com/mattkellyradio/status/1039582150515982336. Accessed 10 Oct. 2022.

Maxwell, Ian. "There's No There There." *Sonic Synergies: Music, Technology, Community, Identity*, edited by Gerry Bloustien, Margaret Peters, and Susan Luckman. Routledge, 2016, pp. 79–89.

McCarroll, Meredith. "Hillbillies Need No Elegy." *The Bitter Southerner*. https://bittersoutherner.com/hillbillies-need-no-elegy-appalachian-reckoning. Accessed 9 July 2020.

———. "On and On: Appalachian Accent and Academic Power." *Southern Cultures* vol. 22, no. 3, Summer 2016. https://www.southerncultures.org/article/on-and-on-appalachian-accent-and-academic-power/. Accessed 24 Nov. 2024.

McCray, Dustin. "Almost Heaven." *The Song That You Sing*. Dustin McCray Music, 2016.

McKelvey, Tara. "Obama Promotes Anti-Heroin Strategy in Coal Country." *BBC News*, 22 Oct. 2015, https://www.bbc.com/news/magazine-33943913. Accessed 24 Nov. 2024.

Me First and the Gimme Gimmes. "Country Roads." *Have Another Ball*. Fat Wreck Chords, 2008.

"Meijer TV Spot: 'Come Home.'" iSpot TV, 10 Nov. 2017. https://www.ispot.tv/ad/wr1I/meijer-come-home. Accessed 24 Nov. 2024.

Melodicka Bros. "Country Roads but It's CYBERPUNK/INDUSTRIAL/SCI-FI wtf." Melodicka Bros. YouTube, 20 Nov. 2019. https://youtu.be/u1_dy1EmV6w. Accessed 24 Nov. 2024.

"Michael Scott Paper Company." *The Office*, created by Ricky Gervais and Greg Daniels, Season 5, Episode 25, NBC, 9 Apr. 2009. https://www.peacocktv.com/stream-tv/the-office. Accessed 24 Nov. 2024.

Milia Malae. "Take Me Home, Country Roads—International Covers." *YouTube* (playlist), 5 Apr. 2013. https://www.youtube.com/playlist?list=PLF1tmPxpsEJcZK8DptgFUHqjWks_fFI-I. Accessed 24 Nov. 2024.

Miller, Roger, "King of the Road." *The Return of Roger Miller*. Smash Records, 1965.

Mistich, Dave. "Hi, How Are You: Remembering Musician, Artist Daniel Johnston." West Virginia Public Broadcasting, 12 Sep. 2019. https://www.wvpublic.org/news/2019-09-12/hi-how-are-you-remembering-musician-artist-daniel-johnston. Accessed 24 Nov. 2024.

———. "West Virginia Has Sharpest Population Decline In U.S., Will Lose A Seat In Congress." West Virginia Public Broadcasting, 26 Apr. 2021. https://www.wvpublic.org/government/2021-04-26/west-virginia-has-sharpest-population-decline-in-u-s-will-lose-a-seat-in-congress. Accessed 24 Nov. 2024.

Moami. "As a German Kid . . ." Tumblr, no date. https://moami.tumblr.com/post/186545057426/as-a-german-kid-i-used-to-wonder-why-our-radio. Accessed 24 Nov. 2024.

Mocedades. "Carretera Del Sur." *Intímamente*. Epic, 1992.

Moipei Quartet. "Country Roads." *In the Land of the Lion*. Arc Music, 2013.

Moracchioli, Leo. "Take Me Home, Country Roads (metal cover by Leo Moracchioli)." Frog Leap Studios, YouTube, 19 Jul. 2019. https://youtu.be/O81XldQHApg. Accessed 24 Nov. 2024.

Morningstar, Mike. "Buffalo Creek." *The Original*. No Date, *Last FM*. https://www.last.fm/music/Mike+Morningstar. Accessed 24 Nov. 2024.

———. "Mountaineers are Always Free." *The Original*. No Date, *Last FM*, https://www.last.fm/music/Mike+Morningstar. Accessed 24 Nov. 2024.

———. "West Virginia Girl." *The Original*. No Date, *Last FM*, https://www.last.fm/music/Mike+Morningstar. Accessed 24 Nov. 2024.

Morris, Jan. "Home Thoughts from Abroad." *The Atlantic*, November 2002. https://www.theatlantic.com/magazine/archive/2002/11/home-thoughts-from-abroad/376703/. Accessed 24 Nov. 2024.

Morris, Jeff. "Gov. Justice Does 'Take Me Home, Country Roads' Book Reading for Kids." *WCHS Eyewitness News*, 1 Mar. 2022. https://wchstv.com/news/local/gov-justice-has-take-me-home-country-roads-book-reading-for-kids. Accessed 24 Nov. 2024.

Mullens, Sarah. Personal interview. 23 Aug. 2021.

Murphy, Eugene Landau. "Come Home to West Virginia." *Come Home to West Virginia*. Hard Knocks, 2016.

Nardella, Beth. "Power, Resistance, and Place in Appalachia." *Cultural Studies ↔ Critical Methodologies* vol. 22, no. 2, 2021. doi:10.1177/15327086211065806.

Nash, Bishop. "Local Support for Sanders Unfazed Despite His Trailing." *Herald-Dispatch*, Huntington, WV, 22 Apr. 2016. https://www.herald-dispatch.com/elections/local-support-for-sanders-unfazed-despite-his-trailing/article_b4bfc342-3618-5f19-8d27-6d6133b6fbd1.html. Accessed 24 Nov. 2024.

National State Tourism Directors Mercury Awards. "The 'Place I Belong WV' Campaign." Us Travel Association, 2021. https://ustravel.secure-platform.com/a/gallery/rounds/18/details/5172. Accessed 24 Nov. 2024.

"Naturalized US Citizens Sing 'Take Me Home, Country Roads.'" *YouTube*, uploaded by Charleston Gazette Mail, 17 Sep. 2015. https://youtu.be/WqQkS3ygeWY. Accessed 24 Nov. 2024.

"New Homecoming Schedule." *Concordian* XLVI.8 (22 Oct. 1970).

Newton-John, Olivia. "Take Me Home, Country Roads." *Let Me Be There*. Festival, 1973.

Nivert, Taffy. Personal interview. 28 Sept. 2020.

Obermiller, Phillip J. "Paving the Way: Urban Organizations and the Image of Appalachians." *Back Talk from Appalachia: Confronting Stereotypes*, edited by Dwight Billings, Gurney Norman, and Katherine Ledford. University Press of Kentucky, 1999, pp. 251–66.

Obermiller, Phillip J., Michael E. Maloney, and Pauletta Hansel. "Appalachians Outside the Region." *A Handbook to Appalachia: An Introduction to the Region*, edited by Grace Toney Edwards, JoAnn Aust Asbury, and Ricky L. Cox. University of Tennessee Press, 2006, pp. 235–58.

O'Brien, Jason. "(Almost Heaven) My Tribute Song to West Virginia." YouTube, uploaded by Jason O'Brien, 6 Nov. 2016. https://youtu.be/cS0eYQeova8. Accessed 24 Nov. 2024.

O'Daly, Britton. "Climate Change Protesters Disrupt Yale-Harvard Football Game." *New York Times*, 23 Nov. 2019. https://www.nytimes.com/2019/11/23/us/harvard-yale-game-protest.html. Accessed 24 Nov. 2024.

Ohio Writers' Program. *The National Road in Song and Story*, University of Illinois Urbana-Champaign, Internet Archive, 1940. https://archive.org/details/nationalroadinso00writ. Accessed 24 Nov. 2024.

"Olivia Newton-John 1972—Take Me Home Country Roads." YouTube, uploaded by Eddie Orz, 26 Mar. 2015. https://youtu.be/Znv9Bvn3x_s. Accessed 18 Oct. 2022.

O'Malley, Frank Ward and Irving Berlin. "Irving Berlin Gives Nine Rules for Writing Popular Songs." Sears, Benjamin. *The Irving Berlin Reader*. Oxford University Press, 2012, 173–81.

"Our Brand." *The West Virginia Company*, 2022. https://thewvco.com/pages/our-brand. Accessed 24 Nov. 2024.

Paisley, Brad. "Taking Requests Live from My House." Facebook, 19 Mar. 2020. https://www.facebook.com/watch/live/?ref=watch_permalink&v=562606067689101. Accessed 31 Oct. 2024.

Panski. "Take Me Home, Country Roads" (feat. Ellena Soule). *A Road Less Traveled*. Panski, 2017.

Parks, Michael. "Country Roads-John Denver WVU 1980 Full Song." YouTube, 8 Jul. 2013. https://youtu.be/Plndo6Rie7E. Accessed 24 Oct. 2024.

Petro, Pamela. "Dreaming in Welsh." *The Paris Review*, 18 Sept. 2021. https://www.theparisreview.org/blog/2012/09/18/dreaming-in-welsh/. Accessed 24 Nov. 2024.

Phillips, Utah, and The Quinaimes Band. "The Green Rolling Hills of West Virginia." *The Quinaimes Band*. Elektra, 1971.

Powers, Christopher. "Why on Earth Are the St. Louis Blues Fans Belting Out 'Take Me Home, Country Roads'?" *Golf Digest*, 22 May, 2019. https://www.golfdigest.com/story/why-on-earth-are-the-st-louis-blues-fans-belting-out-take-me-home-country-roads. Accessed 24 Nov. 2024.

Prelli, Lawrence. "Rhetorics of Display: An Introduction." *Rhetorics of Display*. University of South Carolina Press, 2021, pp. 1–38.

"Presidential Candidate Donald Trump Rally in Charleston, West Virginia." *C-Span*. 5 May 2016. https://www.c-span.org/video/?409094-1/donald-trump-addresses-supporters-charleston-west-virginia&playEvent. Accessed 24 Nov. 2024.

Pretty Lights. "(HQ) Pretty Lights—Country Roads (Remix) [2011 Remixes] (John Denver)." YouTube, uploaded by Sophistefunk, 18 July 2011. https://youtu.be/NAXz2z4giws. Accessed 24 Nov. 2024.

Price, Elizabeth. "Hillbilly Horror: Reckoning with a Genre 15 Years After 'Wrong Turn.'" *100 Days in Appalachia*, 21 May 2018. https://www.100daysinappalachia.com/2018/05/hillbilly-horror-stereotypes/. Accessed 24 Nov. 2024.

Purkey, Elaine. "Keepers of the Mountains." *Revisiting West Virginia, Friends of Pick Up America in West Virginia*. Pick Up America, 2011. https://pickupamerica.bandcamp.com/album/revisiting-west-virginia. Accessed 24 Nov. 2024.

———. "One Day More." *Classic Labor Songs from Smithsonian Folkways*, Smithsonian Folkways Recordings, 2006. *Alexander Street*. https://search.alexanderstreet.com/view/work/bibliographic_entity%7Crecorded_cd%7C367284. Accessed 24 Nov. 2024.

Ramella, Richard. "A State of Music: Songs of Hill and Home." *Goldenseal* vol. 3, no. 2, Spring 2004, pp. 24–28.

———. "West Virginia's Three State Songs." *Goldenseal* vol. 40, no. 1, Spring 2014, pp. 34–39.

Ransom, Heather. "Stockholm State: A History." *Mountains Piled upon Mountains: Appalachian Nature Writing in the Anthropocene*, edited by Jessica Cory. West Virginia University Press, 2019, pp. 107–18.

Reike, Clark. "Extreme Traveler Pro-Tip." Facebook, 5 April 2021. https://www.facebook.com/clarke.rieke. Accessed 10 May 2021.

Restless Road (with Kane Brown). "Take Me Home." *Restless Road*. Sony Music Entertainment, 2020.

Reynolds, Nedra. "13 Cultural Geography and Images of Place." *The Locations of Composition*, edited by Christopher Keller and Christian Weisser. SUNY Press, 2007, pp. 251–65.

Rice, Otis K., and Stephen W. Brown. "History of West Virginia." *e-WV: The West Virginia Encyclopedia*. 10 Sep. 2024. https://www.wvencyclopedia.org/entries/386. Accessed 24 Nov. 2024.

Ridenour, Andy, Bill Wilkinson, and Mary Ellen Griffith. Personal interview. 16 Sep. 2021.

Ritchie, Joy. "Connecting Writers' Roles to Social Roles Beyond the Classroom." *Writing and Sense of Self: Identity Negotiation in Writing Workshops*, by Robert Brooke. 1991, 113–39.

Robinson, Julie. "To the Place I Belong: 'Country Roads' Reminds World Traveling West Virginians of Their Home Far Away." *Charleston Sunday Gazette* 25 Nov. 2012, 1F.

Ryden, Kent. *Mapping the Invisible Landscape: Folklore, Writing, and the Sense of Place*. University of Iowa Press, 1993.

@SaquibSadique (Saquib Qureshi). "Whenever I listen to the song..." Twitter, 9 Mar. 2021, 9:12 p.m. https://x.com/SaquibSadique/status/1369471154600120325. Accessed 24 Nov. 2024.

Satterwhite, Emily. *Dear Appalachia: Readers, Identity, and Popular Fiction since 1878*. University Press of Kentucky, 2011.

———. "Intro to Appalachian Studies: Navigating Myths of Appalachian Exceptionalism." *Appalachia in the Classroom: Teaching the Region*, edited by Theresa Burriss and Patricia Gantt. Ohio University Press, 2013, pp. 3–32.

———. "Objecting to Insider/Outsider Politics and the Uncritical Celebration of Appalachia" in "Appalachian Identity: A Roundtable Discussion." *Appalachian Journal* vol. 38, no. 1, Fall 2010, pp. 68.

Schoening, Benjamin S. and Eric T. Kasper. *Don't Stop Thinking About the Music: The Politics of Songs and Musicians in Presidential Campaigns*. Lexington Books, 2012.

Schoonover, Abe. "Country Roads Performed by Alumnus of 'The West Virginians.'" Facebook, 7 May 2020, 2:24 p.m. https://www.facebook.com/abe.schoonover/videos/10215747764639001/. Accessed 25 May 2020.

Senator Byrd Memorial Service. *C-Span*, 2 July. 2010. https://www.c-span.org/video/?294355-1/senator-byrd-memorial-service. Accessed 24 Nov. 2024.

@Sen_JoeManchin. "Sing along while washing your hands..." *Twitter*, 10 March, 2020. https://twitter.com/Sen_JoeManchin/status/1237453449874354176?s=20. Accessed 20 May 2020.

Shand, Jessica. "The Sound of Occupation: Music and the Spectacle of Collective Action." *Squarespace*, March 2020. https://static1.squarespace.com/static/5c3b71680dbda39a391e9dd5/t/5e78228c4919f8518bf0a4a8/1584931469532/Sound+of+Occupation.pdf. Accessed 24 Nov. 2024.

Shannon, Thomas R. "The Economy of Appalachia." *A Handbook to Appalachia: An Introduction to the Region*, edited by Grace Toney Edwards, JoAnn Aust Asbury, and Ricky L. Cox. University of Tennessee Press, 2006, pp. 67–84.

Shapiro, Henry. *Appalachia on Our Mind: The Southern Mountains and Mountaineers in the American Consciousness, 1870–1920*. UNC Press, 1978.

Shelby, Anne. "The 'R' Word: What's So Funny (and Not So Funny) About Redneck Jokes." *Back Talk from Appalachia: Confronting Stereotypes*, edited by Dwight Billings, Gurney Norman, and Katherine Ledford. University Press of Kentucky, 1999, pp. 154–60.

Shepley, Nathan. "Place-Conscious Literacy Practices in One Appalachian College Town." *Rereading Appalachia: Literacy, Place, and Cultural Resistance*, edited by Sara Webb-Sunderhaus and Kim Donehower. University Press of Kentucky, 2015, pp. 137–56.

Shutika, Debra Lattanzi. *Beyond the Borderlands: Migration and Belonging in the United States and Mexico*. University of California Press, 2011.

Silverman, Ellie, Emily Davies, Steve Thompson, and Ian Duncan. "'Freedom Convoy' Spinoff Rallied in Md. with About 1000 Vehicles and Plans to Drive Around the Capital Beltway." *Washington Post*, 5 Mar. 2022. https://www.washingtonpost.com/dc-md-va/2022/03/05/peoples-convoy-protest-hagerstown/. Accessed 24 Nov. 2024.

6'6 240. "Almost Heaven." *Hard Work and Dedication*. Soundvizion Entertainment, 2009.

Snell, Mark A. "Civil War." *e-WV: The West Virginia Encyclopedia*. 13 Dec. 2016. https://www.wvencyclopedia.org/articles/1193. Accessed 24 Nov. 2024.

Snyder, Todd. *The Rhetoric of Appalachian Identity*. McFarland and Company, Inc. 2014.

———. "The Transition to College for First-Generation Students from Extractive Industry Appalachia." *Rereading Appalachia: Literacy, Place, and Cultural Resistance*, edited by Sara Webb-Sunderhaus and Kim Donehower. University Press of Kentucky, 2015, pp. 77–98.

Sobel, David. *Place-Based Education: Connecting Classrooms and Communities*. The Orion Society, 2005.

"Song Protesting Dollar General Released in Berkeley Springs." *Morgan County, USA*, 15 Feb. 2015. https://morgancountyusa.org/?p=1651. Accessed 24 Nov. 2024.

Sparby, Derek. *Mimetic Rhetorics: Toward a Tool Kit for Ethical Meming*. University of Michigan Press, 2023. https://doi.org/10.3998/mpub.12207107. Accessed 24 Nov. 2024.

Spring, Pam. "The 55 Counties Song." *West Virginia Music and Dance*, MH3WV, 2022. https://mh3wv.org/music. Accessed 24 Nov. 2024.

Staff. "9 Things You Didn't Know About 'Take Me Home, Country Roads' by John Denver." *The Daily Athenaeum Online* [Morgantown, WV], 26 Sep. 2016. www.thedaonline.com/culture/listicles/things-you-didn-t-know-about-take-me-home-country/article_f9d9b8d8-839d-11e6-87e6-5353262785bd.html. Accessed 16 October 2019.

Stimeling, Travis D. *Song Writing in Contemporary West Virginia: Profiles and Reflections*. West Virginia University Press, 2018.

Stocks, Chris. "How to Watch England vs South Africa, 2nd Test: Start Time, TV Channel and Full Fixtures Schedule." *iNews*, 24 Aug. 2022. https://inews.co.uk/sport/cricket/how-to-watch-england-vs-south-africa-2nd-test-start-time-tv-channel-full-fixtures-schedule-series-1813925. Accessed 24 Nov. 2024.

Straw, Richard. "Appalachian History." *A Handbook to Appalachia: An Introduction to the Region*, edited by Grace Toney Edwards, JoAnn

Aust Asbury, and Ricky L. Cox. University of Tennessee Press, 2006, pp. 1–26.

Sunshine. Directed by Joseph Sargent, written by Carol Sobieski, Sony Pictures Television, 1973.

Take me home . . . country roads" (tattoo photograph). *Pinterest*, no date. https://www.pinterest.com/pin/29766047511220707/. Accessed 24 Nov. 2024.

"Take Me Home, Country Roads." *TikTok* (search). https://www.tiktok.com/music/Take-Me-Home-Country-Roads-6744442223464548353?lang=en. Accessed 11 May 2022.

"Take Me Home New York Knicks." YouTube, uploaded by cduzin, 11 Jan. 2007. https://youtu.be/WP1xItPXOiE. Accessed 24 Nov. 2024.

Tate, Linda. "I Hear Appalachia Singing: Teaching Appalachian Literature in a General Education American Literature Course." *Appalachia in the Classroom: Teaching the Region*, edited by Theresa Burriss and Patricia Gantt. Ohio University Press, 2013, pp. 95–108.

Taylor, Kathryn Trauth. "Diverse Rhetorical Scenes of Urban Appalachian Literacies." *Rereading Appalachia: Literacy, Place, and Cultural Resistance*, edited by Sara Webb-Sunderhaus and Kim Donehower. University Press of Kentucky, 2015, pp. 117–35.

———. "Naming Affrilachia: Toward Rhetorical Ecologies of Identity Performance in Appalachia." *Enculturation*, 21 June 2011. http://www.enculturation.net/naming-affrilachia. Accessed 24 Nov. 2024.

Teets, Sharon. "Education in Appalachia." *A Handbook to Appalachia: An Introduction to the Region*, edited by Grace Toney Edwards, JoAnn Aust Asbury, and Ricky L. Cox. University of Tennessee Press, 2006, pp. 119–42.

Ter Horst, Jerald. "No More Pork Barrel: The Appalachia Approach." *Appalachia in the Sixties: Decade of Reawakening*, edited by David S. Walls and John B. Stephenson. University Press of Kentucky, 1972, pp. 31–38.

"Tesla Cybertruck Commercial—Country Roads." YouTube, uploaded by Nat Sharpe, 8 Jan. 2020. https://youtu.be/9NEsBZCJwf0. Accessed 24 Nov. 2024.

Toots and the Maytals. "Take Me Home, Country Roads." *In the Dark*. Dragon Records, 1974.

Tranquility. "Take Me Home, Country Roads by John Denver." Tranquility Burial and Cremation Services, Inc., 29 Mar. 2019. https://tranquilitycremation.com/take-me-home-country-roads-by-john-denver/. Accessed 24 Nov. 2024.

Tribe, Ivan. *Mountaineer Jamboree: Country Music in West Virginia*. University Press of Kentucky, 1984.

Tully-McManus, Katherine. "Two protests in Hart End in Valentine's Day Arrests." *Roll Call*, 14 Feb. 2019. https://rollcall.com/2019/02/14/two-protests-in-hart-end-in-valentines-day-arrests/. Accessed 24 Nov. 2024.

Turman-Deal, Jinny A. "'We Were an Oddity': A Look at the Back-to-the-Land Movement in Appalachia." *West Virginia History: An Open Access Reader*, edited by Kevin Barksdale and Ken Fones-Wolf. West Virginia University Libraries, 2022. https://textbooks.lib.wvu.edu/wvhistory/files/html/17_wv_history_reader_turman-deal/.

Turner, Wyatt. "You Remind Me of West Virginia." *John Wayne*. Masonridge Entertainment, 2015.

u/Bacon-Ranger. "'Country Roads, Take Me Home' was my grandfather's funeral song." Fallout 76. *Reddit*, 15 Nov. 2018. https://www.reddit.com/r/fo76/comments/9xbix7/country_roads_take_me_home_was_my_grandfathers/. Accessed 24 Nov. 2024.

University Relations, Enrollment Management. "Protected Indica." West Virginia University. 2022. https://universityrelations.wvu.edu/services-capabilities/brand-and-trademark-licensing/protected-indicia. Accessed 24 Nov. 2024.

Vance, J. D. *Hillbilly Elegy: A Memoir of a Family and Culture in Crisis*. Harper, 2016.

van Manen, Max. *Researching Lived Experience: Human Science for an Action Sensitive Pedagogy*. Althouse Press, 1997.

Walls, Jeannette. *The Glass Castle: A Memoir*. Scribner, 2005.

Webb-Sunderhaus, Sara. "'Keep the Appalachian, Drop the Redneck': Tellable Student Narratives of Appalachian Identity." *College English*, vol. 79, no. 1, 2016, pp. 11–33.

Webb-Sunderhaus, Sara, and Kim Donehower. "Introduction." *Rereading Appalachia: Literacy, Place, and Cultural Resistance*, edited by Sara

Webb-Sunderhaus and Kim Donehower. University Press of Kentucky, 2015, pp. 1–12.

West Virginia Department of Education. "About the WV Golden Horseshoe Award." *The West Virginia Golden Horseshoe Award*. https://wvde.state.wv.us/goldenhorseshoe/about.html. Accessed 13 Oct. 2020.

West Virginia House of Delegates. "House Concurrent Resolution No. 19: Adopting 'The West Virginia Hills', 'West Virginia, My Home Sweet Home' and 'This Is My West Virginia' as Official State Songs." *Journal of the House of Delegates, 1963*, West Virginia Archives and History: West Virginia State Songs. http://129.71.204.160/history/////symbols/statesongs01.html. Accessed 24 Nov. 2024.

West Virginia House of Delegates. "House Concurrent Resolution No. 40: Designating 'Take Me Home Country Roads' Written by John Denver, Taffy Nivert, and Bill Danoff and initially recorded by John Denver, an Official State Song." *Journal of the House of Delegates, 2014*, West Virginia Archives and History: West Virginia State Songs. http://129.71.204.160/history/////symbols/statesongs01.html. Accessed 24 Nov. 2024.

West Virginia Legislature, Delegate Wright. "House Resolution 17: Commemorating the Passing of John Denver, a Folk and Pop Musician Most Recognized in This State for the Hit Single 'Take Me Home, Country Roads.'" West Virginia Legislature Second Session, 85th Legislature, 1998. http://www.wvlegislature.gov/Bill_Status/bills_text.cfm?billdoc=HR17%20INTR.htm&yr=1998&sesstype=RS&i=1&houseorig=h&billtype=r. Accessed 24 Nov. 2024.

West Virginia Office of Miners' Health Safety and Training. "WV Mine Disasters 1884 to Present." West Virginia Department of Commerce, 28 Mar. 2016. https://minesafety.wv.gov/historical-statistical-data/wv-mine-disasters-1884-to-present/. Accessed 24 Nov. 2024.

"West Virginia's Country Roads Will Soon Be Underwater." *The Late Show with Stephen Colbert*. YouTube, Oct. 19, 2021. https://youtu.be/nBI9QkQphw8. Accessed 24 Nov. 2024.

West Virginia Tourism Office. *West Virginia Vacation Guide,* Oct. 2019. https://wvtourism.com/wp-content/uploads/2019/10/VacationGuide.pdf. Accessed 30 Oct. 2019.

Wheeler, Billy Edd. "Coal Tattoo." *A New Bag of Songs*. Kapp Records, 1963.

———. "Coming of the Roads." *Fifth Album*, performed by Judy Collins, Elektra, 1965.

———. "My Heart Will Always Be in West Virginia." *New Wine from Old Vines–Billy Edd Wheeler Uncorked*. Sagittarius, 2006.

———. "Red Wing Blackbird." *The Judy Collins Concerts*, performed by Judy Collins, Elektra, 1964.

———. "They Can't Put It Back." *Paper Birds*. Kapp Records, 1967.

Whipkey, Charlotte. "Mike Morningstar: West Virginia's Troubadour." *Goldenseal* vol. 45 no. 4, Winter 2019, pp. 12–20.

Whisnant, David. "Appalachian Regionalism: Corollaries to Sheldon Kopp's Eschatological Laundry List" in "Appalachian Identity: A Roundtable Discussion." *Appalachian Journal* vol. 38, no. 1, Fall 2010, pp. 65–68.

Whisper of the Heart. Directed by Yoshifumi Kondō., by Hayao Miyazaki. Studio Ghibli, 1995.

Wilder, Anna, and Thomas Weber. "Mike Pence Holds Non-distanced Campaign Rally in Florida's Biggest Retirement Community." *The Independent Florida Alligator*, 10 Oct. 2020. https://www.alligator.org/article/2020/10/mike-pence-holds-non-distanced-campaign-rally-in-florida-s-biggest-retirement-community. Accessed 24 Nov. 2024.

Wilkerson, Jessica. *To Live Here, You Have to Fight: How Women Led Appalachian Movements for Social Justice*. University of Illinois Press, 2019.

Williams, Hank, with His Drifting Cowboys. "Lost Highway." Single, MGM, 1949.

Williams, John Alexander. *Appalachia, A History*. University of North Carolina Press, 2002.

———. *West Virginia: A History*, 2nd ed. West Virginia University Press, 2001.

WitBlue EX. "Take Me Home, Country Roads by Spank—Fallout 76. YouTube, 16 Feb. 2020. https://youtu.be/2C3JrgVcBZs. Accessed 24 Nov. 2024.

Withers, Bill. "Grandma's Hands." *Just as I Am*. Sussex, 1971.

———. "Lean on Me." *Still Bill*. The Record Plant, 1972.

Withers, Bill, and Anna Sale. "'Wherever You Go, You Take Yourself'—Interviewing Bill Withers." *Appalachian Journal* vol. 42, no. 3/4, 2015, pp. 344–57.

WVU Health. "WVU CORONAVIRUS: Wash your hands for 20 seconds! Sing or hum 'Country Roads' to avoid getting sick." YouTube, uploaded by WVU Health, 11 Mar. 2020. https://youtu.be/yVffxaLSr4U. Accessed 24 Nov. 2024.

@WVU Mountaineers. "Near or far and wherever you are, Country Roads will always make you feel right at home." *Twitter*, 28 Mar. 2020. https://twitter.com/WestVirginiaU/status/1244061711482699779?s=20. Accessed 30 Apr. 2020.

Young, Charles. "State Officials Announce Almost Heaven Swings at Nine West Virginia Locations." *WV News*, 20 Jun. 2022. https://www.wvnews.com/news/wvnews/state-officials-announce-almost-heaven-swings-at-nine-west-virginia-locations/article_a92c09d4-f0a4-11ec-be43-471085a4dcd7.html. Accessed 24 Nov. 2024.

Yu, Charles. *Interior Chinatown*. Pantheon, 2020.

Zelermyer, Karen, and Jamie Zelermyer. *I Was Never There*. Wonder Media Network, 2022, https://www.wondermedianetwork.com/originals/i-was-never-there. Accessed 24 Nov. 2024.

INDEX

Please note that page numbers in italics indicate illustrations.

Abrahams, Roger, 169
Abrams, James, 164–65
absentee land ownership, 67–68, 73, 122
Ackerman, John, 206
activism and protest songs, 118–19, 166–69
Acuff, Roy, 84
Adams, Joey, 100
advertising: commercials, 154–58
affiliative emotions/community ties, 52, 145, 154–55
Alabama (band), 105
Alderson-Broaddus University, 33
Alien: Covenant (film), 153–54
"Almost Heaven" (song by 6'6 240), 100
"Almost Heaven" (song by Dustin McCray), 122
"Almost Heaven" (song by Jason O'Brien), 100
"Almost Heaven" swings, 175
"Almost Heaven" trademark, 8
American Dad! (animated series), 153
"America the Beautiful" (patriotic song), 139
Anderson, Benedict, 18, 52, 116
Anderson, Colleen, 76, 90, 116–18
Anderson, Lynn, 135
anthems, 18, 25, 51
    function of, 183
    national, 163–66, *164*
Antoine, Jonathan, 34
Antonsich, Marco, 48, 154
Apalachee Falls (musical group), 144
Appalachia in the Classroom (Burriss & Gantt), 128
Appalachian Journal, 18–19
Appalachian Magazine, 97
"Appalachian problem," 67
Appalachian region
    Appalachian identity, 35, 120–21
    as commodity, 175–76
    definitions, 62
    diversity within, 107–9
    economic patterns, 73–74
    "holy Appalachia," 70
    literacy, 11
    media representations, 2
    mythical heritage, 69–70
    outmigration from, 73–75
    place-based pedagogy, 188–94
    in popular culture, 67
    problems and challenges, 67, 127–28
    stereotypes of, 2–3, 44–45, 53–54
    See also West Virginia
Appalachian Regional Commission (ARC), 67, 79–80, 130
    Appalachia Proposal, 83
    highway projects, 91
    redevelopment strategy, 82

Appalachian Soul Man (album), 42
Appalachian Spring (Copeland), 86
Appalachian String Band Festival, 87
Arbuckle, Nathan, 29
Area Redevelopment Act, 80
Armed Forces Radio (American Forces Network), 137
Arthurdale (planned community), 66, 111
Artist's Excursion, B&O Railroad (1858), 84
Asia, 137–38
Asleep at the Wheel (band), 87, 89
Augusta Heritage Festival, 87, 88
author's experiences
  "Country Roads" and homecoming, 1–2, 14–15
  "Country Roads" as protest anthem at WVU, 178–79
  family background, 3–4, 52–53, 97
  Hatfield McCoy Marathon, 16–17
  identity formation as West Virginian, 1–2, 192–93
  in Japan, 9, 15
  jukebox and instant community, 170
  West Virginia University (WVU) game day, 160
  West Virginia University (WVU) teaching, 17–18, 198

"Baby Dog" (Jim Justice's dog), 160, 175
back-to-the-land movement, 86, 88
Ballard, Sandra, 71
Batteau, Allen, 69
Bean, Heather Ann Ackley, 27, 35, 105–6
Beckley, West Virginia, 123
Bell, Iris, 95, 117
belonging, sense of, 48, 51–52, 144–45
Bennett, Andy, 107, 125

Berlin, Irving, 131–32
The Beverly Hillbillies (television program), 2, 71
Big Bend Tunnel, 84
Black Diamond Trophy, 160
Black populations in Appalachia, 111–13
Black vocalists singing "Country Roads," 10
Blackwater Falls, 161
Bloustien, Gerry, 155
"Blowin' in the Wind" (song by Bob Dylan), 168
Blue Ridge Mountains, 7, 38, 40
Bobek, Pavel, 143
B&O Railroad, 84
Bradford City Bantam soccer team, 159–60
Brandt, Deborah, 91
Branscome, James, 2, 56–57
Brisbane Lions football team, 159
Brooke, Robert, 9
Brown, Kane, 144
Brumfield, Nick, 142
Brustein, William, 180–81
Buckhannon, West Virginia, 21
"Buffalo Creek" (song by Mike Morningstar), 121
Burge, Todd, 123
Burnside, Jason, 98
Burriss, Theresa, 128, 204
Butler, Judith, 10
Butterflies Are Free (film), 152
Byrd, Robert, 26

Cabin Creek Quilts, 90
Cameron, Charlie, 159
Campbell, Glen, 85
Campbell, Suellen, 189
Cantwell, Robert, 87
Canyon, Christopher, 183–84
Carlile, Brandi, 88, 122, 141, 152

Carlisle, E. Fred, 100
"Carretera del Sur" (song by Mocedades), 143
Casey, Edward, 188
Castells, Manuel, 169
Catte, Elizabeth, 44–45, 50, 194
CBS (television broadcasting company), 54–55
Charles, Ray, 113, 135, 139–40
Charleston, West Virginia
  Capitol steps performance (1971), 89–90
  Trump rally, 46
  West Virginia State Museum, 64
Charleston Daily Mail, 89–90
"Charleston Girl" (song by Tyler Childers), 105
Chenoweth, Erica, 191
Childers, Tyler, 105
"Christmas in Appalachia" (CBS special), 2
church hymns, 24–25
Civil War, 72
Clapp, Elsie, 197
Clarice (television series), 152
Clarksburg, West Virginia, 82
Classic Labor Songs (Smithsonian Folkways album), 118
Clayton, Martin, 29
Clean Air Act, 81
Clean Waters Restoration Act, 81
climate action, 166–67
Clinton, Hillary, 46
The Cloverhearts, 141
Coal (album), 122
Coal House, Williamson, West Virginia, 16
"Coal Miner's Daughter" (song by Loretta Lynn), 105
coal mining. *See* mining
"Coal Tattoo" (song by Billy Edd Wheeler), 108

Cobain, Kurt, 110
Colbert, Stephen, 45
Collis, John, 27
"Come Home to West Virginia" (song by Eugene Landau Murphy), 98
"Come Home to West Virginia" (song by Kathy Mattea), 98, 101–2
"Coming of the Roads" (song by Billy Edd Wheeler), 108
commercials, advertising, 154–58
Concord College, 6
Connell, John, 37, 143, 154, 165
consumer culture, 154–55
Coopers Rock State Forest, 63
Copeland, Aaron, 86
Corden, James, 54–55
Corona beer advertising, 158
Country Music Association, 85
country music traditions, 36–38
  home as theme, 37
  road songs, 84–85
"Country Roads" (Danoff, Nivert & Denver)
  change over time, 199
  chords and harmonics, 29
  as country song, 37–38
  as cultural artifact, contextual aspects, 132–33
  cultural impact, 87–92
  early distribution, 135–36
  as global phenomenon, 43–44, 131–32, 133–46, 183–84, 190
  as international identity marker, 9–10
  as lens, 204–7
  lost verse, 88–89
  as mirror, 201–4
  in multiple genres, 141–44
  new versions, 142–43

"Country Roads" (*continued*)
  origin stories and release, 2, 4–5, 133–34
  outsider perspective of, 7
  "place I belong" line, 134
  political use of song, 45–49
  references to, in media, 146–54
  references to, in other songs, 99–102
  timing of, 90–91
  translations, other languages, 142
  universal appeal, 16–17, 102, 144–45
  as window, 200–201
Country Roads: How Country Came to Nashville (Hinton), 36
Country Roads Political Action Committee, 45
COVID-19 pandemic, 30–34
Creasman, Boyd, 8, 194
Cresswell, Tim, 49, 58–59, 138–39
cricket teams, 159
critical literacy, 197, 207–210
cultural rhetoric, 93
  stereotypes as, 69–72
Cumberland, Maryland, 84
Cummings, Whitney, 54–55

Daily Athenaeum (WVU newspaper), 7
Danoff, Bill, 2, 5, 6, 15, 41, 132
  on commercial use of music, 157–58
  connections to West Virginia, 171
  "Country Roads" lost verse, 88–89
  on covers of "Country Roads," 139–41
  Croatia story, 136
  environmental situation in West Virginia, 81
  generality vs. specificity, 145

  on initial success of "Country Roads," 133, 134, 135
  Jamboree radio show, 86
  Mountaineer Field performance (1980), 180
  on political use of songs, 47–48
  at Vietnam Veterans Memorial, 26–27
Dark Waters (docu-drama), 152
Dawkins, Richard, 146
Dear Appalachia (Satterwhite), 165–66
Deep Mapping, 189–91
DeGraw, Gavin, 105
Del Rey, Lana, 110, 142
Demon Copperhead (Kingsolver), 195
Denver, John, 2
  Charleston State Capitol steps performance (1971), 89–90
  "Country Roads" origin story, 5–6
  funeral, 26
  generality of work, 145
  John Denver's estate and political use of music, 47–48
  Mountaineer Field performance (1980), 180
  religious/spiritual qualities of music, 27
  State Capitol steps, 131
  Take Me Home: An Autobiography, 101
  visits to West Virginia, 6
Devil in the Hills: Coal Country Reckoning (album), 122
di Bari, Nicola, 142–43
Dickens, Hazel, 90, 94, 113–15, 122, 123–24
discrimination
  Black populations in Appalachia, 111–13
  displaced Appalachians, 115

displacement as theme, 114–16
Dollar General stores, 167–68
Donehower, Jim, 58
Door, Daisy, 142
drug addiction, stereotypes of, 55–56
Dubrovnik, Croatia, 136
Dudley, Dave, 85
Dunmire, Harry, 52–53
Dunmire, Mercia, 53
Dylan, Bob, 157, 168

Earth Day, 81, 89
"economic exile/refugees," 74, 113, 115. *See also* outmigration
Elk River chemical spill, 117
Ellison, John, 103–4, 112–13
Engle, Henry Everett, 95–96
Englehardt, Elizabeth, 107
environmental issues
  activism, 80–81, 166–67
  Elk River chemical spill, 117
  See also mining
extraction, history of, 7, 67–68, 72–79, 93. *See also* mining

Facing Future (album), 140
Fairmont, West Virginia, 160
Fallout 76 (online roleplaying game), 25–26, 151–52, 201
Farley, Liam, 51
Farley, Phil, 51
Farmington, West Virginia, 52–53
Farmington Mine Disaster, 81
Fat City (musical duo), 5
Federal Coal Mine Health and Safety Act, 81
Federal Highway Administration, 84
Federal Writers' Project, 68, 84
Ferguson, James, 127
"The 55 Counties Song," 98
#55Strong movement, 168
Fisher, Stephen, 11, 168, 192

Fluharty, Russell, 87
folk festivals, 86–87, 129
folklore of place, 173
folk music
  folk music revival, 87
  folk music traditions, 36–37
  and labor movement, 118
  train and road songs, 84–85
Ford, Tennessee Ernie, 135
"Forever Country" (song by multiple artists), 16, 144
4-H program, 98
"Freedom Convoy" truckers, 166
Fresh, Doug E., 160
funerals, use of "Country Roads," 21–22, 25–26, 27

Galliher, Renee, 191
Gantt, Patricia, 128
Gardner Winter Music Festival, 86
Gaventa, John, 118
Geertz, Clifford, 12, 13
generality, power of, 145
Gerrard, Alice, 94, 113, 114
Giardina, Denise, 194–95
Gibson, Chris, 37, 143, 154, 165
GIS Mapping, 189–91
"glamor shots" metaphor, 104–5, 129
The Glass Castle (Walls), 195
Golden Horseshoe Society test/ Award, 196–97
Goldenseal (magazine), 86–87, 108, 121
Goodyear tire advertising, 156
Google Home advertising, 156
Gotthard (band), 144
"Grandma's Hands" (song by Bill Withers), 123–24
Green Acres (television program), 2
"The Green Rolling Hills of West Virginia" (song by Utah Phillips), 94

grief, experience of, 186. *See also* homesickness
Griffith, Mary Ellen, 5
Groce, Larry, 117, 123
group singing experiences, 28
Gupta, Akhil, 127
Guthrie, Woody, 168

"Hail West Virginia" (song by The Pride of West Virginia), 105
Hard Work and Dedication (album), 100
Harmon, Jeremiah Lloyd, 144
Harpers Ferry, West Virginia, 7, 39–41, 72, 92
Harris, Emmylou, 94, 141
Harrison, Stephen, 51
Hatfield McCoy Marathon, 16
Hathaway, Rosemary, 69, 77, 182, 184–85
Hawker, Ginny, 114
Hawn, Goldie, 152
Hayes, Amanda, 8–9, 11, 49–50, 59, 106
Hazel & Alice (album), 114
Head Start, 80
Hearne, Julian, 95
Hee Haw (television program), 2
Heinonen, Tapio, 142
heritage discourse, 164–65
Hermes House Band, 141
Higgs, Robert, 201, 204
Hill, Jeremy, 85
Hillbilly Elegy (Vance), 195
hillbilly stereotypes, 2–3, 53–55, 191
  "Country Roads" as alternative to, 58–59
  media portrayals, 71–72
  urban hillbillies, 57
  See also stereotypes
Hillshire Farm advertising, 156
Hinton, Brian, 36, 113

hiraeth (Welsh concept of longing), 15, 22–24, 27, 35, 38, 99, 140–41, 154, 165, 187. *See also* homesickness
Hollow and Home (Carlisle), 100
Holt, Homer, 68
home
  existential, 39
  longing for, 15
  meaning of, 33
  place-belongingness, 154
  "place I belong" line, 134
  return to, 39
  theme in country music, 37
  used in marketing, 155–56
  West Virginia as substitute for every listener's home, 35–36
homesickness, 85, 99, 165
  and grief, 186
  and new versions of "Country Roads," 142–43
  outmigration songs, 113–16
  See also hiraeth (Welsh concept of longing)
homesteaders, 88
hooks, bell, 111, 187
hope, 34, 35
  and campaign music, 48–49
Hott, Mary, 122
Hoyt, David, 133–34
Humphrey, Hubert, 80
Huntington High School, 168
hymns, 24–25

identity formation, 7–9
  authentic vs. imaginary, 100–102
  culture and power, 59–60
  and geographical place, 42–44
  identity rhetoric, 9–17, 208
  institutional definitions, 44
  intersectionality, 11
  musical expressions, 109–13

outside vs. inside, 203–4
performative aspects, 12–14, 171
political candidates, 45
renegotiation of identity, 100–101
stereotypes, distancing from, 11–12
symbols and markers, 9, 12
for transplants to West Virginia, 116–17
and university education, 193
visible identity rhetoric, 161–63, *162*
West Virginia, 93, 172
at West Virginia University (WVU), 183
"If You Love My West Virginia" (song by Colleen Anderson), 117–18
imagery, 92–99
authentic vs. idealized, 104–5
imagery production, 69–72
of place, 207–8
Inscoe, John, 70
Interior Chinatown (Yu), 137
In the Land of the Lion (album), 141
invisible landscapes, 24
isolation, 193–94
I Was Never There (podcast), 88
"I Will Always Love You" (song by Dolly Parton), 16, 144

Jamboree radio show, 86
James, E. W., 97
Jamison Coal and Coke Company, 52–53
Japan, 137
Whisper of the Heart (anime film), 142
Jefferson, Thomas, 40, 41
Jefferson's Rock, 40, *41*, 92
Jelly Roll (rapper/singer), 144
Jeong, Jason, 137
J. Marinelli (band), 110

"John Henry" (folk song), 84
Johnson, Lyndon, 80
Johnston, Daniel, 109–10
Jones, Aristotle, 42, 73, 100, 110–12
Jones, Loyal, 72, 78, 204
Justice, Jim, 30, 160, 175, 183–84

Kamakawiwo'ole, Israel, 140
Kawanlama (Indonesian band), 141
"Keepers of the Mountains" (song by Elaine Purkey), 119
Kennedy, John F., 67, 80, 130
Kenya, Africa, 141
Kessinger, Clark, 87
King, Ellen Ruddell, 95
"King of the Road" (song by Roger Miller), 85
Kingsman: Golden Circle (film), 152
Kingsolver, Barbara, 195
Klemt, Barbara, 37
Know Your Meme (website), 147
Kurlinkus, Krista, 47
Kurlinkus, Will, 47

labor union movement, 66, 118
Laforêt, Marie, 143
land
absentee ownership, 67–68, 73, 122
connection to, 8
pastoral themes, 36–38
landscapes
imaginary, 172–73
invisible, 24
mythical, 35
Lanier, Parks, 36
The Late Late Show with James Corden, 54–55
The Late Show with Stephen Colbert, 45
Leach, Neil, 202
"Lean on Me" (song by Bill Withers), 123, 201

"Leaving West Virginia" (song by Kathy Mattea), 115–16
Leonard, George, 29
Let Me Be There (album), 135
"Libertà" (song by Nicola di Bari), 142–43
"Lift Every Voice and Sing" ("Black National Anthem"), 139
Lilly, John, 113–14, 124
Lipton, Michael, 103, 104, 128
literacy
    development, 204–5
    performances, 13–14
    texts and understanding, 92–93
    texts transcending the writer, 91–92
Locklear, Erica Abrams, 11, 185, 194
Loersch, Chris, 29
Logan Lucky (film), 152–53
loneliness, 37, 186
longing as theme, 23, 96. *See also hiraeth* (Welsh concept of longing)
loss as theme, 76–77
"Lost Highway" (song by Leon Payne), 85
Luckman, Susan, 155
Lynn, Loretta, 105, 135

Machine Gun Kelly, 144
Maggard, Sally Ward, 119
Malae, Milia, 142
"Mama's Hand" (song by Hazel Dickens), 124
Manchin, Joe, 31, 45, 55
Mann, Jeff, 196
Manning, Ambrose, 201, 204
mapping, 189–91
marketing, 154–58
    and tourism, 173–76
Marsh, Clay, 30
Marshall University, 6

Maryland as inspiration for song, 5, 6
Massey, Carissa, 12, 35, 78
Massey, Doreen, 189
Matewan massacre, 16
Matheny, William, 95
Mattea, Kathy, 94, 98, 101–2, 114, 115–16, 122
Maxwell, Ian, 124, 172
McCarroll, Meredith, 193
McCray, Dustin, 122
McLennan, Barbara, 189–91
Medicaid/Medicare, 80
Me First and the Gimme Gimmes, 141
Melodicka Bros., 141
memes, 146–52, *148, 149, 150, 151*
memorial/funerary industry, 26
A Message from the People (album), 139
Midler, Bette, 55
migration
    migration patterns and music, 85
    transplants to West Virginia, 88–89, 116–17, 134
    See also outmigration
Miller, Jim Wayne, 204
Miller, Roger, 85
Miltenberger, James, 180
mineral rights, 73
"mine wars," 66
mining, 46, 73
    acid drainage, 80–81
    and colonization, models of, 127
    disasters and dangers, 81, 121–22
    mechanization of, 74–75
    mountaintop removal (MTR), 119, 167
    in Wales, 23–24
The Mitchell Trio, 6, 99
Mocedades (singing group), 143
Moipei Quartet, 141

Monk, Stella, 90
Monongahela River, 7
"Mon Pays est Ici," 143
Moore, Arch, 171
Moracchioli, Leo, 141
Morgantown, West Virginia, 17, 82. *See also* West Virginia University (WVU)
Morgantown High School, 7
Morningstar, Mike, 120–22
Morris, Jan, 23
"Mountain Dew" (folk song), 105
Mountaineers Are Always Free (Hathaway), 182
"Mountaineers Are Always Free" (song by Mike Morningstar), 121
"Mountain Mama" (song by Gotthard), 144
"Mountain Mama" (song by Joey Adams), 100
Mountain Mamas Political Action Committee, 45
Mountain Man (musical trio), 141–42
Mountains of Music (Lilly), 86–87, 124
Mountain Stage (public broadcasting program), 87, 88, 103, 117, 129
mountaintop removal (MTR), 119, 167
"mountain values," 72
Mullens, Sarah, 53–54
Murphy, Eugene Landau, 98
music
   brain, effects upon, 29
   commercial uses of, 155–58
   as embodied experience, 172
   and global consumer culture, 154–55
   and interconnectedness, 99
   popular music, functions of, 101, 124–26
   rhythm and human connectedness, 29
   songs and storytelling, 106
   songwriting, 131–32
   See also country music
"My Heart Will Always Be in West Virginia" (song by Billy Edd Wheeler), 108
"My Home Among the Hills" (song by E. W. James), 97–98, 105

narratives, "tellable," 61–63, 202–3
Nashville Sound (genre), 85. *See also* country music
The Nation (periodical), 53, 78–79, 82
National Environmental Policy Act, 81
National Road, 84
negative stereotypes, 52–56, 194
   "Country Roads" as resistance, 56–61
   origins of, 77
   See also stereotypes
Nelson, Willie, 16
"neonatives," 88
New Deal Guidebook controversy, 68
New River Gorge, 64, 161
   New River Gorge Bridge, 83
Newton-John, Olivia, 135–37, 139
New York Knicks basketball team, 160
1960 political campaign, 80
Nivert, Taffy, 2, 5, 6–7, 91–92, 96, 120, 132, 138
   on commercial use of music, 157
   connections to West Virginia, 171
   on "magic" of "Country Roads," 28–29
   Mountaineer Field performance (1980), 180

nostalgia, 105–6, 124
    media of nostalgia, 165
    and popular music, 85, 124–26, 143
    rhetoric of, 47
Notes on the State of Virginia (Jefferson), 40

Obama, Barack, 45
Obermiller, Phillip, 57
O'Brien, Jason, 100
The Office (television series), 153
Oktoberfest, 137
Old Crow Medicine Show, 42
100 Days in Appalachian (nonprofit newsroom), 71
"One Day More" (song by Elaine Purkey), 118
"On the Road Again" (song by Willie Nelson), 16, 144
opioid epidemic, 195
"othering" of Appalachians, 53, 77
outmigration
    from Appalachia, 3, 73–75
    and music, 85–86
    and "othering," 53, 77
    outmigration songs, 113–16
    and stereotypes in landing places, 78–79
outsider perspectives, 7, 8–9, 12, 93
    economic and political control of West Virginia, 50
    vs. insider perspectives, 128
    "us" vs. "them" in political settings, 49

Pack, Colton, 144
Paisley, Brad, 16, 31–33
Panski (singer), 141
Parkersburg, West Virginia, 82
Parton, Dolly, 16
pastoral themes, 36–38
The Patient (television series), 154

patriotism, American, 163–66
Payne, Leon, 85
Pence, Mike, 45
Peters, Margaret, 155
Phillips, Utah, 94
pilgrimage, 38, 116, 145
Pippi, Jason, 159
Pittston Coal Strike (1985), 118
place
    and Appalachian values, 59–60
    and belonging, 48, 144–45
    concept of, 11
    and discourses of power, 49
    fictionalization of real places, 124–26, 165–66
    "home" and ideological beliefs, 138–39
    imagery, 207–8
    imagined spaces, 172–73, 187
    in marketing and consumer culture, 155–56
    music and place-making, 172
    place-based knowing, 60
    place-belongingness, 154
    place-identity, 170–71
    protest songs and place-identity, 168
    student research concerning, 205–6
    as unifying value, 78
place-based pedagogy, 197–99, 208–9
    Appalachia, 188–94
    West Virginia, 194–99
placelessness, 37
Poems, Prayers, and Promises (album), 27
politics
    1960 election cycle, 80
    2016 election cycle, 45–47
population loss in Appalachia, 3
porches, 111
Potomac River, 40
poverty, 53, 79–80, 130

"Pray for West Virginia" (song by Jason O'Brien), 100
Pretty Lights (electronic musician), 144
Price, Liz, 71
process philosophy, 35
"project identity," 207
protest music, 118–19, 166–69
Purkey, Elaine, 118–19

"quiescence," 118
The Quinaimes Band, 94

racism, 111–13
Rainforest Action Network (RAN), 167
Ramella, Richard, 93–94, 95, 97, 108, 113
Ransom, Heather, 50
Ravenswood, West Virginia, 133
Read Across America Day, 183–84
"Red Wing Black Bird" (song by Billy Edd Wheeler), 108
Reece, Florence, 118
Reg Varney Review (UK variety program), 136
resistance, 168–69
    to negative stereotypes, 56–61
    resistance identity, 169
    See also protest songs
Restless Road (band), 144
Reynolds, Nedra, 207
rhetoric
    rhetorical displays, 145–46
    visible identity rhetoric, 161–62
rhododendron, as state flower, 9
"Rhododendron" (state anthem), 98
rhythm, 29. *See also* music
Ridenour, Andy, 5
rituals
    sports teams, 159–60
    at West Virginia University (WVU), 181
Rivers, Dick, 142
roads
    roadbuilding and infrastructure, 81–83
    road songs, 83–85
Rockefeller, John D. "Jay," 88, 171, 180
Rockwool (insulation company), 167
"Rocky Mountain High" (song by John Denver), 145
romanticism, 35–39, 126–30, 169
Roosevelt, Eleanor, 66
Route 40, 84
Ruby, Chelsea, 173
rurality, 123
    and college attendance, 191
Ryden, Kent, 24, 144–45, 172–73, 174

Sale, Anna, 123
Sanders, Bernie, 46
Satterwhite, Emily, 36, 38, 60, 102, 165–66, 200–201, 207
Scotts Run, West Virginia, 66, 111
self-concept, 9. *See also* identity formation
sentimentality, 86, 98
Shadow of a Martyr (musical group), 100
Shannon, Thomas, 73–74
Shapiro, Henry, 12
Sharp, Cecil, 36
Shelby, Anne, 192
Shenandoah River, 7, 40
Shepherd University, 193
Shepley, Nathan, 197–98, 208–9
Shutika, Debra Lattanzi, 159
Silence of the Lambs (film), 152
Simon, Carly, 157
"Simple Gifts" (Shaker song), 105

6'6 240 (rap artist), 100
"Six Days on the Road" (song by Sawyer Brown), 85
"Sixteen Tons" (song by Tennessee Ernie Ford), 105
Skyline Bluegrass Festival, 86
Slab Fork, West Virginia, 123
Smith, Barbara Ellen, 11
Smithsonian Folklife Festival, 87
Snyder, Todd, 2–3, 53, 57, 69, 144, 185–86, 191, 197
"Some Kind of Wonderful" (song by John Ellison), 112
"Somewhere Over the Rainbow" (song from *The Wizard of Oz*), 140
songwriting
  hit songs, 131–32
  about West Virginia, 122–24
Songwriting in Contemporary West Virginia (Stimeling), 108–9
Soul Brothers Six, 112
Soule, Ellena, 141
Sounds Good to Me (podcast), 111
spaces
  and belonging, 170–71
  created, 35
  physical vs. symbolic, 207–8
Spank (musical group), 201
Sparby, Derek, 150
sports promotion, 159–60, 201–2
Springs, Pam, 98
Stanley, Patrick, 123
Statler Brothers, 135
stereotypes
  compartmentalization and reductive stereotypes, 71
  as cultural rhetoric, 69–72
  distancing from, 12
  education to counter, 195–97
  embracing of, as resistance, 58
  flattening effect, 77–78
  hillbilly, 2–3, 53–55, 57, 58–59, 71–72, 191
  history of, 66–67
  of women, 119–21
  See also negative stereotypes
Steubenville, Ohio, 6–7, 120
Stimeling, Travis, 105, 108–9, 123
St. Louis Blues hockey team, 159
Strait, George, 105
student-driven inquiry, 205–6, 207–8
Studio Ghibli, 153
Sunshine (TV film), 152
swings, statewide installation, 175
Switched on Pop, 137

"Take Me Home" (song by Restless Road/Kane Brown), 144
"Take Me Home, Country Roads." *see* "Country Roads"
Take Me Home: An Autobiography (Denver), 101
"The Talk" (song by Aristotle Jones), 111
Tate, Linda, 193
tattoos, 161–63, *162*
Taylor, Kathryn Trauth, 12–13
Teets, Sharon, 191–192
"tellable" narratives, 61–63, 202–3
"They Built a Railroad" (song), 122
"They Can't Put It Back" (song by Billy Edd Wheeler), 108
"This Is My Home" (song by Larry Groce), 123
"This Is My West Virginia" (song by Iris Bell), 94–95, 101
"This Land Is Your Land" (song by Woody Guthrie), 168
Tiananmen Square protests, 166
TikTok (video platform), 152
Toots and the Maytals, 140
tourism, 8, 173–76

tradition, value of, 8
translations into other languages, 142
Travis, Merle, 105
Tribe, Ivan, 108
Trump, Donald, 45–47
Tug Fork River, 16
Turman-Deal, Jinny, 88
Turner, Wyatt, 100

value systems, 72–73
Vance, J. D., 195
Vandalia Gathering, 87
"Veď Mě Dál, Cesto Má" (song by Pavel Bobek), 143
Vietnam Veterans Memorial, 26–27
Volunteers in Service to America (VISTA), 80, 90, 117

"Wabash Cannonball" (folk song), 84–85
Waits, Tom, 110
"Wake Up Call (Black Like Me)" (song by John Ellison), 113
Wales (nation), 23
Walls, Jeanette, 195
War on Poverty, 67, 80
Webb-Sunderhaus, Sara, 61, 62, 202
weddings, use of "Country Roads," 22, 27–28
Weintraub, Jerry, 134
"We Shall Not Be Moved" (protest anthem), 168
"We Shall Overcome" (protest anthem), 168
West Virginia
  as "alternative America," 93
  as completely Appalachian, 68–69, 79–80
  creation of state, 72
  diversity within, 107–9, 111–13
  exploitation, history of, 66–69
  extraction, history of, 72–79
  identity formation, 3, 109–13, 172, 183–84
  imaginary conceptions, 92–99
  infrastructure, 80, 81–83
  loss of congressional seats, 75–76
  marketing and perceptions of place, 156
  media portrayals, 45–46
  native musicians and "Country Roads," 99–102
  Office of Miners' Health Safety and Training, 81
  outmigration from, 74–75, 77
  place-based pedagogy, 194–199
  population loss and outmigration, 3
  poverty assistance efforts, 79–80
  as proxy home for Americans, 164–65
  radio stations, 133–34
  renaissance (1970s), 91
  state anthems, 8, 25, 64, 94–97, 171, 173
  teacher's strike (2018), 168
  tourism, 8, 161, 173–74
  transplants to, 88–89, 116–17, 134
  Vietnam War, 76
  working class population, 44–45
  See also Appalachia
"West Virginia, My Home" (song by Hazel Dickens), 90, 113–15
"West Virginia, My Home Sweet Home" (song by Julian Hearne), 94–95, 101
West Virginia: A History (Williams), 88
"West Virginia Boys and Girls" (4-H song), 98
"West Virginia Chose Me" (song by Colleen Anderson), 76, 116–17
"West Virginia Girl" (song by Mike Morningstar), 120–21

West Virginia Highlands Conservancy, 81
"The West Virginia Hills" (Aristotle Jones version), 42, 100, 110–12
"The West Virginia Hills" (hymn/anthem), 24–25, 94, 95–97, 101, 105
West Virginia Humanities Council, 129
West Virginia Music Hall of Fame, 103, 123, 128–29
  Exhibits Museum, 103
West Virginia Office of Tourism, 8
West Virginia Public Broadcasting, 88
West Virginia State Folk Festival, 86
West Virginia State Museum, Charleston, 64
"West Virginia State of Mind" (song by John Ellison), 103–4, 112–13
West Virginia University (WVU), 131
  Black Diamond Trophy, 160
  "Country Roads" as community rhetoric, 180–82
  during COVID-19, 33–34
  Daily Athenaeum, 7
  first-generation students, 185, 191
  graduation ceremonies, 28
  identity formation, 161
  Marching Band, 64
  out-of-state and in-state students, 182–87
  promotional materials, 8
  sports teams, 14
West Virginia Wesleyan College, 6, 97
What Happened (Clinton), 46
What You're Getting Wrong About Appalachia (Catte), 194
Wheeler, Billy Edd, 108, 122
Wheeling, West Virginia, 82
  Jamboree radio show, 86
  WWVA, 87

"Which Side are You On?" (song by Florence Reece), 118
Whipkey, Charlotte, 121
Whisnant, David, 18–19
Whisper of the Heart (anime film), 142, 153
"whiteness" as distortion, 107–8
Whitford, Bradley, 54
"Wichita Lineman" (song by Glen Campbell), 85
Wilco (rock band), 110
"Wild West Virginia" (song by Daniel Johnston), 109–10
Wilkerson, Jessica, 119
Wilkinson, Bill, 5
Williams, Buzz, 202
Williams, Hank, 85
Williams, Hank, Jr., 105
Williams, John, 84, 86, 88, 92–93, 118
Williamson, West Virginia, 16
Winterplace Ski Resort, 8
Withers, Bill, 112, 123–24
WMOV radio, Ravenswood, 133–34
women
  contributions of, 119–20
  stereotypes, 119–21
  women's voices, 141–42
"Wonderful World" (song by Louis Armstrong), 140
Wordsworth, William, 37
WOWK13 (news station), 50–51
writing instruction, 198–99
Wrong Turn (film), 71
WWVA radio, Wheeling, 87

"You Remind Me of West Virginia" (song by Wyatt Turner), 100
Yovel, Hanan, 142
Yu, Charles, 137

Zelermyer, Jamie, 88
Zelermyer, Karen, 88

www.ingramcontent.com/pod-product-compliance
Lightning Source LLC
Chambersburg PA
CBHW031424150426
43191CB00006B/392